# RHODE ISLAND POLITICS

## AND THE

## AMERICAN REVOLUTION

BROWN UNIVERSITY STUDIES XXIII

# RHODE ISLAND POLITICS
## AND THE
# AMERICAN REVOLUTION
## 1760-1776

DAVID S. LOVEJOY

PROVIDENCE · RHODE ISLAND
BROWN UNIVERSITY PRESS

STANDARD BOOK NUMBER: 87057-053-6

LIBRARY OF CONGRESS CATALOG CARD NUMBER: 58-10478

BROWN UNIVERSITY PRESS, PROVIDENCE, RHODE ISLAND 02912

*To the Memory of*
EDMUND MATTESON LOVEJOY

## CONTENTS

# INTRODUCTION

A REHEARSAL of the issues, arguments, and incidents which occurred in Rhode Island in reaction to the designs of the British
government is insufficient to explain why the colony left the Empire.
An understanding of what encroachment by Parliament meant to
Rhode Islanders involves an understanding of what Parliament encroached upon in Rhode Island. Such an inquiry has led to a study of
the colony's economy, government, and politics and the reasons for
resistance which were peculiar to the colony itself, in addition to the
more general causes of revolt in the American colonies as a whole.

From the very beginning Rhode Islanders were noticeably independent in their attitude toward the British government. Once the revolutionary movement commenced, this independent attitude became even
more apparent, and, from the crisis over taxation to the Declaration
of Independence, Rhode Island seemed one step ahead of her sister
colonies in defiance of the power of Parliament and the authority of
the Crown. Politically Rhode Island had never fitted very well into
the Empire, and when in the 1760's and 1770's the imperial structure became more sharply defined and more annoyingly restrictive,
King and Parliament recognized that the colony fitted hardly at all.

A close study of Rhode Island reveals that this precocious attitude,
this advanced point of view in regard to the colony's place in the Empire, was not identifiable with a demand for political democracy, except as self-government itself is a principle of democracy. According
to Carl Becker, the issue in New York in the same period was not
only a question of home rule, but also of who should rule at home.
The revolutionary movement there shared the stage with a struggle
between a colonial aristocracy and a disfranchised class which, in the
interest of patriotism and democracy, pushed its way into the political
arena by extralegal means.[1] Rhode Island was also torn by a bitter dispute over who should rule, but the struggle, unlike that in New York,
was not caused by the attempt of one class of people to tear down an-

other and broaden the basis of government. The struggle in Rhode Island over who should rule at home was a struggle between equals, between people who already enjoyed the right to vote and who fought to control the government for their own ends.

The factional struggle and the revolutionary movement, as we shall see, were intimately connected for other reasons. A piecing together of the political history of Rhode Island just prior to the Revolution leads to conclusions similar to those of other historians about political organization in this period. The research of several British and some American scholars, beginning with Sir Lewis Namier a generation ago, has impressed upon us the significance of local issues in the structure of British politics in the eighteenth century. What appear to us today to be political parties in a modern sense were really shifting coalitions and connections uncommitted to any broad principle or program. These factions owed their origins more to local questions and selfish interests than to national or imperial policies. Men went into politics for a variety of reasons, few of which were related directly to the national welfare. Nevertheless, the affairs of ordinary people and their local concerns as reflected in Parliament helped to form the basis of the larger political problems and even contributed to their development. By examining at close hand the House of Commons and the political and economic motives of its members, Namier and his students learned new and valuable answers to their questions about the nature of British politics and the relationship between politics and the larger issues of the day.[2]

The General Assembly of Rhode Island was a far cry from the British Parliament, but it did contain a number of Rhode Islanders whose interest in politics was curiously similar to that of their English brothers in the House of Commons. The dominant characteristic of Rhode Island politics just before the Revolution was the struggle (generally called the Ward-Hopkins controversy) between two factions for control of the government. As we shall see, it was more than a controversy; it was continuous political warfare which had reverberations throughout Rhode Island and which affected in some way most of the inhabitants. But the government and politics in Rhode Island reflected only local concerns, not those which might be called colonial or American. Election to office and participation in the factional struggle had meaning only in local terms. The voters of a town did not send men to the General Assembly to settle imperial or even American problems. They chose deputies to unite with others to bring control of the government to their section of the colony for the advantages this control would produce.

Concern among Rhode Islanders for local issues and personal and community advantages from government became the basis for resistance to Great Britain. Once British interference commenced in the form of a stricter enforcement of trade laws, Parliamentary taxation, extended jurisdiction of the admiralty courts, threatened revocation of the charter, and later the punitive acts of Parliament, Rhode Islanders foresaw an end to the virtual independence their charter allowed. If the new policy became effective, Rhode Islanders would kiss goodbye their whole system of politics which generously rewarded the dominant faction and made elections worth winning. The protection of local rights and accustomed privileges was easily translated into more defensible terms of charter rights and the rights of Englishmen. Although voters in Rhode Island elected deputies and Assistants to the General Assembly to represent their local interests, these political leaders, when necessary, transcended the particular issues, co-operated with other colonial governments, and vigorously resisted encroachment from abroad.

This volume is not a full scale history of Rhode Island; it does not deal broadly with the economic, social, religious, and cultural character of the colony. Rather it treats these aspects of colonial life only insofar as they bear on the colony's politics and the revolutionary movement.

The political development of each British American colony was molded by a number of local conditions which varied from colony to colony—owing to the different types of government; contrasting geographical features which resulted in economic and sectional differences; an assortment of religions, some established, some not; diverse customs and traditions; and a host of other factors. Rhode Island exhibited a unique combination of characteristics which produced the peculiar struggle described here, and an understanding of the peculiar struggle helps to explain why Rhode Island left the Empire in 1776. If local issues and concerns were the basis for larger political problems as experience in Rhode Island indicates, then a closer look at political organization and conditions in other colonies in the eighteenth century would help historians to determine more clearly the origins of the American Revolution.

\* \* \*

This book began as a doctoral thesis at Brown University under the guidance of Professor Edmund S. Morgan, now of Yale. Professor Morgan read the manuscript at several stages, and I am particularly grateful to him for helpful criticism, valuable suggestions, and scholarly supervision which has been an inspiration. Professor James B. Hedges of the History Department of Brown University and Mr. Bernhard Knollenberg of Chester, Connecticut, read and constructively criticized the manuscript.

Several people assisted me generously in locating manuscripts and printed sources and with friendly advice. I wish to thank Mr. Lawrence C. Wroth, Miss Jeanette D. Black, and Miss Marion W. Adams of the John Carter Brown Library; Mr. David A. Jonah of the Brown University Library; Miss Marion E. Brown, formerly of the Brown Library; Miss Mary T. Quinn of the Rhode Island Archives; Mr. Herbert O. Brigham and Mrs. Gladys Bolhouse of the Newport Historical Society; and Mr. Clifford P. Monahon and Mr. Clarkson A. Collins, 3rd, of the Rhode Island Historical Society. Mr. Collins read the manuscript and asked some fundamental questions which demanded answers. I am also indebted to Professor Edward J. Pfeifer of St. Michael's College who aided me in the interpretation of some of the material investigated.

I wish to thank the staff of the Manuscript Room of the New York Public Library for courteous help and the Yale University Library for permission to use the Ezra Stiles Papers. It is a pleasure to acknowledge my gratefulness to the National Society of Colonial Dames of America for a generous fellowship which substantially helped me to continue my research and to the Society of Colonial Dames in Rhode Island whose assistance helped bring the book to publication. To my wife, for her help and patience, I owe more than can be stated here.

A paper, derived from this volume, describing politics in Rhode Island and their relation to the American Revolution, was read at a meeting of the American Historical Association in New York City on December 28, 1957.

DAVID S. LOVEJOY

# CHAPTER I

## RHODE ISLANDISM

THE CHARTER which John Clarke brought back from London to Roger Williams and the people of Rhode Island in 1663 established "The Governor and Company of the English Colony of Rhode-Island and Providence Plantations, in New-England, in America." What is more, it established the Colony of Rhode Island as "a bodie corporate and politique, in ffact and name." The charter has been justly celebrated for the permission it granted the inhabitants "to hold forth a livelie experiment" to prove that a civil state may exist and flourish "with a full libertie in religious concernments." What has not been as justly celebrated is the fact that this charter established also an experiment in colonial self-government which the colony continued for a hundred years with little interference from the mother country. In addition to the opportunity to govern themselves, the people of Rhode Island were guaranteed the liberties and immunities of free and natural subjects "as if they, and every of them, were borne within the realme of England."[1]

The charter of Rhode Island placed control of the government squarely in the hands of the General Assembly, and according to this charter the only check upon that body was that its laws "bee not contrary and repugnant unto, butt, as neare as may bee, agreeable to the laws of this our realme of England, considering the nature and constitutione of the place and the people there." With England 3000 miles distant, this was not much of a check, and as Rhode Island matured politically it developed into a virtually independent state acknowledging, only when necessary, an allegiance to the King.

The legislature combined all the powers of the government in one branch, and neither the Governor, the elected officials, nor the courts could act independently of it. Sovereignty lay in the General Assembly, and control of that body meant control of the government itself. But the freemen chose the members of the Assembly, and since the legisla-

ture was subject to little or no meddling from England, it was a crea-
ture of the voters who twice a year seated deputies in it and annually
selected a Governor and council as part of it. The circumstances, as it
turned out, gave splendid opportunities for politicking—opportunities which were not lost upon those who voted.

I

A hundred years after the establishment of the "bodie politique"
Rhode Islanders were well accustomed to governing themselves. But
freedom to develop their own political system resulted eventually in
government by faction. For almost twenty years just preceding the
Revolution the colony was split into two political camps, one led by
Samuel Ward of Westerly and Newport and the other by Stephen
Hopkins of Providence. The struggle between the two parties was
deadly serious; it involved in some way most of the inhabitants
whether they voted or not. Each officeholder from a justice of the
peace to the Governor himself felt its influence. Often it helped to
make and break friendships and divide families; it set up one section
of the colony against the other, and, like a "Daemon let loose" scattered "every Evil that can make Mankind wretched."[2] The struggle
continued from about 1757 well into the 1770's when one party,
hopelessly beaten, was unable to muster the political strength to carry
on the fight.

The roots of the Ward-Hopkins controversy went deeper into the
history of Rhode Island politics than the particular conditions which
were present when Ward and Hopkins emerged as the protagonists
of two disputing factions. The historian ought to be cautious in as-
signing absolute reasons for all the political actions he describes, particularly when it is a question whether he can really know what went
on in the minds of the men whose political gyrations he is attempting
to reconstruct. But probably the dispute between the leading political
figures in the 1750's and 1760's originated in an earlier generation
and was maturing when the two able politicians, Ward and Hopkins,
found the conditions ripe for effective political leadership.

Samuel Ward was a devout Baptist farmer and village merchant
from Westerly, where he raised a large family on his salt water farm
in that somewhat remote, southwestern corner of the colony. In 1756

the freemen of the town sent him as a deputy to the General Assembly where he commenced a long and busy career in the colony's government. But this was not Samuel Ward's first exposure to Rhode Island politics. Before moving to Westerly he had grown up in Newport, and his merchant father, Richard, had been Secretary of the colony for eleven years when Samuel was born there in 1725. While he was a youngster, attending school and helping in the family business, his father was three times chosen Governor of the colony. Moreover, his older brother, Thomas, a Harvard graduate, stepped into his father's old job as Secretary in 1747 and was annually re-elected to that post until his death in 1760. Young Samuel was no stranger to Rhode Island politics when he made his first trip to the Assembly in 1756.[3]

Samuel Ward's later political troubles stemmed in part from his father's career before him. Richard Ward's rise in Rhode Island politics had not been altogether smooth. He was born in 1689, was admitted a freeman in 1710, and chosen Recorder or Secretary of the colony in 1714, a position he kept for eighteen years.[4] But just prior to Richard Ward's political debut, two brothers, William and John Wanton, also of Newport, burst upon the political scene following several profitable forays at sea as privateers against Britain's and the colony's enemies. Flush with wealth and considerable popularity, the brothers turned their attention to the affairs of government with a good deal of success. On the road to positions of eminence each had served as a deputy, speaker of the lower house, and as a Magistrate or Assistant in the council. On their way to the top, however, the Wanton brothers had tangled with Richard Ward, who, it must be said, had come off second best.[5]

The trouble between the Wantons and Richard Ward came into the open in 1731 when the whole colony was turned upside down over the paper money issue. Beginning in 1710 the government had periodically resorted to this painless method for providing its inhabitants with a medium of exchange, since the unfavorable balance of trade with Great Britain drained specie out of their pockets. Usually these bills of credit were government loans—at interest for stated periods—to the inhabitants who put up land as collateral. When the Assembly voted in 1731 to issue another batch of bills—this time £60,000—a number of merchants, including Governor Joseph Jenckes,

placed their feet down solidly in opposition and petitioned the King to
put a stop to these inflationary practices. As Secretary, Richard Ward
was caught between the powerful Wantons, on the one hand, who bitterly opposed airing the colony's business before the King and ministry
and, on the other hand, a number of conservative merchants and a
Governor who believed the colony had gone far enough on its way
to financial ruin. The Wantons turned on Ward in a rage when, under
instructions from the Governor, he attested copies of the Assembly's
act and several supporting documents for the petitioners to send to
the King.[6]

It is apparent that the Wantons had the support of a majority of
the freemen since at the next election (1732) William was elected
Governor and his brother renamed Deputy Governor. Ward hung
on to the Secretary's job that year but lost it the next after William
Wanton publicly reminded the freemen of Ward's conduct in 1731,
which, he charged, tended to bring about the total ruin of the colony.[7]
The retired Secretary bided his time. William Wanton died in office
in 1733, and the Assembly immediately replaced him with his brother,
John, who served for six years. In 1740 he died, too, but not before
Richard Ward had made a political comeback, was elected Deputy
Governor under him, and was strategically placed to take over John
Wanton's office at his death.[8]

The year 1740 marked the end of an era in the colony's politics.
With William and John Wanton in their graves, Richard Ward had
clear sailing; the Assembly chose him to fill out the deceased Governor's term, and for two years more the freemen elected him to head
the government. At the time Richard Ward succeeded John Wanton
as Governor, William Greene of Warwick succeeded Ward as Deputy
Governor, and there resulted from this administration a political
alliance between the Wards and the Greenes which obtained even
after Greene's death in 1758. Although Ward dropped out of the
government in 1743, William Greene carried on as Governor and preserved the Ward-Greene alliance for Samuel who assumed leadership
of the faction shortly after he came into the Assembly in 1756. Meanwhile, the Wards and Greenes improved their hold on the government when Thomas Ward, the Harvard graduate, and eldest son of
Richard, was elected Secretary in 1747. Like his father before him

and still another brother, Henry, to follow, Thomas Ward found the Secretary's post altogether agreeable; he relinquished it only at his death in 1760 and then to Henry, who kept it in the family for thirty more years.[9]

During the 1740's the Wanton family, without John and William, of course, was not idle. Gideon, nephew of John and William, managed to scrape together enough votes to defeat William Greene for Governor in 1745 and 1747. With the exception of these two instances, Greene's string of victories was unbroken from 1743 to 1755.[10] But it was quite clear that the Wantons in their present political circumstances were no match for the successful Wards and the Greenes. This was not owing to a scarcity of Wantons. Old William had left a very able merchant son named Joseph, an Anglican like his father, who seems not to have been interested in the government and suppressed for a time his political nature until several years later when his friends persuaded him to run for Governor. Meanwhile, there was Joseph Wanton's son, Joseph, Jr., a vigorous young blade of whom we shall hear more, and it was he who next took over the Wanton flag in politics—and the family's dislike for the Wards— after a successful alliance had been arranged with the voters in the northern half of the colony.

Although there is no documentary evidence to demonstrate when the Wantons looked to Providence for political support, it must have been some time in the middle 1750's. Providence was a smaller town, about half the size of Newport, and in the eyes of the Newporters, it had long been a country town. But Providence was rapidly changing from a rural community to a thriving city with a number of enterprising merchants and several ambitious politicians. The Browns of Providence—Obadiah and his nephews, the Brown brothers, Nicholas, John, Joseph, and Moses—pooled their talents and traded and manufactured their way to become as eminent a mercantile family as New England could boast.[11] Their interests extended far and wide, and among their business friends were the wealthy Wantons of Newport, Joseph and Joseph, Jr. Business laid a splendid basis for political co-operation, and as the Wards looked to the Greenes of Warwick for political support, so the Wantons looked to the Browns of Providence.

Not only did the Browns bring votes and vigor into this political alliance, but they brought also Stephen Hopkins, the northern town's most able politician. Hopkins was born in Scituate on the outskirts of Providence in 1707. In his middle twenties he became interested in public office, and between 1732 when he was chosen town clerk of Scituate and 1755 when he was first elected Governor, he had run the gamut of elected offices, having been at various times a deputy, speaker of the lower house, and a justice of the Inferior and Superior Courts. In the early 1740's Hopkins moved into Providence and continued his public career as a deputy from that town, and for five years prior to his election as Governor the Assembly chose him Chief Justice of the Superior Court.[12] In 1754 Hopkins gave evidence of the statesman he was to become, for in that year the Assembly sent him along with Martin Howard, Jr., of Newport, to the Albany Congress where he hobnobbed with Benjamin Franklin, Thomas Hutchinson of Massachusetts, and other farsighted colonial leaders who understood the need and the advantage of colonial union against the French and Indians. Hopkins' enthusiasm for Franklin's Plan of Union cooled considerably when he returned to Rhode Island, where the Assembly, fearing an encroachment on the colony's charter, avoided the document as if it were infected with the smallpox. However, Hopkins lost no ground by his jaunt to Albany, for the next year the freemen elected him Governor.[13]

In addition to public service Hopkins dabbled in commerce, built, owned, and fitted out vessels for trading, and joined the Brown brothers in smelting iron at Hope Furnace.[14] But Hopkins was more comfortable in politics, and most of his energy was spent in the business of government. When the freemen elected him Governor in 1755 they placed in the chief executive's chair a handsome man, not quite fifty, with flowing gray hair, black eyebrows, a large nose, and quiet eyes. Despite his Quaker background—enough of which had rubbed off on him to make him keep his hat on in public meetings— he was a tough, hardy, and resourceful individual who brought to the Governor's office considerable political experience. In the next fifteen or twenty years he was to demonstrate the artistry of the politician which made him the most formidable political character in the early history of Rhode Island. Hopkins, wrote the Reverend Ezra Stiles of

Newport, is a man "of Penetration and Sagacity and very considerable Acquisitions in those Branches of Knowledge that form the Politician and Legislator."[15]

Once the Wantons of Newport merged their political interests with Hopkins and the Browns, the Newporters were overwhelmed and absorbed by the stronger Providence group. The Wanton faction which had for so long opposed the Wards became the Hopkins faction of Providence with Wanton support in Newport. It continued to oppose the Wards and promptly challenged the Ward-Greene party for control of the government.

And all this time young Samuel Ward was establishing himself in Westerly, getting married, and begetting children; in 1758, after the death of William Greene, he took over the leadership of the Ward faction. Ward seems to have been more mildly tempered than Hopkins and was eighteen years younger than his Providence rival. In no way, however, did his youth or good nature impair his political effectiveness; he was a match for Hopkins and three times proved it by walking off with the Governorship at election time. William Ellery, one of his party stalwarts from Newport, found him "well acquainted perhaps no man so well with these particular different Humours"; he knew "what String to touch."[16] Moreover, in order to broaden the basis of his party he succeeded in getting the ear of the Brown brothers' uncle, Elisha Brown of Providence, whom he persuaded to join him in his struggle against Hopkins. Both leaders then could count on a measure of support from the enemy's territory, a circumstance which made it possible for each through his friends to keep tabs on what his rival was doing. Upon the death of Governor Greene the stage was set for a political battle between Ward and Hopkins and their supporters which rocked the colony until the Revolution.

A contributing factor to the Ward-Hopkins dispute was a bitter personal contest between the protagonists which had actually begun before Greene was safe in his grave. But personal bitterness was more a by-product of the struggle than a cause of it. That it was a contest between two political personalities explains several details of the encounter but not its over-all meaning. To be sure, the court case in 1757 was evidence of a personal conflict. Hopkins' opponents accused him of using his influence as Governor during the war with France to feather his own nest and that of his sons. Ward wrote a pamphlet attacking Hopkins with a barrage of arguments underlining these accusations. He declared that the Governor had acted in a "Tyrannical and arbitrary manner" and had subverted the Constitution by "assuming a power not even pretended to by any King of England since James ye second."[17] Hopkins bounced back with a court action for libel and £20,000 damages, but in order to get fair treatment Ward petitioned the Assembly to move the trial out of Providence County where, he said, Hopkins had "a great many relations, and a very extensive influence."[18] The parties first agreed on Rehoboth, Massachusetts, and then Worcester for the scene of the trial, since the case doubtless could not have been fairly tried anywhere in Rhode Island, let alone Providence. James Otis represented Hopkins while Edmund Trowbridge, another Boston lawyer, argued for Ward.[19] After a full hearing, the verdict went to Ward, and Hopkins paid the cost of suit. Although he appealed to the next session of the court, the case was not heard again. Out of the trial came acrimonious charges and countercharges. Several witnesses testified that Hopkins swore he would blow Ward's brains out if he did not get satisfaction at law.[20] The publicity of the trial put a crimp in Hopkins' political career, at least for that year. William Greene, who had been forced out of retirement by the party broils, licked Hopkins at the polls and settled into the Governor's chair for another term. He died in February of the next year, but the Assembly chose Hopkins, not Ward, to fill the vacancy until the next election.[21]

It is doubtful that personal power was an incentive to Ward and Hopkins to seek the Governor's office. Each may have taken satisfaction in finding himself at the head of the government after the struggle of an election. Doubtless there was prestige in being Governor of the "English Colony of Rhode Island, in New England, in America." There was not much else. The office held little official authority, at least in the General Assembly. Without a veto power, the Governor could only sit in the upper house and vote like any other member of that body. Of course, political power was not all official, and strong politicians like Ward and Hopkins found room to exercise their faculties outside the Assembly in guiding legislation, directing appointments, securing new voters, and reassuring old ones between elections. But the Ward-Hopkins controversy cannot be adequately explained as a personal rivalry between the protagonists. It was party against party rather than one individual against another.

Others have tried to explain the political struggle as a clash between social classes—that Ward of Westerly and Newport "represented both patroon and patrician. [He] was a fruit of the world at large; Hopkins, his opponent, was the product of Rhode Island."[22] The facts do not support such a distinction between the two men. Both were products of Rhode Island, products of the political system permitted by the freedom of the charter. Each was a leader of a faction produced by this political system, but to call Ward a champion of the colony's aristocrats in contrast to Hopkins is to misread the facts. True, Ward was backed by some well-to-do gentlemen in the southern counties and several prosperous merchants of Newport. But Hopkins counted on continuous support from successful farmers in the northern half of the colony, prosperous merchants in Providence, and, in particular, from the Wantons of Newport who were probably as aristocratic and wealthy a family as the colony could boast—some spent occasional winters in Bermuda.[23]

Moreover, Ward's most powerful political crony was Elisha Brown of Providence, who served as his Deputy Governor in 1765 and 1766 and would have in 1762, had his accounts as a member of the Committee of War not presented such a mystery to the auditing committee of the General Assembly.[24] "Uncle Brown," as he was unaffectionately called by the Brown brothers, was as unaristocratic a Rhode Islander as ever tracked dung through the broad halls of the Colony House in Newport. A quick glance at some of Elisha Brown's letters must have convinced even his least socially conscious correspondents that he was hardly an aristocrat. To Samuel Ward he once wrote, describing his hard times,

My Enemey are Endevering to Efect Every parson that I am Endet [in debt] to Sue Me which has Causd Maney suts at Cort and My trading Entrust being at See which puts Me to Agudeel of whot the World Cauls truble, yit I trust Providence will so order in Afue munts more to free Me of thos Difekelteys.[25]

Samuel Ward, it will be remembered, was a farmer and small town merchant. By these means he supported a large family and spent as much time worrying about cattle, hogs, and crops as he did about politics. Hopkins, on the other hand, was involved in politics most of his life and was familiar with the business life of the colony. Neither man had accumulated a fortune or was even considered well-to-do. Farmers and merchants alike supported Ward or Hopkins for reasons not directly related to the position either candidate or voter held in society.

The political struggle between the Ward and Hopkins factions in the 1760's and 1770's was not one of political principle. Neither party embraced a political philosophy challenged by the other. In fact, no one would accuse Ward, Hopkins, or their followers of fighting for a principle, political or otherwise, in their annual struggle for control of the colony's government. This characteristic brings to mind some of the conclusions Sir Lewis Namier and others have come to about the structure of British politics in the same period and earlier— that political parties were not parties in the true sense. They were coalitions and factions rather than parties, since they contained politicians who banded together only for specific political purposes which were not necessarily related to national or imperial issues of the day.[26] In this respect Rhode Island's politics show a striking similarity to the politics of England in the eighteenth century.

Neither group claimed to be a party of the "People," for democracy was not an issue in colonial Rhode Island. The reason for this may be that the basis of government was sufficiently broad, theoretically at least, so that no group felt dispossessed. A good piece of evidence which points toward this conclusion is that throughout this period no protests were made nor reform measures attempted indicating dissatisfaction with the representation in the legislature or the requirements for suffrage. During the same period neither party appealed to a disfranchised class with a promise to better its condition.

In twentieth century terms political democracy is a combination of self-government, equitable representation, and manhood suffrage. With respect to self-government, Rhode Island was dangerously democratic, according to the colony's critics both in America and in England. Judge Horsmanden of the *Gaspee* Commission reported with contempt that it was a "downright democracy," that Rhode Islanders paid no attention whatever to the ministry in London or

the British Parliament, and that the government, entirely in the hands
of the populace, was in a state of anarchy.[27] Rhode Island government
was virtually independent of British control and in this sense was
democratic.

An examination of the system of representation leaves some doubt
as to whether the government was equitably based according to
population. While representation in the Massachusetts house was tied
to the number of qualified voters in each town,[28] representation in the
Rhode Island house was fixed by the charter of 1663 and remained
unchanged until after the Dorr Rebellion in 1842. The charter
directed that Newport send six deputies and Providence, Portsmouth,
and Warwick each four; all new towns added thereafter would seat
two representatives in the Assembly. If this proportional representation reflected the population in 1663, it certainly did not in the years
just prior to the Revolution. In 1774, for instance, Newport, the
largest town, with a population of 9208, rightly sent the largest number of deputies (6), and Providence, a little less than half the size
of Newport, sent four. But Portsmouth, about one-third the size of
Providence, and Warwick, a little more than half the size of Providence, continued to send four also. Moreover, fifteen towns at this
time were larger than Portsmouth—three of them twice as large—
yet these fifteen towns sent only half the number of deputies (2)
to the legislature. Five towns boasted more inhabitants than Warwick;
still each sent only two representatives compared to its four.[29] More
curious than this outmoded system of representation was the fact
that no one complained about it. Nor did either of the opposing
factions attack the antiquated representation as a means to rally
political support. What was good enough for Roger Williams and his
friends was good enough for Ward, Hopkins, and their friends, and
equitable representation was not an issue in the colony's politics. The
charter directed that the council consist of ten Assistants, but it was
silent about how they should be divided. Through the years it became
customary for each of the five counties to send two Assistants to the
upper house.

Since both factions showed no tendency to tamper with the suffrage
requirements, it is possible that the property qualifications and the
admission of freemen satisfied most of the inhabitants. But definite

conclusions are hard to come by since colonial census takers were more interested in the total population and ratable polls than they were in the number of adult males and qualified voters. In order to determine whether the structure of government was democratically based, one ought to know what proportion of adult males could vote. It is a comparatively simple task to learn how many people *did* vote, but that, as we shall see, had little to do with the question.

Property qualifications for voting were never very restrictive in Rhode Island. The right to vote was based on the ownership of land, that is, real estate, and in 1729 an adult male in order to become a qualified voter had to possess land worth £200 or land which would rent for £10 annually.[30] At first glance these figures seem high, but money was cheap in Rhode Island owing to frequent emission of paper bills of credit. That a £200 qualification and the method of enforcing it were not restrictive was apparent in 1746 when the Assembly doubled the suffrage requirement since the manner of admitting freemen was lax "and their Qualifications as to their Estates, so very low, that many Persons are admited, who are possessed with little or no Property." Of course, the eldest son of a freeman, if he were twenty-one or over, was also admitted free of the colony.[31]

One would think that a property qualification of £400 would seriously reduce the number of freemen, but a sampling of the rate-makers' reports in several towns reveals that despite this, a large number of the adult males could still qualify. If the number of adult males is close to the number of ratable polls, that is, the number of males over twenty-one who owned taxable property, real, personal, and otherwise—and by several checks these groups appear to be nearly equal[32]—then it is possible to determine the proportion of adult males who owned sufficient property to vote. In five towns examined for 1757—Providence, Cumberland, Glocester, Smithfield, and Little Compton—it was found that from seventy-five to eighty-four per cent (average 79%) of the ratable polls owned enough real property to permit them to vote. Now if ratable polls and adult males are substantially the same group, then about seventy-nine per cent of the adult males, or from fourteen to nineteen per cent (average 16%) of the total population in these five towns, were eligible to become freemen.[33] This does not mean that they *were* freemen, but it indicates that there were no legal obstacles in their way if they wished to vote. Since these five towns were probably typical of the whole colony, it is reasonable to assume that in 1757 a substantial majority of the adult males or about sixteen per cent of the total population were eligible to be freemen on the basis of property. Certainly property qualifications at this time were not oppressive if three-quarters of the adult males could vote if they wanted to.

By 1760 the paper money difficulty had improved and a more stable system of lawful money had been introduced. In that year the General Assembly fixed property qualifications at £40 of real estate or that which would rent for 40 shillings a year. Still, the eldest son of a freeman was admitted free regardless of any real estate.[34] It is doubtful that the reduction in pounds to lawful money had any adverse effect upon the number of eligible voters since no one seems to have complained about it nor did it become a political issue between the factions.

Despite the conclusion that a sizable majority of adult males in the colony could vote, or at least had sufficient property to become qualified voters, the fact is that very few of these people *did* vote. During the political controversy the population increased from 40,676 in 1755 to 59,678 in 1770.[35] But the number of freemen who cast votes during this time was surprisingly small: about 3600 voted in 1760, 3960 in 1764, 4349 in 1765, 3881 in 1766, 3038 in 1768, and 3662 in 1770.[36] In other words, eight per cent of the population voted in 1760 and 1764, nine per cent in 1765, seven per cent in 1766, five per cent in 1768, and six per cent in 1770. In terms of those who probably held sufficient property, fifty-one per cent voted in 1760, fifty-two per cent in 1764, fifty-four per cent in 1765, forty-seven per cent in 1766, thirty-four per cent in 1768, and thirty-eight per cent in 1770. Although the Ward-Hopkins controversy did not end until 1770, the number of voters reached a peak in 1765 and from that point declined. The violent political dispute between the Ward and Hopkins parties, instead of exciting people to participate in the elections, tended to scare them away. By this time Rhode Islanders already had a reputation for political apathy. Ezra Stiles recorded that in 1749 about half the freemen voted, and that only ninety-six of the 450 eligible Newporters turned in proxes that year.[37]

Add to this the curious fact, which will come up again, that during the controversy some people were paid not to vote, others were "silenced by connexions,"[38] and it becomes increasingly clear why so few freemen bothered to cast votes each spring. When Ward or Hopkins took over the Governor's chair after a colony election, he did so at the direction of a very small minority of the people, a minority even of the adult males, taxpayers, and freemen. The government rested on the will of a small segment of the population not because others could not vote, but because others would not vote. And, what is more, neither Ward nor Hopkins nor their friends seemed anxious to do anything to improve the situation. Probably they were wholly content not to disturb the status quo, for a small number of voters was easy to control for their own political purposes.

## II

The Ward-Hopkins controversy was a political dispute between two factions for control of the government. Politics is the interplay of men, money, and morals; the historian must study the political habits of a people in relation to the forces which helped to develop those habits and the particular brand of politics by which the people governed themselves. Indeed, government by faction would not have been possible without the liberal charter which permitted Rhode Islanders to develop their politics unmolested. At the same time geographical and economic forces helped to shape the ruts of faction into which the freemen allowed the wheels of government to slip.

This smallest of the thirteen colonies extended upwards of thirty miles square; its population in 1764 was estimated by the General Assembly at 48,000 people, more than a quarter of whom lived in either Newport or Providence. The colony was split up one side by the large and beautiful Narragansett Bay which allowed several of the towns avenues of ocean communication. The Bay was choked at its mouth by two large islands; in a corner of the larger, Rhode Island, bordering on a spacious harbor, was Newport, the principal town and capital of the colony. At the northern end of the Bay was Providence, the second town, about half the size of Newport.

Unlike Virginia and Maryland with their tobacco and Carolina and Georgia with their rice and indigo, Rhode Island produced no staple crop that either England or any other part of Europe needed. The lack of a fertile hinterland prevented the colony from producing provisions sufficient even for its own consumption. In this way it differed from the neighboring and larger governments, Connecticut and Massachusetts, which possessed a large, fertile river valley and a forest area for the production of lumber. Yet Rhode Islanders needed, as other colonists needed, the manufactures which only England could supply; each year they imported goods worth about £120,000, sterling, from the mother country but remitted in home-grown products only about £5000 in flax seed and oil and an occasional home-built vessel. The balance of trade between the colony and England was overwhelmingly in the latter's favor. The colony's economy was based on an attempt to pay this debt by other means than direct trade.

The bulk of Rhode Island's commerce was with the West Indies and Surinam, a Dutch colony on the coast of South America, to which Rhode Island ships carried small quantities of cheese, fish, some lumber, a few horses produced at home,[39] and larger freights of lumber, beef, flour, and fish acquired from her neighbors. At the British and foreign islands the ship captains took on mostly molasses which, when unloaded in Newport or Providence, became "an engine in the hands of the merchant." Molasses was the cornerstone of the colony's economy; it found its way into most branches of business. Rhode Islanders traded it in Boston, New York, and Philadelphia for British manufactures, food supplies, and return cargoes to the islands and England; they distilled it into rum to supply the fishing and fur trades in other colonies. They bartered rum for slaves in Africa, and they consumed considerable amounts at home. In 1764 there were more than thirty distilleries in Rhode Island alone; several hundred people were directly dependent upon the manufacture of rum for their livelihood.[40] It is apparent that, lacking a staple commodity, Rhode Islanders were forced into a "circuity of commerce"[41] and a carrying of other colonies' products in order to secure for themselves the means to buy manufactured goods from England. It was a difficult struggle; moreover, it was not always successful.

The business of making a living depended to a large extent, directly or indirectly, upon coastal and foreign trade. There were, however, merchants and shopkeepers in Newport and Providence and plenty of farmers in the country towns who depended upon an intra-colony trade. In 1761 Ezra Stiles, minister of the Second Congregational Church in Newport, estimated that there were eighty-four shops in that town which sold a third of their goods to the local inhabitants and two-thirds to customers who came from out-of-town. The bulk of these goods, of course, came from outside the colony. Newport was not only the entrepôt for the towns in southern Rhode Island but also for Dartmouth, Taunton, and Swanzey, Massachusetts, and Voluntown and Canterbury in New London County, Connecticut.[42] Peter Harrison designed, and several lotteries helped to build, a market at the foot of the parade to facilitate trade between Newport and the outlying towns. Providence, on the other hand, had less foreign trade than Newport but, like its rival, carried on a "vast Home Trade in its own Bowels"[43] and became the trading center for the northern towns. As early as 1721 Nathaniel Sessions opened a cart road west from Providence, serving several Rhode Island towns, to Windham County, Connecticut, with which in 1768 there was "a great and beneficial intercourse."[44] The rise of Newport and Providence as centers of economic activity split the colony in two; half the towns depended upon Newport, the other half upon Providence for economic leadership.

Political leadership went hand in hand with economic leadership. The freemen who looked to Providence as a center for their business interests found it also to be a center for their political interests. The southerners found a similar focus for their politics in Newport. Most freemen in the North supported the Hopkins party because it had their interests in mind when it controlled the government. This was equally true of the southern counties in their support of Ward.

The economic causes of government by faction so far discussed were of long standing, and over a period of years they helped to shape the business of politics in the colony. More immediate economic factors, however, helped to quicken the party spirit which already existed. At the close of the French and Indian War Rhode Islanders found themselves in the middle of a serious depression. The colonists had fought a long and costly war, and, although some managed to improve their lot by devious means, many were adversely affected.

Providence alone lost sixty-five vessels from 1756 to 1764; forty-three of these the enemy captured, and the rest were either plundered, castaway, or lost at sea.[45] A year after the war ceased the government estimated that the colony staggered under a tremendous debt "contracted solely by carrying on the war, of near £70,000, sterling."[46] In addition, the struggle with the French threw the colony's trade out of joint, particularly in the West Indies, and scotched the chief source of income. On top of the damaging effects of the war to the already shaky economy, the colony suffered long and costly drouths in the summers of 1761 and 1762 which "cutt off most of the Crops." A severe winter occurred between the two dry summers; "Numbers of Cattle died for Want of Hay and the People themselves must have perished if large Supplies had not been procured from the other Colonies."[47] Land prices sank "nearly or quite one half in their value."[48] Moreover, the vigorous enforcement in 1763 of the old Molasses Act undercut what little trade was salvaged from the havoc of war. Rhode Islanders were victims of a serious economic depression at the very time that they were bitterly contesting the control of their government. It is not surprising that the freemen should look to government to ease the burdens of their hard times. The farmers and merchants of one section set up in faction against the farmers and merchants of the other.[49] Each candidate for Governor relied heavily upon his own backyard for the bulk of his support; from Newport and Providence radiated the waves of political influence set in motion by Samuel Ward and Stephen Hopkins and their friends.

### III

For a faction to be successful it had to be in power. Control of the government meant the winning of a majority of the freemen's votes, and so the spring election became the focal point of Rhode Island politics. Although the *Newport Mercury* might declare that the "institution of annual elections is the great foundation—the chief cornerstone of English constitutional liberty—" honest Rhode Islanders would have to admit that the blessings of annual elections had been "greatly impaired in this colony, by that accursed enemy to the public virtue, party-spirit."[50]

Elections in Rhode Island in the last half of the eighteenth century were divided into two parts. Each town held an annual meeting on the third Wednesday in April when the freemen chose their town officers for the coming year, their deputies to the General Assembly, and cast votes for Governor, Deputy Governor, ten Assistants, Secretary, General Treasurer, and Attorney General. The newly elected deputies then carried the votes for the general officers to the Assembly which met for what was called the general election on the first Wednesday in May. Here the new deputies convened with the old Governor, Deputy Governor, and Assistants in grand committee and officially inspected and counted the freemen's votes. After the new general officers were determined and engaged, the Assembly settled down—still in grand committee—to the business of electing the colony officers for the coming year: sheriffs, justices of the peace, judges, and clerks.

Although preparations for each election usually began directly after counting the votes of the last one, more intensive planning ordinarily commenced about the middle of February or the first of March and continued until the last justice of the peace was tolled off by the Assembly in May. Political preparation took many forms; it was a time for letter writing, newspaper articles, broadsides, jaunts into the country towns, and party caucuses. Party heroes were extolled and mud was slung; encomium and calumny lay side by side on the same page. "Rancour and Malice" divided the political stage with "Speaches [which] fair Exceeded Lord Campdeen or Mr. Pitt."[51] The methods and practices were "abominations" to the sensitive; to the hardened campaigner they were the pleasures of battle.[52]

A curious characteristic of each election was that during even the hottest party struggles, one side or the other proposed a plan of peace between the factions—usually a kind of coalition—supposedly to heal the breach between the opposing parties. Peace proposals were talked about from 1761 to 1768 when finally each side accepted a plan to join forces and together support a neutral government. Between 1761 and that time part of each party's preparation for the annual contest was spent in discussing these plans of peace to "accommodate the unhappy Differences which had so long distracted the Colony."[53] To say that these schemes were insincere would be an injustice to those freemen who conscientiously hoped to rid the colony of faction. But the plans always favored the party which proposed them, and for that reason they were unacceptable to the opposition.

An example of a disingenuous scheme to end the party strife occurred in 1764 when John Gardner, who had served as Deputy Governor under both Ward and Hopkins, died in office. "His Death," Ezra Stiles knowingly observed, "will cause considerable Change in our little System of Politics."[54] Stephen Hopkins seized upon this vacancy under him to promote, he said, a peaceful settlement of the party differences; with a typical gesture he magnanimously offered Ward the Deputy Governor's job. Ward was indignant; in a pamphlet he declined the offer adding that his acceptance would by no means end the dispute, for, he said, there could be no peace in Rhode Island until Hopkins was out of the chair.

A customary proposal was that both Ward and Hopkins resign all pretensions to the office of Governor, and that the parties select the Chief Magistrate from one town and his deputy from the other— the Assistants to be chosen evenly out of the two contending parties. During most of the controversy the faction which would be deprived of naming the Governor never agreed to this scheme, and no successful plan for compromise was possible for several years. Moreover, some inhabitants were outraged by the "insolence of these popular tribunals" in their bold-faced attempts to end the dispute by dividing the government from stem to stern and dictating who should hold office. One critic loudly charged, "That two parties had for a long time contended for the government; that they at length grew tired of the quarrel; and were now about to share the prize, and enslave the people."[55]

Each party in preparing for an election, after it had exhausted, sometimes half-heartedly, the possibility of a compromise in candidates, printed a prox, or ticket, listing the candidates it proposed for the election. The word *prox* doubtless was derived from proxy or proxy vote, which was what a Rhode Islander cast when he voted in his town meeting for general officers of the colony instead of traveling to Newport to vote at the general election. The charter directed the freemen to vote each year at Newport. When the population and the number of towns increased, it became customary for the freemen who lived some distance from Newport to vote at home by "proxy" for the general officers. In 1760 the Assembly resolved that the free-holders could only vote for general officers at their town meetings in April, eliminating altogether the trek to Newport each spring which, the legislators decided, was injurious to the welfare of the colony "at a Season of the Year when their Labor is absolutely necessary for preparing the Ground and planting the Seed."[56] To prox—Elisha Brown spelled it "procks"—was to vote. A prox, sometimes proxy, was the printed list of candidates a party submitted for the approbation of the freemen. The voter did not necessarily have to approve all the names listed on a party's prox. He could cross out names of candidates whom he did not wish to vote for, and he could write in names which did not appear on either ticket. On occasion a prox was headed by what the party leaders considered an appropriate motto, such as "Seekers of Peace," or "American Liberty."[57] Cantankerous Elisha Brown, with no end of political tricks up his sleeve, printed and distributed, according to his opponents, a spurious Hopkins prox in 1764 to distract an already confused electorate. "You will therefore be cautioned," Stephen Hopkins warned the freemen, "to examine your Votes, before you put them in."[58]

Campaign expenses ran high, probably as high for one party as for the other. However, the historian is not as well informed about the financial arrangements of the Ward party as he is about its opponents. Nicholas Brown & Company served as exchequer for the Hopkins party, and the Browns very obligingly saved every scrap of paper that had ink on it. Each year the Browns listed the contributors to the campaign together with the amounts subscribed. The purpose of the contributions was clearly described on the subscription of 1763:

We the Subscribers Promise to Pay the Sums we have Severaly freely set to our Names, in such articles as may be the most Usefull in procuring the free Votes of the poorer sort of Freemen in this County to be Delivered in for the General Officers, and More particularly them Who's Surcumstances does not admit their Time to the Injury of their Familys Tho for the good of the Government.

Twenty-three of the party faithful subscribed £5023-17-6, old tenor; Stephen Hopkins was high with £800, followed by Daniel Jenckes with £500. The Brown brothers together accounted for £1550 of the total.[59] Rum, fish, and corn were used to procure the free votes of the poor and lazy in Hopkins' own county. Votes in towns in the enemy's territory were purchased with cold cash. In 1767 the Browns warned Gideon Tripp of East Greenwich to expect on Monday next the money for the men he and his friends had engaged "to Vote for our Deputys & to put in Mr Hopkins's prox."[60] That same year the financial committee in Providence sent a hundred dollars to Beriah Brown of North Kingstown to be used with what their good friends there would add to obtain "both Deputies and a Considerable Majority in the Proxies in fav$^r$ of Mr. Hopkins."[61]

The Hopkins party had no monopoly on the timely use of money. Henry Ward often served as campaign manager for his brother, and one year, at least, there is a record of how he and William Ellery scurried around the southern towns lining up subscriptions from the party faithful. They did very well, too, extracting promises of round sums from a number of supporters. On the eve of the election Henry Ward reported to his brother that several of their friends would "assist generously." In fact, he wrote, "Mr. Redwood says he'll give as much as any Man," and Mr. Bannister will advance £5000 "rather than you should suffer by that Scoundrel."[62]

Occasionally it was prudent for a party merely to buy a freeholder's silence at election time when it was known that if he voted it would be for the other party. Ezra Stiles reported that in 1758 only four hundred out of six hundred freemen in Newport went to the polls—"one third lie still, silenced by Connexions."[63] In the hotly contested election of 1764 the Browns complained that Ward and his friends were beating the bushes and taking "Great Pains to Keep our friends at home by paying for their Work &c." If a party leader could not persuade a man to change his vote, it was sometimes possible to pay him to keep away from the town meeting.[64] Indeed, there were several ways to skin an opponent. Purchasing votes was an accepted procedure on both sides, and although lamented by some, it was eagerly practiced by others. Bribery was elevated, if not to an art, at least to a proficiency.

After all the speeches had been made and forgotten, letters written, the newspaper articles, pamphlets, and broadsides read, the peace proposals rejected, the proxes printed and digested, and the campaign funds spent, the weary freemen—at least those who did not "lie still"—struggled to the annual town meetings on the third Wednesday in April and cast their votes. They signed their proxes on the back and delivered them one by one to the moderator of the town meeting who kept a fair register of the names. When all the votes were cast, the Town Clerk certified the number of the proxes for each candidate, sealed up the votes, and presented them to one of the deputies, or an Assistant, if the town happened to have one, who carried them to Newport and delivered them to the Governor or Deputy Governor on the first Wednesday in May.[65]

The procedure was simple, but the chances for fraud—or "alterations" according to Nicholas Brown—were many. It was not unusual for a desperate candidate, in towns where the vote was against him, to take "off a list of all who proxed in order to scrutinize [such] as had no legal right." Nicholas Brown in 1763 advised a party friend who was running for Secretary to do just this, hoping, of course, that the candidate would find fifty or sixty proxes for his opponent which the Assembly could throw out. No doubt, Brown said candidly, some of our votes will be flung out too, but,

as we are strongest when we are joined in Grand Committee we shall do all that Lays in our power to prevail on our Friends to Vote out as many of their proxes and as fue of ours as Can be done Consistently. . . .[66]

General elections were held in Newport "or elsewhere, if urgent occasion doe require."[67] No "urgent occasion" occurred before 1775, and from 1663 until that time Newport was the scene of the meeting of the General Assembly on the first Wednesday in May. The newly elected deputies met with the old Governor, Deputy Governor, and Assistants, counted the votes for the general officers and engaged them; the new Assembly then chose the colony officers for the coming year. Although both houses were not ordinarily full at other sessions during the year, all the deputies and Assistants usually managed to get to this first meeting of the legislature in the Colony House in Newport.

The most exciting general election during the Ward-Hopkins controversy took place in 1761 when Hopkins, supposedly ahead by a handful of votes, was boldly challenged by Ward and a southern dominated House of Deputies. Ezra Stiles reported that between 750 and 800 people were jam-packed in the Colony House when the legislature first sat, and another 400 waited outside in the street. Each candidate stood ready with his friends to avail himself if necessary of the hand voters who milled around the parade awaiting a call for their services. To be sure, hand voting was illegal according to the new election law passed the year before, but both sides would have accepted the proxes, said Stiles, since many freemen "were incensed at the Act as an Abridgmt of their Liberty."[68]

The outcome hung on a "scrutiny" by the Assembly, that is, an examination of the new freemen's qualifications and of the proxes to determine the legality of the votes. Since the Ward faction dominated the new lower house, Hopkins, who controlled the old council, worked to avoid a scrutiny; and when on May 8 the deputies, according to custom, respectfully invited the upper house to join them in order to get on with the business, the upper house just as respectfully declined. Hopkins' stratagem was to insist that his council sit separately in this affair and enjoy a negative on the activities of the deputies. The lower house was enraged at the innovation and argued that a negative voice by the council for scrutinizing the votes was "unconstitutional unprecedented & contrary to the Charter & utterly subversive of the Priviledges & Freedom of the Freemen of the Colony." Moreover, the deputies declared, the Assistants were candidates themselves in this election, and a negative voice put "it entirely in their Power to Establish themselves in their Offices against the Voice of the Freemen."[69] Although the deputies threatened to proceed alone with the election if the council would not join them, Hopkins called their bluff since the proxes were securely locked in the council chamber. Message after message was exchanged; for seven days Hopkins kept the two houses dangling until he wearied the whole lot. The enthusiasm of the hand voters had flagged by the third day, and they soon abandoned Newport for their farms and businesses before either party had occasion to use them. Rumors circulated about the effect of the stalemate. Some people declared that the election was void because it was not accomplished on the day appointed by the charter; others claimed that the election was a fact but simply had not been declared. Still another group whispered that the charter was forfeited; said Ezra Stiles, who saw a bishop behind every tree, the Episcopalians "especially propagated this sentiment."[70]

At the close of the second week of May the deputies were on the point of breaking up the marathon in disgust when Hopkins "let slip a proposal" to the effect that each house—which in this instance meant each party—should choose vote counters to take a list of the proxes for each town and return them to the Assembly. The members willingly seized upon this plan, and when the committee of counters reported, the proxy list indicated a narrow majority for Hopkins. Ward's people had no stomach for continuing the wrangle; the Governor was proclaimed, a new council was formed, and everyone gladly went home.[71] Despite the peaceful conclusion, the Assembly did not settle the main issue. Was the upper house entitled to review the actions of the lower house with respect to admission of freemen and a scrutiny of the proxes? Hopkins, by a combination of compromise and fortitude, had managed to steer the Assembly around the main point and win the election. The next year the same impasse confronted the legislature, and the same expedient—a committee of vote counters—was resorted to. This time, however, Samuel Ward had a majority of the proxes which, his friends took pains to see, did not get lost in the council chamber but were safely lodged with the clerk of the lower house.[72]

Once the general officers had been determined, the first order of business in each new legislature was the election of the colony officers. When the strength of one faction approached that of the other in the Assembly, the struggle remained tense right down to the moment when the last clerkship was decided; the party leaders proceeded with great caution, weighing each move and trying to outguess their opponents. The election of 1764 was extremely close from the choice of Governor to the justices of the peace. Hopkins was the victor by twenty-four of the freemen's votes; four members of the Superior Court took their seats at the bench by grace of three, the fifth by only one vote. Even the militia offices were decided by dangerously small majorities. In fact, said Moses Brown, who was pulling the strategical strings with difficulty, "Some of our Guns Getting very Crooked whereby Gould [,] Randal & D. Mowry Got Shot we Thot propper to Adjurn the House to this Morning 9 O Clock Least we Should Slay many more of our friends."[73]

A faction out of power was as useless as a last year's prox. In order to control the government a party had to win at the polls, and so the spring election became the crux of Rhode Island politics. A faction's success depended upon the wealth of its campaign and the extent to which it was willing to go to secure a majority of the freemen's votes.

This was politics in Rhode Island in the two decades prior to the Revolution. The Reverend David Rowland, minister of the Congregational Church in Providence, branded it "Rhode Islandism" and remarked that a "Surer method cannot be taken to ruine a people." It was characterized by name calling and calumny, political tricks, bribery and corruption; it warped legislation and tainted the courts of justice. "These are practices as detestable to me as can be," Rowland lamented, "For these abominations our land mourns."[74]

The Reverend Mr. Rowland was not alone in his condemnation of factional politics and party spirit; others shared his lament. One has only to scan the colony's newspapers to become acquainted with the ubiquitous complaint against the "baneful influence of party." Englishmen, too, deplored the same evil in their politics; George III frequently denounced the "wicked machinations of faction" and labeled it the "greatest Enemy of this poor Country," while William Pitt wished "to dissolve all factions & to see the best of all partys in Employment."[75]

The words "party" and "faction" were synonymous in the early years of George III's reign,[76] despite Edmund Burke's self-righteous attempt in 1770 to distinguish his "party"—which he identified with the national interest—from the iniquity of faction, connection, and cabal.[77] Either Burke was far ahead of his time or merely deceiving himself, for most Englishmen and Americans would agree with James Madison who saw no difference between party and faction and defined the latter in 1787 as "a number of citizens . . . who are united and actuated by some common impulse of passion, or of interest, adverse to the rights of other citizens, or to the permanent and aggregate interests of the community."[78]

Yet, despite the general condemnation, faction continued unabated particularly in Rhode Island. Although often disgusted by its sordid manifestations, many freemen defended it as part and parcel of self-government, hoping each year to correct it by electing honest men to office—which meant, of course, men of one's own party. More important, Rhode Islanders bore up under factional government because it rewarded handsomely the party in power. Doubtless condemnation was well intended, but after all, Rhode Island freemen, as we shall see, were shrewdly aware of where their immediate interests lay. These were the political conditions which existed in the 1760's when Great Britain decided to remodel her colonial policy in North America.

# CHAPTER II

# MOLASSES BEGINS THE DISPUTE

## I

THE DETERMINATION of the British Ministry in 1763 to enforce vigorously the Navigation Laws and particularly the old Molasses Act came as a complete surprise to the people of Rhode Island. The act which Parliament passed in 1733 laid a prohibitive duty of six pence on each gallon of foreign molasses and four shillings per hundredweight on foreign sugars imported into the American colonies. But it had never been troublesome since it was only infrequently enforced. Rhode Island's commerce which depended primarily on foreign West Indian trade had expanded by ignoring the duties. That Rhode Island was a trading center of importance in 1763 was owing mostly to evasion of the Molasses Act. The collection of duties prescribed by the act was as often winked at by the customs officials as it was by the colony's merchants.

The first blow came on May 1, 1763, when Parliament authorized the naval officers of His Majesty's ships operating along the coasts to make seizures of vessels and goods for violation of the laws of trade. The ships and cargoes seized by the King's officers were to be sold by the court condemning them to the highest bidder, and the net result was to be divided equally between the seizing officers and His Majesty's Exchequer.[1] Rhode Island traders never had much fear for customs officials already in the colonies; but now, in and about their own ports, were armed vessels whose officers, with all the authority of customs officials, were more than willing to board colonial ships and make seizures.

In consequence of the act of 1763 the colonial Governors received fresh instructions directing them to suppress all illicit trade in any shape or manner. Naval vessels, some already in the colonies and some from England, were ordered to the various ports. In all, twenty of these ships of war with a total of 2380 men took up positions in the colonies for the protection of trade.[2] His Majesty's ship, *Squirrel,* with twenty guns, Captain Richard Smith, sailed into Newport Harbor just before Christmas, 1763. Orders from Lord Colville, Commander-in-Chief of His Majesty's sea forces in North America, stationed at Halifax, directed the Governor and all civil magistrates to give the captain "their best assistance in the execution of his duty."[3]

The first reaction, and in most cases the only reaction in Rhode Island, was that the enforcement of the burdensome molasses duty would lead directly to economic ruin. But one thinking individual in the colony saw, too, the danger of robust enforcement to the liberties and rights of the people. When military force was used to compel obedience to law, he wrote, the rights and liberties of the people were in danger. The regular officers of government could exact a general obedience, he concluded, "without the concurrent Assistance of *Swaggering Soldiers* or insulting *Captain Bashaws,* I mean Captains of War ships."[4] This protest was unique in Rhode Island where so much depended upon trade with the foreign West Indies; pocketbooks were ordinarily consulted before liberties and rights.

The original stimulus for official remonstrance against the Molasses Act came from a committee of merchants in Boston early in January, 1764, who sent to the Newport merchants a letter, or "State of Trade," describing the activities in the Bay Colony in opposition to an enforcement of the Act. Its purpose was to unite opposition in order to "defeat the iniquitous schemes of these over grown West Indians."[5] Shortly after the arrival of the Boston letter, Stephen Hopkins published in the *Providence Gazette* "An Essay on the Trade of the Northern Colonies."[6] It was a comprehensive treatment of the peculiar circumstances and difficulties to which the trade of the northern colonies was subjected. Hopkins' essay was popular; William Goddard, printer of the newspaper, reported that it had met with "such universal Approbation," that several neighboring governments reprinted it for the benefit of their people.[7] A few days later several Providence merchants, probably including Stephen Hopkins, put their heads together and produced a draft of a "State of Trade" which specifically described the nature of Rhode Island commerce, "especially so much as relates to the County of Providence."[8] This they sent to Newport where a committee from both towns, drawing on all three of the documents, hammered out a remonstrance and presented it to the General Assembly in special session at South Kingstown on January 26, 1764.[9]

The Rhode Island Remonstrance was a concise statement objecting to the Molasses Act; it clearly described the economic problems of the colony and how the merchants attempted to surmount them.[10] The colony depended upon molasses as the handle of its economy. A six pence duty on the importation of it from the foreign islands was prohibitive and would stop the trade immediately. Moreover, Rhode Islanders imported about 14,000 hogsheads of molasses each year, only 2500 of which came from the British Islands. There was insufficient molasses in all the British Islands to support Rhode Island alone for a single year. What is more, these same islands could only absorb a small part of all the goods and provisions traded each year for molasses. Not only would the enforcement of the duty cripple the economy of the colony and all of New England, but it would prevent the inhabitants from securing the means to buy British goods. The Remonstrance challenged the "horse sense" of such an act.

The Assembly directed the Remonstrance, not to Parliament, but to the Lords Commissioners of Trade and Plantations; it was the first official colonial protest against renewal of the Molasses Act. Before the Assembly met in January it was generally thought that the projected enforcement of the act would excite several legislatures to send home "proper Representations" of the colonies' circumstances.[11] However, none of the legislatures, not even the Bay Colony's, whose "State of Trade" first awakened the Rhode Island merchants to remonstrate, got around to protesting until after the Rhode Island Assembly had approved and voted to send home its objections.[12]

For all the hurry and bustle in Rhode Island, from the arrival of the Massachusetts "State" to the day the Assembly resolved to transmit the Remonstrance to the agent, the subsequent fate of this first protest to the renewal of the Molasses Act was an unfortunate anticlimax. The Assembly adjourned its special session on January 27, 1764. Before returning up the Bay to Providence, Governor Hopkins admonished Henry Ward, the colony's Secretary, to forward as soon as possible an attested copy of the Remonstrance to him at Providence so that it might go home without delay. The Secretary promised speed in this vital matter, and members of the Assembly returned to their homes.[13]

But Henry Ward delayed sending the Remonstrance to Providence for nineteen days. Merchants in that town wrote frantic letters to the Secretary demanding his obedience to the Assembly's act and the Governor's order. Either through habitual negligence or political design, the document did not arrive in Hopkins' hands until February 15. "This was the fatal stroke!" wrote William Goddard; the Remonstrance so long delayed "did not reach home till after the Act for imposing the most grievous duties, &c. upon us, was passed, and everything relating to our trade settled to its ruin, which the *Memorial* had the Secretary done his duty, might possibly have been a means of mitigating."[14]

It is improbable that Henry Ward's conduct can be blamed on his dilatory habits. Ward recognized the importance of the colony's protest and the desirability of its hasty transmission, for he had signed the petition requesting the Governor to convene the Assembly which approved it.[15] It is even more improbable that Ward deliberately intended to thwart the success of the colony's Remonstrance; he must have disliked the molasses duties as much as the next man. Ward had no pro-British sympathies which could have dictated his conduct. The Secretary probably delayed the Remonstrance not long enough—he thought—to injure its over-all effect in England, but long enough to embarrass Hopkins politically in the colony. If the Remonstrance arrived in England soon enough to be effective, yet not so early as to reflect considerable credit in the eyes of the freemen on Hopkins, who was as much as anyone the guiding spirit behind the protest, a political purpose would be served. Henry Ward's conduct, whatever his reasons may have been, was an issue in the election of 1764. The Hopkins faction with the aid of Goddard's newspaper made political fodder of the Secretary's misconduct. To imply that a member of the rival party had deliberately injured the colony's cause against Great Britain was good political ammunition. Henry Ward, however, weathered the storm and mustered enough proxes in April to keep his job as Secretary.[16]

## II

Merchants, customs officials, and naval officers were at each other's throats from the very first attempt to force Rhode Islanders to obey the customs regulations on imports from the foreign islands. The trouble began in January, 1764, when John Temple, Surveyor-General of the Northern District, who was responsible for enforcement of the acts of trade, stormed into Rhode Island from his headquarters in Boston and declared his firm resolution that the Molasses Act of 1733 should be executed with the utmost rigor. This announcement particularly infuriated the molasses traders because two months earlier he "caused it to be given out to the Merchants, that they might expect the same Indulgence . . . as had been heretofore usual." Many suspected a trap, for in consequence of the former statement a number had discharged their ships to the islands. In January, however, Temple visited both Newport and Providence, assembled the customs officials, dictatorially issued new orders, and forced fresh oaths upon them, even on those who had been sworn before.[17] He reserved several oaths of another kind for Governor Hopkins, whom he insolently sent for to administer the oaths to his subordinates.

Temple's plan was to bolster the authority of the customs officers by having the colony's civil magistrates tender the oaths and in that way involve the colonial government in enforcing the acts of trade. Temple may have been successful in this stratagem in other colonies, but he had as yet little experience with the Rhode Island government. The Assembly beat him to it and shortly before his arrival forbade the Governor to swear any customs officials without its bidding; its bidding was not forthcoming in response to Mr. Temple's demands. After damning both Governor and government Temple headed for Boston in a rage vowing that "he would lock up all the Ports in this Colony, in such a Manner, that not a Vessel should come in or go out."[18] One reason for his sudden burst of anger was that while in Newport he had ordered the seizure of the sloop, *Rhoda,* from Surinam, for breach of the acts of trade. Neither he nor the King's Exchequer was the richer for his trouble, for the *Rhoda* two days later after sundown was "got under Sail and carried off by Persons unknown." Temple posted a reward of fifty pounds, sterling, for the discovery and conviction of the offenders, but there were no takers.[19]

The affair of the *Rhoda* set a pattern for what was to follow. From this time Rhode Islanders, and particularly Newporters, kept the colony constantly embroiled with the home government, the customs officials, and the Royal Navy. From the initial attempt to enforce the old Molasses Act, to the repeal of the Stamp Act, the history of Rhode Island is the history of hardheaded resistance to the new enforcement of the laws of trade, to impressment by the Royal Navy, and to Parliamentary taxation. Rhode Island's answer to all of these was a thumping "NO," and although no blood was spilled in the physical struggle, it was not owing to the colonists' lack of vigor.

Trouble with the Royal Navy began in the spring of 1764. Rhode Islanders resented the presence of His Majesty's vessels because these ships and men, in addition to impressing colonial seamen, made smuggling more hazardous than usual. Resentment flared into acts of violence on several occasions, one of which involved the schooner, *St. John,* whose crew got into trouble with the Newporters over some hogs and poultry they had stolen. Before the situation was settled, the gunner at Fort George, with an order in his pocket from two members of the colony's council, had opened fire on the schooner; he was promptly joined by about fifty of the inhabitants who gladly contributed to the cannonading. Gunner Daniel Vaughan later reported that he would have sunk her "had he been so disposed but fearing his orders would not support him in so violent an act he threw the shot accordingly."[20] Captain Richard Smith of the *Squirrel,* another royal vessel at anchor in the harbor, along with one of his lieutenants, immediately called upon the Deputy Governor and council "to demand a proper acknowledgement of the insult" the Crown and the Royal Navy had received. Joseph Wanton, Jr., and as many of the Magistrates as he could scare up, admitted "that the gunner acted by authority, and that they would answer for it, when they thought it necessary." I found them, Captain Smith reported, "a set of very *ignorant council.*" Smith believed that the mob guided the hands of the Magistrates, and he wrote to Lord Colville, his superior at Halifax, that he was certainly sorry they ceased firing "before we had convinced them of their error." He hoped, however, that through Lord Colville's representation the insurrection would "be a means of a change of government in this licentious republic."[21] When Daniel Vaughan, the gunner at the Fort, waited upon the council "to make return of his orders," they wanted only to know why he had not sunk the schooner.[22]

Eleven months later the Governor of Rhode Island received a communication from the Lords Commissioners of Trade "concerning certain disorderly proceedings in Newport" with the explicit orders to return immediately to His Majesty "an exact account of the whole proceeding, authenticated in the best manner. . . ." The Lords of Trade asked discomfitting questions about the efforts of the government to suppress the tumult; what protection did the government afford to His Majesty's vessels; and what, if anything, did the government do when the mob ran loose over Fort George?[23] Samuel Ward's answer to the Lords of Trade was a worthy example of Rhode Island's procrastination in matters which were embarrassing to confront.

Ward, who had replaced Hopkins as Governor for the second time in May, 1765, probably had his finger as close to the pulse of Newport as anyone. When he sat down on June 28 to write to the Lords of Trade in obedience to the King's mandate, he wrote as though he had spent his lifetime on a farm in north Smithfield. Ward agreed as soon as possible to collect an account of the incident. But, he wrote, "as I was not in the administration last year, and was out of town when the affair happened, it will require more time for me to acquaint myself with and prepare a statement of the case properly authenticated, than if I had been present at the time of the transaction." He informed the Lords that the General Assembly did not meet again for the colony's business until the next September. He promised to lay before it a statement of the affair, and at the first opportunity, "with their approbation," to transmit it to His Majesty.[24] The matter ended there. Events occurred in Rhode Island during the summer of 1765 of greater significance than an investigation of a year-old riot. The General Assembly which met in September was busy considering a more serious threat to the colony than punishment for an attempt to sink His Majesty's schooner, *St. John.*

On another occasion the Newporters tangled with the Navy over the impressment of seamen. His Majesty's ship, *Maidstone,* Captain Charles Antrobus, arrived in Newport Harbor early in December, 1764. She had an insufficient number of crewmen aboard, and like other British naval officers her captain resorted to impressment of colonial sailors. The sheriff of Newport County had extracted Antrobus' word that he would not seize townspeople, but the *Maidstone's* crew became careless, and in the spring of 1765 they operated the "hottest Press ever known" in Newport. The people claimed that the threat of impressment by this "Set of Myrmedons" prevented the wood boats from delivering fuel for the town against the next winter. Coasters from the neighboring colonies shunned the port for fear of losing their crews. Fishermen whose vessels the *Maidstone* had fired upon were afraid to leave their berths and so deprived the town of an important food supply. Seamen's wages had advanced almost a dollar and a half a month. The inhabitants could take no more of these arbitrary measures and decided that if Captain Antrobus could not be persuaded to desist from "impressing in the very Bowels of the Town" the people would take positive measures to insure the safety of life and property.[25]

On June 4 shortly after the *Maidstone's* officers had impressed the entire crew of a brigantine from Africa by the way of Jamaica, a mob of about five hundred incensed inhabitants seized one of the *Maidstone's* boats, dragged it to the upper end of town, and there in great tumult burned it to ashes. At the same time the crowd seized Lieutenant Jenkins, one of the ship's officers, and, as Antrobus reported, would have murdered him if it had not been for two men who interfered and prevented any serious personal injury.[26] Governor Ward, who inherited a number of problems when he took over from Hopkins in May, 1765, went to bat for the irate citizens and demanded that Antrobus return all the Rhode Islanders he held aboard his ship. The burning of the *Maidstone's* boat, Ward said, caused him great uneasiness. "Upon proper application"—applying the remedy he was ever willing to use after the damage was done—he would take measures to prevent any similar violent proceedings and to discover and punish the offenders.[27] Antrobus bitterly charged that the Governor and Magistrates were "not at home" at the time of the riot and that he was unable to receive any redress whatsoever.[28]

A few weeks after the burning of the boat Antrobus released the sailors, and Ward agreed to drop the dispute, not without a final retort. The immediate cause of the riot, Ward told Antrobus, was the "extravagant height of imprudence and insolence" of the *Maidstone's* crew in boarding and carrying off from a wood boat one of its two men and hounding the vessel right up to the wharf. And all this, Ward added, on the King's birthday. In justice to the town Ward found it necessary to report that the mob which burned the boat and abused Lieutenant Jenkins consisted "altogether of the dregs of the people, and a number of boys and negroes."[29] The Captain of the *Maidstone* did not agree with Governor Ward in attributing the destruction of the boat to the people's rancor over impressment. Antrobus in his report claimed a seizure he had made was the cause of the riot.[30] But it would have been as unwise for Ward to claim that a legal seizure of illegal molasses was responsible for the riot as it would have been for Antrobus to cite kidnapping of Rhode Island seamen as the cause.

The Captain wrote home that the colony was in such a confused state that no one could expect redress for these licentious acts. The Magistrates, he said, echoing the words of Captain Smith in the affair of the *St. John* the year before, were "a very ignorant and turbulent set of people." Instead of preventing the outbreaks, they were "the planners and countenancers of these riotous measures." Many of the offenders were electors of the Governor, Antrobus added; if the Governor attempted to bring them to justice, he and his Magistrates would be turned out at the next election.[31] The royal customs officials, who had been silent during the affair, reported to their superiors that the firing on the *St. John* and the burning of the *Maidstone's* boat sprang from the lawlessness of the people and "from the principles of the constitution of the government, which is the most popular that can be formed." Certainly what had provoked these outrages could cause other riots and disturbances in the future.[32]

The truth of Antrobus' charge that the officers of the government were the "planners and countenancers of these riotous measures" was evident in the case of the *St. John,* for two of the council had ordered the gunner at Fort George to prevent the schooner from leaving the harbor. If the officers of the colony instigated the burning of the *Maidstone's* boat, they profited by their earlier experience and covered up their tracks. If they did not instigate the later riot, they did nothing to prevent it.

III

Instead of renewing the Molasses Act of 1733, Parliament in March, 1764, enacted the Sugar Act in order to produce a revenue in the colonies for "defraying the expences of defending, protecting and securing the same." The new regulations became effective on September 30, 1764. The act reduced to three pence the duty on foreign molasses. It levied a duty of £1-2 per hundredweight on all white or clayed sugars of the foreign islands carried to the colonies and laid new duties on foreign indigo, coffee, pimiento, Madeira wines, and several kinds of cloth goods. It stopped the importation of rum and spirits from the foreign West Indies and required that American iron and lumber headed for Europe must first go to England. All duties were to be paid in sterling money of Great Britain which was to be entered separately by His Majesty's Exchequer to be disposed of by Parliament as it saw fit for the defense and protection of the American colonies.[33] Rhode Islanders were quick to see that, although the new act cut the duty on molasses in half, three pence was still prohibitive. A gallon of molasses which was worth twelve pence could not bear an import duty equal to one quarter its value. The resolutions passed in Parliament preparatory to the Sugar Act contained also the suggestion that it might be proper to charge certain stamp duties in the colonies.

In November, 1764, the Assembly addressed the King in a succinct statement of grievances against the Sugar Act and the impending stamp duty.[34] The Assembly devised no new arguments against the economic burdens of the Sugar Act but repeated those in the Remonstrance showing that the importation of foreign molasses was the foundation of the colony's commerce. The destruction of this commerce by the three pence duty prevented Rhode Islanders from marketing their exportable goods, from slave trading in Africa, and from making remittances to England for manufactured goods. The petitioners prayed that the King return to their trade its former freedom, and that it be "no further limited, restrained and burdened, than becomes necessary for the general good" of all His Majesty's subjects.

It is curious that the Assembly did not object to a renewal of the Molasses Act and the Sugar Act on constitutional grounds as illegal taxes but complained of the economic unfairness of a prohibitive duty on foreign molasses. Rhode Islanders were not blind to the fact that Parliament was after their money; the recent rigid enforcement of the old act and the preamble of the new act, which described it as a means of obtaining a revenue from the colonies, made this quite clear. It is probable that the Assembly confined its argument to economic reasons against the tax, first because molasses duties had the faint smell of a regulation of trade which the colonists believed was within Parliament's power. Then, in 1733 they had got nowhere objecting to the Molasses Act on constitutional grounds. In fact, at the mention of their charter, members of Parliament had denied that such a charter exempted colonists from regulation by Parliament.[35] Rhode Islanders doubtless believed it was unwise to expose their charter to unnecessary danger when their point could be so strongly made against the import duties on economic grounds, by showing that the tax would destroy their commerce and prevent them from purchasing English manufactured goods. (However, when it became apparent, with notice of an impending stamp duty, that Parliamentary taxation was no isolated experiment in finance but a definite intent with far reaching consequences, and that the new tax had not the slightest connection with the regulation of trade, the Assembly clearly denied Parliament's right.) In the case of the molasses duty the Assembly saw no need to become entangled in a constitutional argument with Parliament which would involve charter rights, when it might accomplish its purpose by focusing on the economic folly of the act. Unfortunately neither an economic nor a constitutional argument staved off Parliament's determination to levy taxes on the inhabitants of America.

Enforcement of the old Molasses Act and the new Sugar Act involved more than molasses traders, customs collectors, and naval officers; it involved, too, the admiralty court in Rhode Island. Since the colony's courts of law were controlled by the General Assembly, it is reasonable to assume that Rhode Islanders were not anxious to be saddled with a permanent admiralty court over which they would have no authority. This was not the case; in fact, the merchants had requested a resident judge during the French and Indian War. These merchants, whose privateers returned to the colony with their hulls laden with booty, could not legally claim their spoils until the cargoes had been judged by a lawful court of admiralty. The existing Rhode Island court had only a deputy judge whose powers his superior in Boston controlled and restricted. The merchants, eager for their prizes and tired of the damages and delays of an inefficient system, requested a resident judge for the colony. On the recommendation of Governor Hopkins, the Lords of the Admiralty appointed Colonel John Andrews of Providence judge of the admiralty court of Rhode Island in May, 1758.[36] The selection of John Andrews insured satisfactory decisions even in a court which had no jury.

As part of the new stringent colonial policy the Commissioners of Customs in London appointed John Robinson Customs Collector of Rhode Island in 1763—although he did not arrive in Newport until the last week of May, 1764. The new Collector, a native of England and a career man in His Majesty's customs service, took his time in getting to his post despite the fact that some months earlier the Lords of the Treasury and Commissioners of Customs had resolved that "every Collector shall reside on his Benefice."[37] Robinson was hardly comfortable in his new quarters in Newport when one of His Majesty's naval officers, Lieutenant Thomas Hill of the schooner, *St. John,* seized ninety-three hogsheads of contraband sugar near Howland's Ferry at the other end of the island. Infuriated that the lieutenant should have cut him out of a prize, Robinson reseized the vessel and cargo, claiming Hill had not taken the proper oaths for this business, and brought the case promptly to the colony's admiralty court. But the Collector should have known better; at least he should have known Rhode Islanders better. Robinson never realized a shilling from his seizure. The court sold the sugar—probably to its original owner—but never demanded the price of it, and although he fussed and stewed over the affair, the Collector never received his share. Later the court took eight months to pay him money due on another account; even then he received only a fraction of the sum.[38] When a customs officer of the Crown met in court a judge recommended by the colony, it was the King's cause which usually suffered.

Owing to loopholes in the statute of 1696 which established admiralty courts in America, the area of their jurisdiction was not precise and was frequently encroached upon by courts of common law in Rhode Island and other colonies. Sometimes a colony court with na-

tive judges and jury would usurp jurisdiction in cases involving violations of the Navigation Acts. Or, if a case did go to the admiralty
court, a local court under colony control might issue a writ of prohibition preventing execution of the judge's decree. Merchants and shipowners, accused of violating the laws of trade, might commence actions in a colony court against the Customs Collector or prosecutor
and in this way delay the procedure of the court of admiralty.

To overcome these difficulties Parliament specifically declared in
the Sugar Act that penalties and forfeitures under the new act or *any*
act of trade could be sued for in the future in a court of record *or* a
court of admiralty. Furthermore, the Sugar Act authorized a Vice Admiralty Court for all America which was established during the summer of 1764. The Lords Commissioners of the Admiralty appointed
William Spry, LL.D., judge of the court and sent him on his way to
America with a "currence of powers with the several judges of Vice-
Admiralty courts already appointed or to be appointed in each province."[39] The people of Rhode Island did not worry themselves as much
about the identity of the judge as they did about where he would set
up court. If under the Sugar Act a prosecutor could choose in which
court he wanted his case tried, Rhode Islanders, like other colonists,
believed that the location of this court would be a matter of great importance. With dismay they learned in October, 1764, that Dr. Spry
and his family disembarked at Halifax, Nova Scotia.[40] There, a thousand miles away, a judge without a jury could determine cases which
heretofore had been settled at the port in which the offense occurred
and often in a court of common law.

Definition and expansion of the courts' jurisdiction did not end
here. Hitherto colonial merchants enjoyed the protection of local
courts when their goods were illegally seized by suspecting officials,
or as Stephen Hopkins remarked, "if seizures were made, or informa-
tions exhibited, without reason, or contrary to law, the informer, or
seizor, was left to the justice of the common law, there to pay for his
folly, or suffer for his temerity."[41] But the Sugar Act seriously under-
mined this protection. If the judge in an admiralty court trial believed
(or as Rhode Islanders put it, could "be prevailed upon to certify") that
there was probable cause for seizure, an innocent merchant, having recovered his vessel and goods, was charged the costs of the trial and

prevented from bringing action against the seizor in one of the colony's courts.[42] The burden of proof was on the colonial merchant, not upon the Collector or prosecutor.

In its petition to the King, the General Assembly complained that the extension of the jurisdiction of the admiralty courts unhappily distinguished Americans from their fellow subjects in Great Britain where the same courts had less power. Furthermore, Rhode Islanders pointed out, this increase in admiralty court authority tended to "deprive the colonies of that darling privilege, trials by juries, the unalienable birthright of every Englishman." A review of the history of the admiralty court in Rhode Island indicates, as we have seen, that the extension of the court's jurisdiction would encroach upon more than constitutional principles. Such an extension would not only deprive Rhode Islanders of reliance upon their own colony courts when necessary, but it would make mincemeat of the carryings-on of an admiralty court which for several years had been in the colony's control and sympathetic to its merchants and shipowners.

In other words, Rhode Islanders had local, peculiar reasons for objecting to the new powers of the admiralty court, because these new powers would cut deeply into local interests—because this new authority, if translated into action, would cost Rhode Islanders money. Constitutional rights are seldom invoked until they are violated, or about to be violated, and constitutional principles are sooner invoked if the violation of them costs people money or renders property insecure. Common law courts under the Assembly's control had for years come to the rescue of colonists subjected to admiralty court jurisdiction. The new law, by allowing prosecutors to sue in an admiralty court for *any* breach of the laws of trade, rendered property, including smuggled property, no longer secure. A single admiralty judge might decide the issue without a jury in *any* admiralty court in America including one as far distant as Halifax, Nova Scotia. Self-interest and constitutional principle lay side by side. From self-interest sprang a constitutional complaint which other colonies could share, and the extensive powers of the admiralty courts under the Sugar Act went into the record as a common grievance.

Rhode Islanders, confronted with the new system of admiralty jurisdiction, did not, at first, suffer as much as they feared they would.

They got their share of molasses despite the pains of John Robinson and the Lords of Admiralty to prevent it. One method of beating the King's officers was clearly indicated in the case of the *Wainscott* and the *Nelly*.

Early in March, 1765, John Nicoll, Comptroller of Customs at Newport, and Lieutenant Jenkins of His Majesty's ship, *Maidstone*, which had arrived in Rhode Island waters the previous December,[43] seized at Providence the brig, *Wainscott*, and the sloop, *Nelly*, for illegally running cargoes of molasses. Collector Robinson, along with Nicoll, who prosecuted the case, could have carried the business to Halifax; but they submitted it for trial in Rhode Island despite disastrous experience with the court there. Probably a trial in Halifax would have been as inconvenient for Robinson and Nicoll as for the owner of the vessels, and since it was notorious that the molasses regulations had been ignored by the ship masters in this case, the Collector doubtless assumed there was little risk in settling the issue in Rhode Island. Robinson, it seems, was slow to learn. There followed a long controversy involving the customs officers, the admiralty court, Governor Ward, and the Commissioners in England which is significant for the light it throws on Rhode Island's defiance of the King's officers in their attempt to enforce the laws of Parliament.

John Andrews, judge, and James Honeyman, advocate, of the admiralty court, thwarted at every step the efforts of Robinson and Nicoll to try the case fairly. They ordered the trial at three days' notice in Providence, not Newport, where the customs officials had every right to expect it. They failed to execute a court order for the examination of witnesses—the only means by which Robinson and Nicoll could assure the appearance of witnesses on the day of the trail. Moreover, the advocate refused even to attend the trial, and Nicoll, the comptroller, was obliged to leave his duties in Newport and stand his own advocate in the court at Providence. When the court did issue a new process to summon witnesses, it was returned unexecuted because the witnesses could not be found, or as one report claimed, because they had absconded. Notwithstanding all this, Judge Andrews pronounced the decree and acquitted both vessels.[44]

Robinson and Nicoll, hopelessly stifled in their attempt to carry out their duties, wrote home to the Commissioners of Customs in

June, 1765, complaining of the conduct of the judge and the advocate of the Rhode Island court. The affair reached the ears of the Commissioners of the Treasury who ordered the Governor to investigate and explain the whole business.[45] Samuel Ward, who was becoming facile in delaying explanations, informed the Lords in November that he woud lay the matter before the General Assembly at the next session when he was sure the Assembly would pursue measures wholly satisfactory to their Lordships.[46]

Collector Robinson and John Nicoll demonstrated great impatience about the whole matter. They complained bitterly to Governor Ward that the trying of cases at no stated time or place had often been a grievance on the part of the subject; but certainly it was an extraordinary state of affairs when customs officials, prosecuting in the name of the King, were obliged to mention it as an inconvenience that they had "laboured under in every Instance when [they] . . . had any Business before the Court." Robinson and Nicoll could conceive that the judge might "discretionally Act his Own Pleasure, as well as to Time as place" for holding court, but "to hold it at his own House, in the Woods, or any other less private place, at any hour of any Day in the Year," was beyond their comprehension. Not satisfied with frustrating the King's officers by admiralty court procedure, Judge Andrews added to their difficulties by suing them for defamation in a court of common law for the letter they had written home in complaint. Not only did Judge Andrews win this case, but he commenced another against Robinson personally for complaining to the Governor.[47]

The affair dragged on for months and even years. The Assembly appointed several committees which failed to act until late in 1767 when one of them, after making "due inquiries," dismissed the customs officials' charges as not having the "slightest ground or foundation."[48] By this time interest in the case of the *Wainscott* and *Nelly* had flagged in both England and America, and when the Commissioners of Customs removed Robinson from Newport to Boston, the colony promptly forgot the whole affair.[49]

Although Collector Robinson was often the object of criticism and abuse, probably the financial reward for his tasks at the Customs House in Newport was well worth the discomfort. Ezra Stiles reported that

Robinson gave his salary of £100, sterling, for his office. William Vernon, a Newport merchant, told Stiles that Robinson pocketed six thousand dollars a year, and the officers under him received half that amount. Vernon added that the merchants at Newport would gladly compromise with the Customs House for £70,000, old tenor, annually.[50]

Defiance of royal officers had become popular in Rhode Island. Twice the people of Newport had committed violence against His Majesty's ships and officers with impunity. The colonial government at the time of the riots, it appeared, was powerless to prevent them and deliberately negligent in discovering the offenders and bringing them to justice. Investigation into these outbreaks at the command of the King or ministry was conveniently thwarted. Royal officers could write home and complain all they pleased about Rhode Island's licentious government and ignorant magistrates. By the time such reports circulated through the ministerial channels and an investigation was attempted, attention became focused on new offenses, and the old ones dropped out of sight.

The Sugar Act was a tax levied by Parliament over which the people of Rhode Island had no control. But Rhode Islanders saw to it that government in the hands of the freemen prevented the enforcement of the tax in Rhode Island. And, what is more, if evasion of the tax meant violence, their control of the government prevented its officers from stopping them or bringing them to justice. For, as Captain Antrobus remarked, a Governor and council who punished their electors would find themselves out of office at the next election. So too, the admiralty court in the colony's hands ignored the violations of the Sugar Act. And in the case of the *Wainscott* and *Nelly*, when an investigation was commenced into the conduct of the judge and advocate, it was hindered at every turn. By deliberate negligence and by playing a waiting game Rhode Island had won out over the King's officers. Self-government meant more than control by faction of the colony's government; it meant an immunity to punishment for violent resistance to the authority of Parliament.

CHAPTER III

OTHER MOTIVES THAN LOVE OF GOD AND COUNTRY

I

ON NOVEMBER 4, 1764, in Providence, Governor Stephen Hopkins called the members of the upper and lower houses of the General Assembly into joint session in order to speak to them. Such an occurrence was not frequent, and Hopkins apologized for imposing upon the members in this way. The dangers which threatened the people's liberty, he said, obliged him to lay before them some "alarming circumstances" with the hope that the Assembly would do all in its power to "avert the impending mischiefs." Hopkins laid before the members a reminder of the burdens of the Sugar Act, passed by Parliament earlier that year, which, he said, were already severely felt. He reported also that a new threat, a stamp tax, then pending before Parliament, would be a still heavier burden. Neither of these "alarming circumstances" were the members hearing for the first time. Both had been topics of earnest conversation among Rhode Islanders for several months; what they had not heard discussed among their friends they doubtless had read in the newspapers.

To this Hopkins added a piece of information that apparently he had lately received. A number of men in the colony, he reported, had petitioned the King to revoke the colony's charter and introduce an entirely new form of government. Upon hearing this there was a great stirring among the members of the Assembly. They directed the Governor to write immediately to the colony's agent in London instructing him to "use his utmost endeavors to prevent the evil intended." Moreover, the Assembly requested the agent to secure, if possible, a copy of the petition with the names of the subscribers.[1]

It is understandable that ominous news about the Sugar Act and stamp duties would provoke the Assembly to action—the legislature dispatched an address to the King complaining about them during this same session. But why did a petition against the colony's charter throw such a scare into the General Assembly? What was there about this charter which made it so valuable in the eyes of the Assembly and most of the inhabitants of the colony? On the other hand, why should a group of men within the colony want the King to revoke it?

That there were several people in the colony who were professed enemies of the charter and Rhode Island's political system was a grim fact frequently thrust in the faces of the two factions. At Newport in 1764 a small group of men, firm defenders of Parliamentary supremacy and tight control over America, formed a cabal in opposition to the virtual independence of the colony. Martin Howard, Jr., an Anglican lawyer, Doctor Thomas Moffat, a Scotch physician from the University of Edinburgh, George Rome [pronounced room], agent for a London mercantile firm, and probably the King's officers stationed in the colony were the principal members of this little "knot of thieves, beggars and transports" as James Otis called them.[2] None of these gentlemen was closely involved in the politics of the colony, although Martin Howard, Jr., attended the Albany Congress of 1754 with Stephen Hopkins and unsuccessfully ran for Attorney General in 1761 on a prox with Samuel Ward.[3] The members of this group in 1764 and early 1765 got the ear of Samuel Hall, printer of the *Newport Mercury,* and frequently contributed to his newspaper essays and letters annoying to the colony's political factions and leaders of the opposition to Great Britain. As early as March, 1764, Ezra Stiles was aware of the hungry Europeans, "nourished in our Bosoms," he said, who "have ingratefully transmitted to the mother Country inimical Accusations which they cannot support."[4] The value of the Newport Junto—however embarrassing its criticism was to the patriotic cause and to government by faction—was that its members often told the truth.

In April a letter printed in the *Newport Mercury* clearly explained the Junto's purpose.[5] A charter, this group believed, was sufficient for the government of an infant state; but when "simplicity of heart, and mutual confidence," was replaced by "licentiousness of manners and universal distrust," then a coercive power was necessary to control and confine the power of the state within its bounds. The charter of Charles II was satisfactory a hundred years ago, but in 1764 this very charter was the source of all Rhode Island's troubles. The people had too much power, Howard's cabal argued; the Crown had too little. Men, by a display of popular talents, rose out of the disorder of the people to rule parties and factions. The pernicious influence of party government permeated every corner of the state; courts and judges were not spared. Can anyone, asked the charter enemies, love so well charter privileges which serve only to thrust forward ambitious and proud men who rule by the folly and weakness of the people who vote for them? Moreover, it was these vain, artful, but powerful leaders "who are loudest in the sound of liberty and charter privileges; and it is truly in their interest to be so." But the people had neither the strength nor the wisdom to effect a change, for a change in leaders in Rhode Island was but a change of faction. "Our distemper is radical," the Newport Junto declared, "and so must be the remedy." Every honest man who truly believed in the welfare of his country should join in facilitating the general reformation in the colonies, which, this group was convinced, Parliament was already seriously considering.

Beginning on September 3, 1764, the cabal published in the *Newport Mercury* a number of letters and essays ostensibly written to encourage the cultivation of hemp, flax, and the raising of sheep within the colony. By taking advantage of the popular attention given to colonial agriculture and home manufacturing since the passage of the Sugar Act and notice of the eventual stamp duties, Howard and Moffat thrust upon the people their own loyal and unpopular ideas about dependence and necessary submission of the colonies to Parliament. Along with technical advice on the improvement of agriculture, a writer, who signed himself O.Z., criticized the spirited remonstrances and exhortations which the colonies had sent to England in opposition to the Sugar Act. It would have been better for all of us, he wrote, if many of these had been suppressed and the illiberal and indecent abuse of the supreme and sovereign power stopped. He suggested "more Moderation & Civility, more Meekness and better Manners."[6] O.Z. had much to say about the profligate politician who, just before election, outdid himself in an attempt to curry favor with the freemen. The money which he spent "debauching the health and conscience of the voter" might serve a better purpose if he dispersed it in small amounts as bounties to his daughters for learning to card and spin wool.[7] Rhode Islanders, O.Z. remarked, were a lazy lot, passionately devoted to rum, sugar, and molasses, but they grew sick at the sight of flax and hemp. Learning to cultivate these plants would be much easier "than playing at Cards, Billiards or Backgammon."[8]

Articles, letters, and essays promulgating the arguments already described appeared in the *Newport Mercury* from early September until March, 1765. The writers alienated their Newport Junto from the inhabitants of Rhode Island by severely critizing not one but both factions which divided the colony into two hostile political camps. Moreover, Martin Howard, Jr., Thomas Moffat, and their friends antagonized the freemen by charging that the source of the party evils was the liberal charter which permitted them through self-government to form these factions. The freemen considered an enemy to the colony's charter a party to all oppressive British regulations; they were not far from right as later events will show. It was the Newport Tories who petitioned the King in the fall of 1764 to revoke the charter of Rhode Island.

Why should Rhode Islanders react so strongly to the Newport Junto? Obviously one reason was because the Newport Tories objected strenuously against colonial resistance to the sugar and stamp taxes. Parliamentary taxation not only violated a constitutional right, according to the colonists, but it also was economically injurious, since it heavily burdened the West Indian trade and by stamps was about to wring sterling money from the normal daily activities of a busy people. Had the Junto only defended Parliament's action in this respect, it would have been enough to make the members the object of bitter resentment. But Howard, Moffat, and their friends were guilty of more heinous crimes; they attacked the charter and system of government and petitioned the King to alter drastically the whole political character of the colony. Even more than taxation Rhode Islanders feared a change in government. A loss of the charter would annihilate a political system which they had nursed along for years to their own advantage and profit. Ward, Hopkins, and their followers fought annually for control of the government for very real reasons. What was there about government and politics in Rhode Island which the Junto hoped the King would alter and which the colonists were ready to defend at all costs?

II

### THE GENERAL ASSEMBLY AND POLITICAL PATRONAGE

The Ward-Hopkins controversy was a political dispute, but its roots were firmly tangled with the economic life of the colony. Since Rhode Island's economy was poor at best, the lack of a staple crop put each inhabitant on his mettle to derive a sufficient income either directly or indirectly from trade or agriculture. Indeed, there were several wealthy merchants in Newport and Providence who had successfully pursued a "circuity of commerce" and pocketed healthy profits. But the general run of people had difficulty supporting their families by trading other people's goods and operating small farms. Samuel Ward was a prime example. Rhode Islanders were constantly on the lookout for new sources of income. Over the years it became habitual for a number of freemen to look to the colony government as a means of support. Moreover, if the government could be shaped to ease the lot of the freemen in one section at the expense of the freemen in another, then that government was worthy of encouragement.

Men in politics group together in order to accomplish a political purpose. In this case the political purpose of each party was the same: to control the government for the rewards this control offered. It was a political system in which jobs with fees were distributed as rewards to the party faithful and to others to insure their votes and loyalty. A General Assembly captured by a faction could shift the burden of taxes for the benefit of a town or section. Lastly, political victory meant an excellent opportunity for the dominant party in the legislature to elect courts of justice which would look kindly on plaintiff or defendant who toed the party line. According to one contemporary observer, Ward, Hopkins, and the top men in their parties "had nothing in view, but to keep or acquire to themselves and adherents all the profits and emoluments of the government."[9]

To obtain an office if one's party was in power was probably not a difficult task. The critics of government by faction emphasized this point and chided the officeholders for prostituting themselves to the "baleful influence of party." "To be a thorough party man, as the phrase is," remarked one bitter critic, "comprizes all that merit necessary to obtain a place of profit and trust in the government."[10] "To commence a party man," another commented, "is to renounce Honour and Honesty and to gain an *Office* is to become a *Rascal*."[11] But to obtain the emoluments of government and the places of profit and trust, one had to be on the winning team each May. William Ellery of Newport put it simply in a letter to Samuel Ward: "If our Enemies should have a Majority in the Lower House at the Next Election the consequences will be that your humble Servant with your other friends will be turned out of Office."[12]

When one faction replaced another at the May election the change was felt from the Governor himself to the Captain of Fort George in Newport Harbor, from a justice of the peace in Smithfield to a clerk of the Inferior Court in Kings County. Such a change in control did not mean that all the incumbents lost their jobs. But a number of offices was subject to the will of the faction in power, and a shift in these offices altered significantly the complexion of the government.

Ward and Hopkins struggled annually for the governorship, probably the office most sensitive to the will of the freemen. (During their ten year rivalry Ward was successful in only three elections.) But the Governor sat only as a member of the council, and he had no veto power over the doings of the legislature. Control of the government meant control of the General Assembly, and a faction, in order to wrest this control from its opponent or keep what it had won in a previous election, was obliged to scramble to secure deputies and Assistants in the party's favor. This brought politics right down to the town meetings where these officers were elected by the freemen. The turnover in the General Assembly accurately reflected the frequent shift of parties in this period of "intestine broils."

## DEPUTIES

The House of Deputies was elected twice a year by the freemen in their town meetings. According to the charter, Newport sent six representatives, Providence, Warwick, and Portsmouth, four each, and the remaining towns two apiece. From 1759 to 1765 twenty-seven towns theoretically sent sixty-four deputies to the lower house each May and October.[13] Not all of these deputies were present at each session, and in May the number was consistently larger than in

October.[14] Election of deputies was as much a party affair as the struggle to choose a Governor. But because of the inconsistent attendance of the members of some of the smaller towns, particularly New Shoreham on Block Island, and because the deputies were elected twice a year, it is difficult to determine exactly the turnover of members when the factions changed. For instance, if a deputy from Warwick elected in April of any one year acted against the wishes of his constituents, he could be replaced in October, although a major party shift might not come until the next annual election six months later.

Nevertheless, a larger turnover in Assembly seats occurred each spring when a colony-wide election was held; and, moreover, the number of changes usually jumped when one faction replaced the other. The significant point is that during the sharpest party struggle the lower house was in a state of continual flux. When Ward took over the government for the first time in 1762, thirty-one (48%) changes occurred in the house which then contained sixty-four members. Hopkins bounced back in May of 1763 and along with his victory thirty-one seats again changed hands. Probably the hottest campaign of the whole controversy was waged in 1767 when after two years of Ward the northern faction outdid itself, and Hopkins took the prize by a larger majority than either had previously won. Accompanying this victory was a 59% shift in the lower house: thirty-nine of the sixty-six members were newcomers.[15] In 1769, after a coalition government had failed miserably to end the controversy, a Hopkins-backed candidate took over the Governorship, and *forty* of the last year's crop, or 61% of the deputies, found themselves without seats. This was faction, good and earnest.

The first duty of each new house after greeting old friends from previous administrations was to choose a speaker and clerk. During the most pressing party struggles between 1761 and 1767, the speakership shifted frequently in favor of the faction in power. But in 1767 with the election of Metcalf Bowler, a Ward man from Portsmouth and Newport, the contention ceased. Probably he performed his function so well that even the most staunch party men did not dare to suggest a replacement regardless of which party was in power. Anyway the deputies elected him biyearly until 1777.[16] Nor did the clerk's job respond to faction; Josias Lyndon of Newport served faithfully in that post for almost a generation.

## ASSISTANTS

There was no doubt about the effect of government by faction on the ten Assistants who sat with the Governor and Deputy Governor as an upper house. The freemen, it will be remembered, chose the Assistants or Magistrates each spring at the annual election. When the freemen re-elected Hopkins in 1761, they replaced only two of the Assistants who had served with him. From 1761 to 1770 the government changed hands six times. In none of these six elections were there less than six changes among the Assistants. On three occasions, 1765, 1767, and 1768, the whole upper house was replaced. In 1769 the more stable, Hopkins-dominated government headed by Joseph Wanton placed eight new men in the upper house when it rescued the colony from the evils of coalition. From then on the number of new Assistants diminished rapidly, there being but five replacements in the next three years.[17]

## OTHER GENERAL OFFICERS

Three other general officers were annually elected by the freemen: the General Treasurer, Attorney General, and Secretary. These were important positions in the business of government, and although it was the privilege of the freemen to elect them, the same men were returned to office year after year. In the case of the General Treasurer and Attorney General the qualifications were probably sufficiently specialized to warrant a continuation in office of the same people. What is more, the General Treasurer had to give bond with good securities to the tune of £10,000 "for the true and faithful Discharge of his office." This may have discouraged some takers. Although he received no fees, the General Treasurer was one of the few salaried officers in the colony receiving for his pains £38, lawful money, a year. The government paid the Attorney General no salary but allowed him fees for his several duties, one of which was ten shillings "For every Criminal executed to Death."[18]

## The Secretary

The office of Secretary was a coveted position and bears more looking into than some of the other offices, for the Secretary carried considerable weight in the political affairs of the colony. He sat with the upper house, kept its journal, and carried on a large portion of the colony's business which was not actually transacted on the floor of the Assembly. The freemen elected the Secretary each spring along with the Governor and other general officers, but, despite the fact that each party struggled continuously to put its candidate behind the Secretary's desk, the Ward group enjoyed a monotonous success in filling the position. In fact, from 1714 to 1797, with the exception of a fourteen year period from 1733 to 1747, either Samuel Ward's father or one of his brothers was Secretary of the colony. For reasons that are not altogether clear the Secretary's post stayed in the Ward family for almost seventy years.

That the Secretary's job was politically important to each faction is indicated by the scramble for the job which resulted when Thomas Ward died in office in late December, 1760. Samuel Ward went promptly to work in behalf of his other brother, Henry, whose integrity and capacity for the job, said Samuel, "will not be disputed." Samuel Ward barked orders like a party whip, and the Ward machine clanked and groaned in several southern towns, for it was general knowledge in Newport, he recorded, that two members of Hopkins' party "went out yesterday Morning to ingage the Members of the Gen'l Assembly in their Interest." He also wrote to his wife in Westerly asking her upon receipt of his letter to request one of his lieutenants "to take his Horse next Morning" in order to rouse the friendly members of the Assembly in the southern towns and prepare them for battle in the coming session. This was an affair, he wrote, of great consequence, not only to his brother Henry but to all their political friends, "for should the opposite Party obtain a Secretary in their Interest It would be a vast Damage to the main Cause next Spring."[19] What Ward meant was that victory in the coming election would be extremely difficult without one of their faction in the Secretary's chair. Eight days later the Assembly met in Providence and chose Henry Ward Secretary for the remaining part of the year "in the room of Thomas Ward, Esq., deceased."[20] The freemen re-elected him annually to the same position for the next thirty-six years, and only death deprived him of it several years after Rhode Island condescended to join the federal union. Try as they would the Hopkins gang could not dislodge him, and they finally ceased to try.

As Secretary, Henry Ward was a key figure in the colony's politics. He had his finger in every pie, and doubtless his political influence was as extensive as that of the Governor. There was no salary connected with the job, but no record survives to show that Ward complained of the fees he received for his varied duties. The digest of laws listed seventeen in 1767, one of which was eight shillings a day for attendance at the General Assembly.[21] Accounts of the General Treasurer indicate that considerable sums of money were paid out to the Secretary "at Sundry Times."[22] There is little doubt that the Secretary's post was as lucrative as any within the gift of the freemen.

In the eighteenth century Rhode Island did not produce a more thoroughgoing party man than Henry Ward. We have already seen that his delay in forwarding to Providence the Remonstrance against the old Molasses Act became a political issue in the campaign of 1764. Several other instances demonstrate a calculated intent on the part of the Secretary to serve the interests of party and friends at the expense of the public good. In 1762 he collaborated with Samuel Hall, the Newport printer, to cheat William Goddard of the Providence press out of any share of the government's printing—and this contrary to the direct vote of the legislature.[23] About this time he delayed sending the acts and resolves of the Assembly to towns in the northern half of the colony, although some people, including William Goddard, were convinced that it was more design than negligence on the Secretary's part. Matters came to a boil when Ward was late forwarding a new election law to Providence and other towns where the clerks were not in his party. The consequence was that a number of freemen were unable to vote in the next election because the new law arrived too late for them to be legally propounded before the annual town meeting. This did not happen to Henry Ward's friends, however, because they received the law in *printed* form in plenty of time to qualify properly for voting. The *Providence Gazette* hit hard in its criticism of such goings-on and remarked that the exposure of his conduct would be as popular with the Secretary as "letting in the Light of the Sun upon a Nest of Owls."[24]

Ward and Elisha Brown were good party friends—so good that in

1763 the Secretary certified an unpassed bill of the legislature allowing Brown to adjust a large and long standing debt with the colony
at a startling reduction without interest. Several inhabitants were
shocked to learn that the government "should be taken in by such a
Piece of Artifice of Mr. *Brown* and his Friend the Secretary."[25]

But Henry Ward lived a charmed political life. He could aid a
party friend to cheat the government out of funds; he could deliberately delay the distribution of acts of the Assembly to towns which
did not vote for his brother; he could flout the will of the legislature
and favor the Newport printer over Goddard of Providence. He could
do all these things and more; yet at each election he managed to poll
a majority of the freemen's votes regardless of his opponents' efforts
to pry him loose from his post. As a politician, Henry Ward was a
huge success.

III

The charter which Charles II granted to Rhode Island in 1663
gave the General Assembly power "to elect and constitute such
offices and officers, and to graunt such needfull commissions, as they
shall thinke ffitt and requisite," for managing and dispatching the
affairs of the government. The Assembly exercised this power
liberally and by 1764 it elected each year, including judges of the
courts and militia officers for each county, about 250 officers.[26] On the
first Wednesday in May the Assembly met in the Colony House in
Newport at the head of the parade in joint session of both houses
and tolled off the votes for sheriffs, justices of the peace, judges, and
a number of other public servants. Control of the Assembly, of course,
was absolutely necessary for the successful carrying out of party
purpose in doling out jobs where they would do the most good. The
turnover in some of these jobs will indicate their importance in the
eyes of the party generals.

SHERIFFS

The Assembly annually elected a sheriff for each of the five
counties at the general election in May. A sheriff's office in Rhode
Island was not a salaried position, but in the digest of laws for 1767
there was a list of twenty-three separate fees which a sheriff was

entitled to in line of duty. Among these were one shilling, six pence, for each day's attendance at court and four pence for "turning the key on every person committed."[27]

Sheriffs' jobs were sharply contested in the General Assembly. In 1764 Hopkins beat Ward by twenty-four votes out of 3960.[28] The majorities were small all the way down the line. Of the five sheriffs elected not one went home with a larger majority than six; John Brown of Bristol was possessor of his office by grace of one vote.[29] This was not always the case. After two years of the Hopkins faction the freemen switched to Ward and his friends in 1765. Ward won by a comfortable margin and the sheriffs placed in office under his party were elected by majorities of at least twenty votes.[30]

A sheriff's office was important politically. Hopkins and his sponsors, the Brown brothers of Providence, carried on vigorous political business with Beriah Brown of North Kingstown who was regularly sheriff of Kings County when Hopkins was in power; for Sheriff Brown was one of the few political links Hopkins had with this southern county which was consistently Ward territory.[31] Forty dollars was not too much to assist Walter Chaloner in his debut as sheriff of Newport County in 1767, and the Hopkins faction paid that sum to a Mr. Browning, "for not being in his Way."[32]

The election of sheriffs during the years of the controversy followed a definite political pattern. When the factions shifted, the slate of sheriffs shifted with it. When the faction remained in power, all, or a majority of the sheriffs, remained in office. For instance, when Hopkins was Governor from 1758 to 1761, not one sheriff budged from his spot. When the government was stabilized in 1769 by the Wanton-Hopkins regime, the shift in sheriffs was negligible, there being but one change in the next four years. From 1761 to 1769, however, each faction upon coming to power brought its own sheriffs with it.[33] A curious exception occurred in the election of 1762. Ward topped Hopkins at the polls by a slim margin but only one sheriff— Providence County—was replaced. The reason for this lay in the fact that although Hopkins won the Governorship the year before, the Ward faction had succeeded in placing a sizable majority in the lower house.[34] Out went the sheriffs of the preceding Hopkins administration; out, too, went the Chief Justice of the Superior Court and Samuel Ward, himself, took his place. So when Ward completed the turnover by winning the Governorship in 1762, the party's work, as far as sheriffs were concerned, was already accomplished. Only one change took place that year; the Assembly chose Paul Tew, sheriff of Providence County, to replace Elisha Brown who probably was too proud to take the job after having run hard for Deputy Governor and lost.[35]

Sheriffs frequently reappeared on the scene with party regularity. Beriah Brown of North Kingstown was elected to the office each spring from 1757 to 1776 except for the four years the Ward faction controlled the Assembly. Allen Brown held the office in Providence County for four years, three of them under Hopkins, until 1761 when the Ward group captured the Assembly but not the Governorship. He appeared again in 1763 with the return of Hopkins. Other men were similarly rewarded at election time when the party was successful. The Ward faction had its favorites, too, but only three political victories and an extra year's control of the Assembly did not give an opportunity for the same regularity their opponents enjoyed.[36] It is obvious that the election of sheriffs in the General Assembly was strictly party business. The offices were the rewards of victory, and both parties took advantage of the opportunity to serve their friends.

### JUSTICES OF THE PEACE

The officers of government elected by the freemen or chosen by the General Assembly for the most part were fixed in number either by the charter or by act of the legislature. There was only one Governor, and no one was so presumptuous as to suggest that there be more. The charter fixed the number of Assistants at ten; it also determined the number of deputies which each town could send to the Assembly. The only way to increase the number of deputies in the lower house was to establish new towns in the colony. This was twice accomplished in the Ward-Hopkins period, once in 1759 and again in 1765, when Johnston and North Providence were set off from the town of Providence.[37] The number of sheriffs, judges, and clerks was settled by law, and the freemen did not look to the Assembly to increase them.

The General Assembly by its own act had power to choose

annually "so many Justices of the Peace, for each respective Town in the Colony as to them shall seem needful and requisite, for the better Administration of Justice." The authority of a justice of the peace extended throughout the county in which he lived in criminal affairs and for the preservation of the peace. In matters of a civil nature his jurisdiction was confined to the town for which he was elected. In addition to this the justices in each county, or any five of them, were a Court of General Sessions with power to try cases from which appeal could be made to the Superior Court.[38] The Assembly did not fix the number of these justices, and one would expect that as the population of the colony grew larger, the number of justices would increase. This was exactly what happened, but the rate of increase took some curious spurts during the Ward-Hopkins controversy, particularly when the Hopkins party was in power. In 1761 under Hopkins the Assembly chose 138 justices of the peace for that year. When Ward replaced him in 1762 the number of justices increased only slightly to 141. However, when Hopkins returned in 1763 the Assembly added ten more to bring the number to 151. Doubtless believing that re-election in 1764 was confirmation of its administration, the legislature jumped the number of justices to an all time high of 167. The Hopkins faction in two years' time added twenty-six justices of the peace to the list of civil offices. Each justice, of course, received fees for his labors; the number of separate fees listed by the Assembly in 1767 was sixteen including three shillings for "marrying persons."[39]

On Ward's return in 1765 the Assembly put its foot down on the spiraling increase, promptly reduced the number of justices to 164, and even chopped off another the next year. The Hopkins faction when it recovered the government in 1767 doubtless realized that the game had ended, for the number of justices elected remained about the same as the previous year.[40]

The turnover in justices of the peace followed the shift in parties. One might expect a considerable change in these officers anyway because of the large number chosen each year. But the big changes came when one party replaced the other. At Hopkins' comeback in 1763, ninety-nine new justices of the peace, or sixty-six per cent of the total, took office. Upon his re-election in 1764 only thirty-eight changes were made (23%). A similar turnover (55%) took place in 1765 when Ward and his friends won at the polls. The next year the freemen re-elected Ward, and the Assembly replaced only forty-four of the justices. The record for 1767 is not complete since neither the Providence nor the North Providence figures are available. But without these, eighty-five new justices, or more than half of the total, were commissioned to serve.[41]

There is no doubt that the offices of justice of the peace were political jobs and reflected the will of the party in command. What is more, many of them doubtless wielded political influence in their respective towns which would make it important to the ruling faction that the offices be placed in friendly hands. Politicking between Providence and North Providence suggested this in 1767. Benjamin West of North Providence requested in a letter to Moses Brown, a Providence deputy in the legislature, that a Mr. Foster be made a justice of the peace. He will not, wrote West, oppose "rejunction of the Two Towns"; he thinks that if he "acts in any way it will be in favor of it." The rejoining of a section of North Providence to Providence was a hot political issue in the election of 1767 and dear to the heart of Moses Brown who took personal responsibility for it in the next session of the legislature. A justice of the peace on his side in the town involved would be a distinct advantage. In addition, West reported to Moses Brown that Foster "has likewise intimated to me that he shall not oppose Mr Hopkins for the future."[42] This was probably sufficient to insure Moses Brown's interest in Mr. Foster, but unfortunately the list of justices for North Providence for that year is omitted from the printed schedules of the session. Since the Hopkins party won by a comfortable majority, it is very probable that he got the job. When the factions were fairly even in the legislature, election of justices was keenly contested. For example, when Hopkins nosed out Ward in 1764, two justices from South Kingstown won their offices by margins of two votes.[43]

## MISCELLANEOUS OFFICERS

During the Ward-Hopkins controversy there were several officers elected each May by the Assembly who did not reflect the shift in factions. These were the Grand Committee, or trustees of the colony, who signed the bills of public credit, the mortgage officer, the sealer of weights and measures, and the public notary for the town and county of Providence. The same men served in these positions year after year with monotonous regularity.[44] This does not mean that these offices were not contested at the general elections. Henry Paget, for example, who was chosen public notary from 1760 to his death in 1771, won his first election by a margin of only twelve votes.[45] Henry Paget did not rely solely on whatever compensation he received for his notary job, for in 1765 the Surveyor-General appointed him Searcher and Preventive Officer of His Majesty's Customs in Providence.[46] Edward Thurston served as a colony trustee, mortgage officer, and sealer of weights and measures from 1761 to 1776. One of these jobs returned him a salary, but it is impossible to determine from the treasurer's accounts which it was. Anyway, he received £100, old tenor, a year, until 1771 when the Assembly began to pay him in lawful money. It is doubtful that Thurston's salary turned his head, for in lawful money it amounted to three pounds, fifteen shillings, *per annum*.[47] The Assembly did not re-elect Edward Thurston to his three offices in 1776. Instead it ordered the sheriff—who doubtless received a fee—to bring him before the Assembly to answer for his conduct as a Tory.[48]

The lower house was jealous of its power as part of the Assembly to choose the colony's officers, and it continuously defended its right to exercise this power in grand committee of both houses as directed by the charter. The reason for this is understandable when it is remembered that the lower house consisted of sixty-six members in 1765 and the upper house of twelve, including the Governor and his deputy. A faction with a reasonable majority in the lower house could always outvote the council and in that way thwart even the wishes of the Governor.

The reluctance of the General Assembly to share the power of appointing officers can be seen in the fact that the Governor had only one office in his pocket to dispose of as he pleased. This was the Naval Office; the man holding it was a local customs officer who was charged with taking entries of vessels. He was responsible, too, for the observance of the Navigation Acts and the maintenance of Beaver Tail lighthouse on the southern tip of Conanicut Island. There was no salary connected with the appointment, but the officer was entitled to a number of fees for such tasks as entering and clearing vessels, taking bonds for enumerated goods, and signing certificates. The value of his fees equalled those of the King's Customs Collector in the colony.[49] Probably the chief source of the Naval Officer's profits was not fees but gratuities and other payments made by the merchants and traders for services rendered.

Since the Governor alone appointed the Naval Officer, the office was bound to be a political plum. A glance at the list of incumbents is sufficient to indicate that they shifted with the same regularity as the sheriffs and justices of the peace.[50] It is apparent, however, that all the profits of the Naval Office, which must have been considerable, did not always find their way into the pockets of the man who held the post. It was customary for the Naval Officer to share his profits with the Deputy Governor; in fact, such an arrangement was the only condition under which Darius Sessions would accept second place on the ticket in 1769. The next year when the Ward faction sounded out Samuel Nightingale about running for the Deputy Governorship, he was willing, he said, only if a proportion of the profits of the Naval Office "be applyed to ease the Burthens of this and no other Gent.ᵐ."[51]

## MILITARY OFFICERS

In addition to civil officers the General Assembly chose at each general election thirty military officers for the five regiments of the colony. The appointments ranged from colonel to ensign; each received a commission from the Governor.[52] Neither salary nor fee was attached to these offices, but considerable prestige was associated with a commissioned office in each county regiment. Like many of the civil offices, these appointments hinged on politics, and it became prudent to dole them out to political friends throughout the colony. Party subordinates in the towns brought pressure to bear on the members of the Assembly to insure the appointment of the right people to the right places. "Don't fail putting Jos. page Leuit," one party adviser wrote to Moses Brown in 1764; "he Says he is yet True for hopkins."[53] Doubtless Moses Brown could not resist such acceptable qualifications.

## IV

### SALARIES AND FEES

Political jobs meant more than votes and loyalty to the faction in power; political jobs meant remuneration to those who accepted them. There were few offices in the government of Rhode Island which did not compensate the incumbents with either salaries or fees. True, the deputies and Assistants received no fixed payments for their services or attendance, but a glance at the *Colony Records* and the General Treasurer's Accounts is sufficient to indicate that sums of money were frequently paid out to committee members, of which there were many, for particular duties, services, and expenses by the day. The thirty military officers in the five counties were forced to get along on the respect paid to them by their friends and neighbors.

The offices of Governor and Deputy Governor may still have been places of honor, but they were hardly places of profit as far as salary was concerned. In 1761 the General Assembly paid Stephen Hopkins £1400, old tenor, that is, inflated paper currency, "for his Salary and extraordinary Service, for the Two Years Last past."[54] In 1768 the Assembly began paying the Governor in lawful money and voted him that year an annual salary of thirty pounds.[55] If the Deputy Governor intended a career in public office, it was a good thing for his dependents that he derived some of the profits of the Naval Office. Elisha Brown, who was Deputy Governor under Ward in 1765 and 1766, received only six pounds a year for his pains.[56] This was raised to fifteen pounds in 1767,[57] but Brown was no longer in the government.

The Governor of Rhode Island was not entirely dependent upon his salary for his income. Like other officers he was entitled to fees for some of his duties. Chief among these was a shilling, sixpence (1767), for "every Commission he shall sign for any Officer in the Colony."[58] The freemen and the Assembly chose yearly more than 250 officers, and each received a commission from the Governor. If the Governor's hand was tired after each general election in May, he might have comforted himself with the fact that his pockets were full. In 1763 the General Treasurer paid Stephen Hopkins £329-10, old tenor, or almost half the value of his salary, for signing commissions. During January, 1766, Samuel Ward received a total of £219-10, old tenor, for the same reason. Joseph Wanton had been in office only six months when the treasurer paid him £30-1, lawful money, a sum equal to his salary, for the commissions he signed during his first administration.[59]

There were other ways for a Governor to clear expenses than to sit in office and wait for salary and fees to come to him. Few of the following activities of Stephen Hopkins were facts by his own admission; rather they were accusations from the pen of Samuel Ward leveled at Hopkins for his conduct during his wartime administrations. Ward accused Hopkins of using "every art to gain for himself and his family, posts of profit," and since he made the most of every employment, "it is natural to believe such a man is influenced by other motives than Love of God and Country." Ward claimed that as a member of the Committee of War Hopkins received large sums from the government, and that his two sons enjoyed lucrative jobs during the war. Hopkins demanded and got, Ward argued, fifty to sixty pounds for each letter of marque and even more for commissioning privateers when Governor Greene during the last war had been content with only five. Who, then, were the best friends to their country, asked Ward, "those who have maintained themselves and their Families out of the publick money, or those who have generously served the Colony without any way, Consulting or promoting their own Private Interest?" For the above statements Hopkins sued Ward for libel—and lost.[60]

There was also the affair of the sugars in 1761 which involved Stephen Hopkins up to his ears. A large cargo of sugar, illegally imported into the colony, was seized by the government and put up for trial. Hopkins got more than his share of the cargo by taking the King's third for himself. The affair did not rest well with a number of the inhabitants who believed he had "acted a Very Singular part and What no other Would have Done."[61] Hopkins seemed safe until the Ward faction captured the government, when the Assembly ruled that he forfeit £10,665-12-6, old tenor, and he reluctantly paid that amount to the General Treasurer in April, 1762.[62] Hopkins lost the election which took place a few days later.

The Governor, Secretary, Attorney General, sheriffs, justices of the peace, naval officer, judges and clerks of the courts, and clerk of the lower house were all dependent upon fees allowed them by the General Assembly. But fees which remained static year after year were inadequate returns, it seemed, for the annual struggle a faction underwent to win an election. At least that was what must have crossed the minds of the Hopkins faction after their boss was re-elected in 1764. The legislature had not touched the fees since March, 1757, when they were regulated under Hopkins who was then Governor.[63] One of the items of business in the May session, 1764, following the general election, was the passage of an act which hoisted the fees all along the line from the Governor to the clerks of courts and established them in lawful money.[64]

The homemade ink, manufactured from rain water and other ingredients by Henry Ward,[65] was not dry in the journal of the upper house when a lengthy protest against the act was presented to the Assembly signed by ten of the members. The protest complained that the fees were unfair because they came out of the "poorer Sort of People," and, what is more, they "were full high before." Secondly, it appeared that the act was passed "just at the Rising of the General Assembly, when there was but a thin House." Furthermore, the ten complained, the act passed this rump session of the Assembly by a majority of only eight votes out of but forty-four members. (The lower house numbered sixty-four at this time.) Lastly, the deputies declared, "a great Number of them were Judges of the several Courts, and Justices of the Peace, and were voting Money into their own Pockets, which in our Opinion is unjust."[66] Not only did a faction work hard to win the profits and emoluments of office, but once in power it was good policy to improve these emoluments and profits of office. The ten deputies who signed the protest were representatives of towns in the southern part of the colony which were consistently Ward areas.

Those who protested the raising of the fees did not have long to wait for relief from what they considered an injustice. In October, 1764, a new house of deputies was elected by the freemen, and twenty, or almost a third, of the representatives were replaced. Immediately the new Assembly repealed the act, provided that it be continued only until a new table of fees could be established. The next month the May act was repealed outright, and a new table enacted in its place lowering slightly the whole list of fees. But this did not satisfy the Wardites, for when that faction moved into the Assembly in 1765, it voted a further reduction, placing the fees close to what they had been before the Hopkins group tampered with them.[67] It was the fashion, the Brown brothers complained, "for one party to oppose whatever the other party proposes."[68]

## V

By the time the Tory Junto petitioned the King to revoke the charter, Rhode Islanders were well accustomed to factional politics whereby the profits and emoluments of office, the privileges and fruits of political victory, were absorbed by the party in power. If the charter were recalled the house would fall. The establishment of a new government under a Royal Governor would dissolve the party practices which were indigenous to Rhode Island politics. Factional government by the freemen may have been biased and corrupt and shot through with unhealthy politics, but it was their government which they operated as they pleased; they were prepared to defend it against all comers. It is no wonder, then, that the champions of faction—and these included almost all the freemen in either party—manifested an intense disapproval of Martin Howard, Jr., Dr. Thomas Moffat, George Rome, and other members of the Newport Junto. Upon hearing Governor Hopkins' weighty message, the Assembly immediately directed him to request Joseph Sherwood, the agent in London, to do all in his power to avert the intent of the petition. For an obvious purpose they asked the agent to return a copy to the colony with the names of the men who signed it.[69]

The petition from the Tory Junto was by far the most serious threat directed at the colony's charter up to this time. Heretofore, any danger in this respect had come from Parliament and the ministers, and there had been several instances in the colony's history when the British government contemplated infringement of the charter rights and privileges.[70] But this time the complaint came from within Rhode Island itself, and who knew but what the King might believe all these grievances the Newport Tories bleated about. Doubtless it was well known, too, that Benjamin Franklin was on his way to England in November, 1764, to persuade the Crown to take over the government of Pennsylvania from the proprietors.[71] With encouragement from the Junto, George III might think that this was an opportune moment to bring other colonies under a closer control.

Politicians were not the only Rhode Islanders who jealously defended the charter against its enemies. It did not require much political insight to realize that the charter was the basis of the virtual self-government so long enjoyed in the colony. "Our Charters are dear to us as our Lives," Ezra Stiles wrote home to a friend, and later this staunch Congregationalist admitted that he would rather see Rhode Island politics in the hands of the Baptists than a loss of the colony charter.[72]

While Parliamentary taxation stared them in the face, Rhode Islanders were further threatened with a serious change in their government. The future looked even blacker a few months later when two members of the Tory Junto sailed to England to complain directly about the outrageous conduct of the "licentious republic." If the King revoked the charter, Rhode Islanders would certainly know whom to blame; but this would be little enough consolation for loss of their independence and the opportunity to fight among themselves from "other motives than Love of God and Country."

# CHAPTER IV

I

S O FAR Rhode Islanders had been fairly successful in thwarting the design of Parliament to tax their molasses trade. But more alarming than the Sugar Act was Parliament's intent to derive a stamp tax from the American colonies. A stamp duty, the people soon learned, would levy taxes in sterling money on all legal documents such as wills, deeds, mortgages, and licenses, on pamphlets and newspapers, on ships' clearances and business papers. Very few activities of colonial life which involved paper of any kind would escape these onerous stamps. It was a method of taxing the colonists at their very doorsteps, and if executed, the *Newport Mercury* declared, adieu liberty and every other privilege our ancestors came here for and enjoyed until lately.[1] If Parliament, Rhode Islanders believed, could force a stamp duty on the colonies, it could impose taxation of any kind. There would be no end to the parade of taxes passed off on the Americans. "You'll soon have a Parcel of Myrmidonian Ravens," the newspapers warned, "who will feed upon and rip up your very Vitals, such as Officers of Stamp Duties, Appraisers of Lands, Houses, Furniture, Ec." The ministry, the papers continued, had decided to make the colonists pay for the peace because it did not dare load Great Britain with any more taxes.[2]

The imposition of taxes on the Americans by Parliament stimulated some Rhode Islanders to examine more closely the relationship between Great Britain and America. One outspoken citizen of Providence concluded that the relationship consisted only in that the subjects of both countries had the same King. He denied that the people of New England were any more dependent on the people of Great Britain than the people of Great Britain were dependent on those of New England. These taxes were means for keeping the colonies poor, a scheme to prevent them from gaining strength. The late acts of trade, clogging commerce, he charged, were not only unnatural but highly injurious. Every act which pertained to America proposed an advantage to England. Just once, this writer concluded, it would be a pleasure to see an act with a preamble reading, "for the good of our plantations."[3]

The petition to the King which protested the burdening of the West Indian trade also protested the impending Stamp Act and stated that Parliament's intent tended to deprive the colonists of their just and long enjoyed rights. Rhode Islanders believed that they were entitled to rights and freedom equal to subjects living in Great Britain who were governed by laws to which they had consented in some way. Only by these laws could subjects in England be deprived of their property. The petition did not explicitly deny Parliament's right to tax the colonies; it implied it, however, and asked that Rhode Islanders be taxed as their fellow subjects in England were taxed, by their own representatives. The Assembly concluded with a complaint against the economic burdens of a stamp duty. The colony's trade, which was overwhelmingly in Great Britain's favor, drained cash out of the colony. Shortly, as a consequence of import duties, the post office, the stamp duty, and other internal taxes, what little money did accrue would be entirely drawn off leaving the people incapable of paying their British debts and purchasing British goods.

It is significant that the Assembly addressed the petition to the King and not to the Parliament which enacted the Sugar Act and resolved to charge stamp duties. The original agreement of the early settlers, the petitioners pointed out, was made with the King; the colonists promised to remain subject to him and dependent on the kingdom of Great Britain. The petitioners beseeched the King that their rights be preserved inviolate, that their trade be restored to a former condition, and that the admiralty courts in America have no more scope than the law gives these same courts in England. Lastly, they asked that the colonists be taxed only with the consent of their own representatives as subjects in Great Britain were taxed. The petition did not mention the Parliament which by enactment had or was about to thrust these grievances upon the inhabitants of Rhode Island. It did not ask for representation in the Parliament which passed these laws concerning the colonies; it asked that the Rhode Island Assembly alone continue to tax the people of Rhode Island. As far as the petition is concerned it would seem that Parliament had nothing to do with the colony. Joseph Sherwood, the colony's agent in London, close to the fountain of power, wrote to the Governor after receiving the address, informing him that he had delivered it to the Secretary of State, "that being the usual and proper Channel." He had little hope, he remarked, that any benefit would result from addressing the King on affairs of trade and commerce, which were left to the Board of Trade and Parliament.[4] The business of levying a stamp duty, Sherwood might have added, would be confined wholly to the House of Commons.

Had the Assembly addressed the petition to Parliament instead of the King, it would have fared no better. Sherwood told Hopkins that the Commons refused to admit the Virginia and Connecticut petitions because it was against an established practice to hear petitions against money bills.[5] No sooner had the House rejected Richard Jackson's Connecticut petition than he presented one from Massachusetts which shared the same fate. Protests from New York, South Carolina, and the West Indies were either rejected or never presented owing to their agents' inability to find members who would introduce them. This treatment discouraged other agents from attempting to present petitions.[6] The only publicity the colony's address received in London was mention about the middle of January in the *Evening Post,* which reported that the Rhode Island Assembly complained against stamp duties and internal taxes and entreated that the colonies' long enjoyed rights be preserved.[7]

## II

The Rhode Island petition which ignored Parliament is better understood if it is read in conjunction with Stephen Hopkins' pamphlet, *The Rights of Colonies Examined.* Without doubt Hopkins was Rhode Island's most skillful politician; he was at home in all the intricate byways of the colony's politics and probably exerted more influence in the business of factional government than any of his friends or rivals. On occasion, however, Stephen Hopkins exhibited attributes of statesmanship; the writing of *The Rights of Colonies*

*Examined* was one of these occasions. This pamphlet was before the Assembly in an unfinished state when that body approved the address to the King. Upon completion it was sent to Joseph Sherwood for publication in London.[8] William Goddard first printed it in Rhode Island by order of the Assembly on December 22, 1764.[9]

Hopkins' pamphlet at first glance is confusing to the historian who wishes to determine exactly where the colony stood in regard to the power of Parliament. He denied Parliament's right to tax the colonies; that was explicit. He denied also Parliament's right to legislate for the colonies; since the people of Great Britain had no authority over America, they could not give that authority to their legislature. At the same time he modified his bold stand by admitting the need of an authority in Parliament to control problems of the whole Empire. This authority, according to Hopkins, included regulation of commerce and currency—"Indeed, every thing that concerns the proper interest and fit government of the whole commonwealth." Just what Hopkins would deny Parliament in addition to taxing the colonies, he did not make crystal clear. But legislation for the colonies, other than acts for the general good of the whole Empire, Parliament could not legally enact. Between the power of taxation which he denied and the power to enact laws for "all these general matters" which he admitted, there was a middle ground upon which Parliament could not tread—a middle ground of legislative authority reserved to each local government within the commonwealth. In addition to being a tax, the Sugar Act was an unfair prohibition, falling heaviest on the northern colonies and particularly on Rhode Island which was most deeply involved in the molasses trade. Certainly it was not legislation for the general good. Similarly the Stamp Act was a tax and therefore unconstitutional; but also it was specific legislation aimed at taking the property of one part of the Empire for the good of another part, and thereby hardly within the purview of Parliament whose authority was limited to "general concerns." Although Hopkins' pamphlet was somewhat ambiguous, one fact is clear: he denied more than Parliament's power to tax Americans.

The petition and Hopkins' pamphlet were supplementary; one blandly addressed the King for redress of grievances, and the other, by way of explaining that Parliament had very little to do with the colonies, explicitly denied its right to tax America or legislate in any other than a general way. The British Empire, according to Hopkins, was a commonwealth of nations, all subject to the same King. Each state or colony had its particular privileges for internal government including Great Britain. But none of these governments had power over more than its own people. Parliament, the supreme legislative body, was an integrating mechanism. It controlled problems such as trade and commerce "of the whole British empire, taken collectively." Beyond this it had no power to interfere with the government of the several colonies and least of all a power to tax them.

When *The Rights of Colonies Examined* reached Sherwood's hands in London, it suffered a fate similar to the Remonstrance sent over almost a year earlier. It arrived in England after the stamp duty which it protested had become law. Sherwood informed the Governor that he had tried effectively to apply it, but since the act had already passed, and because there were a number of other pamphlets printed on the same occasion, the colony could derive no benefit from its publication at that time. Sherwood claimed that even if he were to extract "the Quintessence of the whole" and print it for the perusal of the members of Parliament, as Hopkins had suggested, it would do no good. We must wait until next year, Sherwood remarked, "as it is too late to carry into Execution a scheme of this sort this Session."[10] In America the pamphlet was popular. The *Massachusetts Gazette* advertised it as a treatise which "breathes a true Spirit of Liberty."[11] In New York it met "with the highest Approbation."[12] Goddard reported in May, 1765, that almost every colony in North America had reprinted it from the Providence edition.[13]

Rhode Island's official position in regard to the power of Parliament is more clearly understood when it is considered in light of the colony's accustomed attitude toward the supreme legislature and Great Britain as a whole. The charter itself, as we have seen, established in effect a self-governing colony, and events had occurred during the eighteenth century which strengthened in Rhode Islanders an independent attitude toward the mother country.

In 1731 the Assembly enacted a law emitting £60,000 in paper money which Governor Joseph Jenckes believed was unwise and promptly vetoed. The Assembly was incensed and declared that the

Governor had no power to veto an act of the legislature. Both sides appealed home for judgment in the matter. His Majesty's Attorney and Solicitor General returned the opinion that according to the charter the Governor could not veto an act of the Assembly; he could sit merely as a member of that body. Moreover, the Crown had "no discretionary power of repealing laws made in that Province." The validity of the colony's laws depended upon their not being contrary to the laws of England.[14] During a boundary dispute with Massachusetts in 1746 the Bay Colony's agent reported to the Privy Council that in "Rhode Island government they deem his Majesty's royal authority to be entirely given up by their charter."[15] Reports like this did not endear the colony to King, ministry, and Parliament.

In connection with the libel case in 1757 when Hopkins sued Ward for what the latter had published in a pamphlet attacking the Governor, it came out that in addition to expressing his opinions about Samuel Ward, Hopkins had expressed his opinions also about the power of Parliament in America—the connection, if any, between the two was not explained. Two witnesses testified that Hopkins publicly declared that "the King and Parliament had no more right to pass any Acts of Parliament to govern us than the Mohawks."[16] About this same time Hopkins charged also that "nothing could be more tyrannical, than our being Obliged by Acts of Parliament To which we were not parties to the making, and in which we were not Represented."[17]

Rhode Island's conduct during the French and Indian War further indicated an independent attitude toward Great Britain. A large proportion of the trade carried on by the colony throughout the war was not only a violation of the Molasses Act but—more reprehensible in British eyes—it was a brisk trade with England's and the colonies' enemies. The extent to which the colony traded with the enemy came to the attention of the King. William Pitt warned Governor Hopkins of His Majesty's orders directing him and the Assembly to "make a strict and diligent inquiry into the state of this trade [and to] use every means in their power to discover the persons concerned in it...."[18] General Amherst complained bitterly to Hopkins about this illicit commerce. He found Rhode Island to be one of the principal offenders. The only aim of New England merchants, he claimed, was to make money regardless of the welfare of their country.[19] Rhode

Islanders were apprehensive of the reports about this trade promulgated at home by army and naval officers who served in the colonies during the French war. There was reason for anxiety over the observations of the famous ranger, Major Robert Rogers, who, upon his return to England, published *A Concise Account of North America,* containing few complimentary remarks about Rhode Island.[20] The people of this colony, he wrote, were not at all scrupulous in confining themselves to the limits of their charter. During the late war they trafficked with the enemy with impunity, often carrying to the French many material articles.

Even the courts reflected the precocious attitude of Rhode Islanders. In 1761 Aaron Lopez and Isaac Elizur, two Jewish merchants of Newport, applied to the Superior Court for naturalization after seven years' residence under an act of Parliament. The Court did nothing about the application, and Lopez and Elizur appealed to the Assembly for help. The Assembly promptly threw the matter back into the lap of the Superior Court as being its business to determine. In March, 1762, the Superior Court under Samuel Ward considered the application and dismissed it on grounds that the act of Parliament authorizing the naturalization of foreigners was enacted only for increasing the number of inhabitants in the colonies. Rhode Island, the Court declared, was already overpopulated; in fact, many who were born in the colony had moved to and settled in Nova Scotia because of this. Furthermore, the charter directed that the full and quiet enjoyment of the Christian religion was a principal purpose of settling the colony, and owing to this the Assembly enacted a law in 1663 refusing admission as freemen to any inhabitants not professing the Christian religion.[21] The Court's decision would seem to indicate that laws of Parliament were acceptable as long as they "bee not contrary and repugnant unto, butt, as neare as may bee, agreeable to the lawes of this our"[22] colony of Rhode Island.

Protests against the Sugar Act and stamp duty must be considered in light of this stubbornness toward external control over the colony's affairs. It will be remembered that the Assembly addressed the Remonstrance against renewal of the Molasses Act to the Lords of Trade, not to Parliament. Moreover, it sent the petition in protest against the Sugar Act and proposed Stamp Act to the King, not

Parliament which dealt with both these matters. Also Hopkins' pamphlet not only denied Parliament's right to tax the colonies but went further and denied that body legislative authority over the colonies except in general matters for the good of the whole Empire. Further evidence of this independent attitude will be found as the dispute between Great Britain and the colonies became sharper and more bitter.

## III

*The Rights of Colonies Examined* did not go unchallenged in Rhode Island. Samuel Hall informed his readers in the *Newport Mercury* on February 18, 1765, that he had just published *A Letter from a Gentleman at Halifax to his Friend in Rhode-Island,* which was a serious attack on Hopkins' pamphlet. Supposedly this letter originated, as its title indicated, in Halifax, Nova Scotia. Although it appeared anonymously, Rhode Islanders soon guessed the author to be one of the Newport Junto which had petitioned the King to vacate the colony's charter. Later in the year it was generally known that the writer was Martin Howard, Jr.[23]

The *Halifax Letter* was a direct answer to Stephen Hopkins. Howard's convictions supporting the supreme sovereignty of Parliament were diametrically opposed to Hopkins' principles of colonial self-government within the British Commonwealth. The Rhode Island charter, Howard argued, did not preclude Parliament's jurisdiction nor did a grant from the King lessen in any way this jurisdiction which was based on the common law and therefore antedated charters and grants. The authority of Parliament followed an Englishman wherever he went; moreover, it is not divisible, but "transcendent and entire." Of course, Howard granted, the colonists had the privilege of writing pamphlets, petitioning, and remonstrating when they felt that they were imposed upon unreasonably. But let them not, he warned, invoke the cause of liberty to "cloak maliciousness." He hoped Englishmen would ignore Hopkins' pamphlet against the stamp bill, because if it caught the eye of the ministry, the colonists might expect measures calculated to increase their dependency rather than mitigate the grievances supposedly imposed upon them.

The *Providence Gazette* bristled with resentment for the author and his *Halifax Letter*. An answer to Howard's pamphlet appeared anonymously in three succeeding issues of that newspaper beginning on February 23, 1765; without doubt it was written by Stephen Hopkins.[24] But it is a disappointing answer to Howard's attack, for Hopkins pulled in his horns. In "A Vindication of a Late Pamphlet," as it was called, Hopkins did not defend the bold constitutional theory he developed a few months before but insisted that in the earlier pamphlet he contended only against the Parliament's right to tax the colonies. He claimed in the "Vindication" that he "advanced no contrary position" to what Howard had said was Parliament's right, but that the Halifax writer had deliberately pretended to confute him in order to embroil America with the mother country. The writer of *The Rights of Colonies Examined,* Hopkins continued, never questioned Parliament's authority, "but only said, that taxing the plantations, in their interior police, would be, in his opinion, such an exercise of that authority, as was not conformable to British principles of government." Furthermore, although in *The Rights of Colonies Examined* Hopkins never advocated colonial representation in Parliament, in the "Vindication" he suggested that the colonies would never complain if they received the same advantages as Scotland to which they were certainly entitled.

It is impossible to lay these statements alongside those of Hopkins' first pamphlet and not conclude that he had changed his mind. True, he still spoke of the colonies as "municipal states" incorporated by the Crown, and since they were taxed heavily by the several Assemblies for their own support, they ought not to be taxed by Parliament. But this related only to taxation and is a far cry from the imperial state described earlier which contained several separate governments of equal power subject to the same King and only the general legislation of Parliament.

Why is there a disagreement between the pamphlet and the newspaper articles? Only three months elapsed between them. Doubtless Stephen Hopkins came to see that the statements set down in the pamphlet were too extreme for the time. He may have believed them then; he may still have believed them when the "Vindication" appeared. But he may also have believed that it was imprudent to push these arguments at a time when Parliament was considering the stamp bill. If a denial only of Parliament's right to tax America would prevent a stamp act—as many colonists believed it would—why should Rhode Island deny Parliament's right to legislate at all for the colonies other than in a general way for the good of the Empire? Whatever Hopkins' reasons, it is clear that the two documents were contradictory. One of the first persons to recognize the contradiction was Martin Howard, Jr. He later chided the Governor for denying that the colonists had rights independent of Parliament in his second paper when he had insisted upon it in his first. In fact, Howard claimed, the Governor had watered down his whole argument and pretended to object only to Parliament's right of taxation over the colonies.[25]

The pamphlet controversy begun by Hopkins and Howard did not end here. In March, 1765, James Otis of Boston picked up his lance to protect the British colonies from the aspersions of the gentleman from Halifax.[26] But instead of defending Hopkins' pamphlet, Otis tried ineffectually to explain it away. At the same time he disavowed some of the arguments of his own pamphlet, *The Rights of the British Colonies Asserted and Proved,* which had made him a national hero only a few months before.[27] In attempting to explain Hopkins' first pamphlet Otis wandered further and further from the original argument and ended in a tangle of ideas much closer in content to those of Howard than of Hopkins. It is probable that Martin Howard, Jr., was delighted to have provoked two such distinguished persons as Hopkins and Otis who, in their answers to him, recanted arguments which they had expressed earlier. Doubtless, too, Howard and his friends enjoyed several chuckles over the fact that he had not only provoked Hopkins and Otis to disagree with him, but he had provoked them to disagree with each other. Spurred with success, Howard tried again in April and published *A Defence of the Letter from a Gentleman at Halifax;*[28] Hopkins refused to bite this time, but Otis dashed off *Brief Remarks on the Defence of the Halifax Libel, on the British-American Colonies.*[29] Otis would have better served his purpose had he kept his mind on what was going on in Boston. He surrendered—not without several scurrilous remarks—to most of Howard's arguments. The gentleman at Halifax never answered Otis' last pamphlet; there was little more to say. With a few insignificant exceptions they were arguing the same side. The pamphlet controversy which began with *The Rights of Colonies Examined* and the *Halifax Letter* on the high level of political theory, was reduced to gossamer arguments punctuated by abusive and scandalous personal remarks.[30]

IV

The publication of the *Halifax Letter* caused a local political reaction. The supporters of Hopkins in Newport seized upon it as a club with which to beat their opponents. According to Martin Howard, Joseph Wanton, Jr., Hopkins' Deputy Governor, attempted to persuade the General Assembly to take official action against the *Letter.* Late in February, 1765, when the Assembly was sitting in East Greenwich, Wanton appeared before the lower house, waving a copy of the *Letter* in his hand, and strongly urged the members to take measures against the pamphlet or the printer. Those who supported Wanton pushed the plan and a warm debate followed. Some declared that the pamphlet was a libel and that the Assembly should summon the printer to answer for his conduct. Others wanted it publicly burned by the common hangman. A more moderate group claimed that they saw nothing offensive in it and voted down the Deputy Governor's scheme. Howard became apprehensive of the liberty of the press in Rhode Island and criticized the zealous members of the Assembly for their disavowal of the true principles of the British Constitution.[31]

Although the General Assembly did not call up Samuel Hall, the printer of the *Halifax Letter,* the Superior Court, which was in Hopkins' control, did, and after questioning him and letting him sweat for a while, the judges sent him back to his shop. This was sufficient to arouse the Newport hemp writers. O.Z., in the next issue of the *Mercury,* screamed in protest against this "dangerous stretch of power, more threatening to the liberty of the press, and of the subject, than anything we have yet heard of in America." He exploited the incident for political purposes and used it to discredit the party in power. It is high time, he wrote, we turned these overseers out. Who cannot see that "extensive liberty verges on servitude"; too often, he warned, tyranny is built on the ruins of freedom.[32]

The Hopkins faction tried hard to identify the enemies to the charter with the southern faction, hoping it would get them votes. (Martin Howard, Jr., was doubtless a supporter of Ward, for in 1761 he had appeared on a Ward prox as a candidate for Attorney General in opposition to Augustus Johnston, a Hopkins man and victor over Howard in that election.) In 1764 rumors had circulated that members of the Junto were writing accusing letters home to England against the colony's charter. Moses Brown, in preparing the campaign that year in Hopkins' behalf, was eager for party purposes to get hold of any evidence sent home "being signd by any principal people in the opposition."[33] A year later just before the election the Hopkins faction accused the Newport Junto of attempting for some time to undermine and destroy the government and effect a total subversion of the charter and the colony's privileges. They were trying desperately, Hopkins' friends charged, to tear the reins of government from the Governor's hands along with the liberties of the people so "that they may commit them to a *Ward* of their own."[34] It is possible that Ward and his friends were not averse to accepting support from the Newport Junto, willingly forgetting for the time being that the Junto's criticism was general and aimed at all factions, whereas theirs was specific, leveled only at the party in power.

On the other hand, Hopkins' friends in 1765 paraded the Governor as the great defender of the colony's rights. They praised him for informing the Assembly of the evil plot to revoke the charter, a deed for which their opponents, Hopkins' people charged, "have fell upon him and intend to turn him out."[35] Hopkins saw his party as the protector of the people's liberties and during the campaign drove home the fact "that we are generally thought to be the friend to the Colony and the Constitution, and that our opposers at present are not. This being true," he wrote to Beriah Brown, "should be much insisted on, and will probably have some influence with the people."[36] Moses Brown beat the drum about Hopkins' patriotic zeal, which, he said, sparkled in both the petition and *The Rights of Colonies Examined*. The freemen, he declared, could not "Discharge their obligations Better than Continuing his Administration."[37]

In spite of the Hopkins faction's attempt to smear their opponents as enemies to the colony's rights, liberties, and charter privileges, the freemen in April elected Samuel Ward Governor for the coming year. The causes of Hopkins' defeat can only be surmised, but it may be that in the spring of 1765, his strong stand on the limitations of Parliament's power, spelled out in *The Rights of Colonies Examined,* was more suspect in the eyes of some of the freemen than it was admired. Hopkins, himself, alluded in his pamphlet to the opinion held by some that the colonies' vigorous claim to rights would only provoke the resentment of Parliament. Yet a man on a wreck, he added, "was never denied the liberty of roaring as loud as he could." Martin Howard, Jr., in the *Halifax Letter* had warned that the surest way to bring on a stamp tax was to deny Parliament's right to levy it. It was possible that a number of Rhode Islanders agreed with him and shifted their support from Hopkins to Ward who had not opened his mouth about the rights, privileges, and liberties of anyone. Ezra Stiles declared that Hopkins' "defense of the Colonies was said to procure the Stamp Act &c which lost" him some of the votes.³⁸ The Governor doubtless had the election of 1765 in mind when he answered the *Halifax Letter* in the *Providence Gazette.* In "A Vindication of a Late Pamphlet," we have seen, he abandoned his bold theory which challenged the legislative authority of Parliament and settled for a denial of its power to tax the colonies. In March Hopkins had occasion to comment on the petitions and pamphlets of the colonies against the sugar and stamp tax; Rhode Island's, he said, were bold and free, "but imperfect and incorrect, &c."³⁹

Hopkins gave evidence of statesmanlike character in his brave pamphlet which wrestled with the power of Parliament over the colony of which he was the Governor. It may be that he wrestled too hard and roared so loud that the freemen questioned the prudence of his courageous attack. In that case, the good politician was forced to take over from the imperial statesman and modify the doctrine to conform with the will of the voters. While Hopkins grappled with his conscience and the principles of government, Samuel Ward won the election.

But it would be wrong to imply that the election of 1765 was won or lost over the issue of Parliamentary taxation. Local demands and local intrigues as usual influenced the outcome. After all, the Tory Junto was small in number, and although the Ward people accepted the Junto's votes, they shunned their principles despite the claims of the faction to the north. Granted the imperial issue may have changed a few votes, the struggle continued in the accustomed manner, strictly along factional lines.

It was John Brown's turn this year to propose a scheme to end the political warfare, and just before the election he declared that

Mr Ward and Uncle Brown have Kept the Government in a Rage for this 7 or 8 yars past by [opposing ? illegible] Mr Hopkins prox when at the same time they have known the Majority of the Freeholders in the Colony have bin in favour of his Administration. . . .

John Brown suggested that the only way "to prevent their Usual Manner of Inflaming the Colony any Longer," was for all honest men, who had heretofore kept quiet and were impartial enough to judge the conduct of both parties, to vote unanimously this year—of course for Hopkins—and so overpower the "Contentious party" that it would be ashamed to struggle any longer.[40] (The majority of the freeholders were so much in favor of Mr. Hopkins' administration that a few days after John Brown wrote those lines, it will be remembered, they elected Mr. Ward Governor of the colony.)

Campaign expenses for 1765 ran unusually high. About twenty-five of the Hopkins party faithful subscribed £6167-4-2 to the party fund. But this proved too small, and eight men on the subscription list paid £417-14 more to take care of the deficiency. Typical expenditures were a barrel of rum worth £69-15 paid to Timothy Wilmarth of Glocester, along with one quarter hundred weight of cod fish to John Davis of the same town. A Mr. Sails of Cranston received fifteen bushels of corn for his co-operation during the trying days of the election. John Dexter picked up the liquor bill of £88-10 "for Govr Hopkins friends," and at the close of the town meeting in Providence £18-8 was paid out in damages for three bowls, two case bottles, a window sash, and four squares of glass.[41] Although the Browns were meticulous in their accounts, they did not record who or what made an exit through the window of the town house.

As usual the Hopkins party was not alone in the timely use of material goods to persuade the electorate, but unfortunately the Ward party's records are not as complete as those kept by the Browns of Providence. To be sure, Hopkins and his friends were well aware of their opponents' activities in this respect; in fact, wrote Hopkins, the Wards "have as little to avail themselves of this year as they ever had except that mortal weapon MONEY, and being sensible of this, no doubt they will furnish as much of it as they possibly can."[42] It would be difficult to determine whether Hopkins' bold stand in the face of Parliament or the effective use by Ward of that "mortal weapon MONEY" was the decisive factor in Hopkins' defeat. Anyway, Ward took over the Governorship for the second time in the course of the controversy, and both parties immediately began preparations for 1766.

Although Hopkins recanted the stand he took in *The Rights of Colonies Examined,* that pamphlet and the petition to the King went on record as Rhode Island's official statement against the Sugar Act and the pending stamp tax. According to the General Assembly which approved both documents and sent them to England, the molasses duty was an unfair prohibition of the colony's trade; the extension of admiralty jurisdiction in America subjected the colonists to different treatment from their fellow subjects in Great Britain. Parliament could not constitutionally levy a stamp duty in America; the colonists who enjoyed equal rights with subjects within the realm could not legally be deprived of their property by laws to which they had not given their consent. Had Rhode Island ended its objections there, its protest would have joined the main stream of American opposition to Great Britain's new colonial policy. But it went beyond its sister governments and denied Parliament's right to legislate for the colonies other than in a general way for the good of the whole Empire. The British Empire was an accumulation of many states, each with its own legislature and each responsible for its own internal government and police. No one government had power over another. Each was subject, however, to the Parliament of Great Britain for legislative authority in general matters such as the regulation of trade. Beyond this Parliament could not go. Rhode Island advanced a constitutional theory of the British Empire in 1764 which was not generally accepted in America until the next decade when the Continental Congress supported a similar policy upon which it based the union of the colonies.

# CHAPTER V

# TAXATION WITH REPRESENTATION AND JUSTICE OF THE COMMON LAW IN RHODE ISLAND

BEHIND the constitutional protests against Parliamentary taxation and admiralty justice lay local and particular reasons for Rhode Island's strenuous objections to the new revenue acts. An understanding of why Rhode Islanders reacted as they did to Parliamentary encroachment depends upon an understanding of the taxing and judicial systems that Parliament encroached upon; for taxation with representation and trial by jury in a local court had peculiar significance in the colony of Rhode Island.

## I

### LOCAL TAXATION

All taxation was burdensome; Rhode Islanders were no different from human beings all over the world. But taxation by Parliament in the form of a Sugar Act and a Stamp Act was not only burdensome; it was relatively equal. A tax on imported foreign molasses, which was the cornerstone of the colony's economy, if paid, was felt by a large proportion of the inhabitants. The importers shared the burden with the merchants and the distillers and all who became involved in the rum trade and, of course, rum consumption. The long arm of Parliament in levying a stamp duty would reach into the homes of the colonists, increase the price of their newspapers and playing cards, and tax all the official papers in business and practice of law. Taxation by the General Assembly, on the other hand, was burdensome; but it was not equal. Since control of the government was in the hands of one faction or the other, the levying of taxes was quick to respond to the prejudices of party.

The power to tax is an accepted right of self-government. In the colony of Rhode Island where self-government meant government by faction, the power to tax was not only an accepted right of the General Assembly, but the right of each faction to shape the government's taxing policy to its own ends. "If ever the Time Should happen," a group of Rhode Islanders remarked about their government in 1766, "when the Passions of any prevailing Administration should be the Rule of their Government, a Matter of Taxation, without any other Rule or Guide than mere Arbitrariness [,] would be the Object of their particular Attention." This was no idle comment but "deduced from Fact and Experience."[1] A review of the tax legislation during the Ward-Hopkins controversy will indicate to what extent this statement was true.

In June, 1761, Stephen Hopkins had been in office for three successive terms, and the month before the freemen had returned him for his fourth term. Each year the Assembly had levied taxes upon the towns, and each year protests and dissents were heard against them. Protests and dissents throughout the controversy usually were of two general types. One pleaded an inability to pay, as Newport did in 1758, when the merchants had lost "upwards of Two Millions of Money" owing to the war.[2] The other, which was more frequent, claimed that the taxes levied were incorrectly proportioned and therefor unjust. It is significant that a report submitted by the General Treasurer to the Assembly at this June session indicated that eleven towns were delinquent in tax payments; nine of these towns were in the southern half, or the Ward half, of the colony.[3] Hopkins taxes were not popular with the Ward voters.

During the second session of the legislature in June, 1761, the Assembly passed an act for "enquiring into the Value of Rateable Estates . . . in order that a just Proportion of the Rates and Taxes may be assessed and levied on the Inhabitants."[4] A general estimate of ratable estates, as it was called, was an estimate of the value of all the real and personal property belonging to the inhabitants of the colony. To accomplish this formidable task, the Assembly appointed several committees which were authorized to inquire into and list the value of property including land, buildings, works, ships at home and at sea, slaves, stock, and any other real or personal property.[5] Once the returns were made they would be "liquidated" or reduced to one grand list which the Assembly would use as a measure for proportioning future taxes—"so material a Part of civil government"—on counties and towns.[6]

Which faction was responsible for the act to determine a new general estimate is not certain. Although Stephen Hopkins was Governor, Samuel Ward's friends enjoyed a majority in the lower house. Since nine southern towns were delinquent in tax payments under the existing tax rate, it would appear reasonable to assume that the southern faction demanded the general estimate to be taken. From what occurred after the estimate made its appearance in the Assembly, the assumption loses some of its reasonableness. It is possible that members of both factions were dissatisfied with the existing proportion of taxes and therefore supported a new estimate of the value of ratable property.

In 1762 the new estimate of ratable estates became effective, and between this time and 1770 a bitter fight occurred between the two factions over proportioning taxes according to it. When Ward and his friends were in power, the Assembly, obviously displeased with the new estimate, completely ignored it—in fact, declared it null and void in 1766—and apportioned taxes through committees appointed for that purpose. The northern towns protested vigorously these high acts of "Arbitrary Power and Despotism," and several flatly refused to levy or collect the new taxes. When the Hopkins faction recaptured the government, it taxed the towns according to the general estimate, and then it was the southerners' turn to howl. They claimed that the new rates were unjust and particularly burdensome to towns in the southern half of the colony. There was little that a town could do to change the mind of the faction in control of the Assembly. The alternatives, of course, were either not to pay the tax or to defeat the faction in power at the next election.[7]

A comparison of the tax rates of 1764 and 1765 reveals how each faction apportioned taxes in favor of its own section. The 1764 tax was apportioned by a Hopkins legislature according to the general estimate, and the Ward Assembly apportioned the 1765 tax in committee without benefit of any fixed rule. The whole rate in the first year was £12,000; in the second tax the total amount was £12,468-15. This meant, of course, that were both amounts equally apportioned each town would have paid a slightly higher rate in 1765, or the 1764 rate plus a small proportion of the difference between the two taxes. In every town in Newport, Bristol, and Kent counties the latter was slightly higher. For instance, Newport, the largest town in the colony, paid £95 more for the second tax;[8] the difference between each rate for New Shoreham, the colony's smallest town, was only £5. Similarly Jamestown paid £9 more in 1765 and Tiverton £15. Bristol and Warren each paid £10 more in the second tax; Warwick and East Greenwich in Kent County were increased £21 and £11 respectively.

Kings County, always Ward territory, presented a different picture. The tax for Westerly, where Samuel Ward resided, was £12 *less* in 1765; South Kingstown's was reduced by £60, Charlestown's by £32, Exeter's and Hopkinton's both by £19. North Kingstown's tax increased only £8, which was less than other towns of similar value and population. On the other hand, in Providence County, Scituate was ordered to pay an increase of £52 in the second tax, and Cumberland's second rate was £67 higher than the first. According to the rates of other towns similar in value, Scituate and Cumberland should have paid £17 and £10 respectively. But the town of Providence afforded the most striking example of tax shifting. In 1764, according to the estimate, Providence's apportionment was £766. Between the time of the two taxes, North Providence was set off from Providence as a separate town. In 1765 the apportionment for Providence was £660 and North Providence was £277. This meant that the total amount expected from both towns paying separately was £937, or £171 more than what the same number of people had paid in 1764 before the towns were separated. It is clearly evident that the Ward faction's apportionment reduced the taxes of six towns in the southern section and increased those of three towns in Providence County. The other towns' apportionment remained about the same.

But Providence, Cumberland, and Scituate never paid the 1765 tax or the 1766 tax—which was levied in the same manner—despite the fact that the Assembly resolved to sue them if they didn't. (The Scituate tax collector did suffer from the southern faction and was later thrown in jail for refusing to do his duty.) The three towns were just as stubborn as the Assembly, patiently waiting and hoping for the northern party to return to power. They were not disappointed. In May, 1767, Hopkins won the election by the largest majority either candidate had ever polled. The new Assembly promptly relieved Providence, Scituate, and Cumberland from their burden and let them pay their taxes according to the general estimate of 1762. Moreover, the sums taken off these three towns the Assembly voted to apportion among the towns which were lightly assessed in those years according to a new estimate to be taken that year.[9]

One can well imagine that this last resolve was warmly protested. Twenty-seven deputies, every one of them from the southern half of the colony, dissented from the vote of the legislature. Nothing but fatal consequences would follow this new action of the Assembly, they said; every town which finds that it paid more than its due proportion according to this estimate will demand a refund out of the general treasury. What is more, the towns that must take on the burden thrown off by Providence, Scituate, and Cumberland, with the help of the Assembly, will have reason to follow their example and simply refuse obedience to the acts of the Assembly. Then, they concluded, the authority of the government will be seriously weakened, the collection of future taxes will be extremely precarious, and the whole affair will end in the total ruin of all public credit.[10]

The twenty-seven gentlemen from the southern section spoke more truth than they knew. At the same May session, 1767, the Assembly called for a report of tax delinquencies and was quite surprised to find that in addition to Providence, Scituate, and Cumberland, which owed all of the 1765 and 1766 taxes, Newport also owed all of the 1765 and 1766 taxes and part of each tax assessed the two previous years. In addition, Portsmouth and East Greenwich each owed most of the 1765 tax, while Jamestown, Exeter, Middletown, and Hopkinton —all southern towns—had paid only about half of their rates for the same year. Only Bristol, Little Compton, and North Providence had paid anything toward the 1766 tax.[11] This was a fine situation. The Ward Assembly in 1766 had sued Providence, Scituate, and Cumberland for failure to levy, assess, or collect the two taxes but completely disregarded the fact that Newport owed not only these taxes but parts of two others. And six other southern towns owed at least half of the rate levied in 1765. The colony's tax authority had obviously broken down; the Ward faction exploited this general breakdown to favor its own section of the colony. The tax rate in Rhode Island was a political issue until 1770. Had the contest for control of the government continued, the fight between factions over taxation would probably have continued with it. From 1770 until the Revolution one faction predominated and decided the question of taxation without opposition.

The conclusions drawn from a study of tax legislation during the Ward-Hopkins controversy are simple. The faction in control of the Assembly made it a policy to apportion taxes in favor of the area from which it derived its support and to shift the burden to sections which supported the opposition. Towns which were favorably affected paid their taxes—if they could—and kept quiet. Towns which believed they were unjustly assessed had two alternatives: they either suffered the abuse until their own faction regained supremacy and then accepted relief, or they refused to pay the taxes with impunity, knowing full well that a political victory would solve their problems, excuse their delinquency, and relieve them of that portion of the tax which appeared to them to be unjust. The loser was the colony itself; tax delinquency became increasingly prevalent, and the authority of the General Assembly diminished as the towns openly defied the taxing power of the legislature.

One purpose for which Rhode Islanders elected a Governor and council and sent deputies to the legislature was to enact tax laws favorable to the section in which they as voters lived. No wonder, then, that they had special interest in opposing taxes levied in England. Manipulation of taxing policies would be impossible if Parliament were calling the turn, particularly if the taxes were vigorously enforced. The sphere of political influence of a Hopkins or a Ward would have little effect in the halls of Westminster. Taxes by Parliament would be burdensome to the point of having to pay them.

## II

### THE COURTS OF JUSTICE

Samuel Ward took over the government of Rhode Island in May, 1765. About this time the inhabitants learned that Parliament in March had definitely passed the Stamp Act which would become effective on November 1. The fact that the news was not a complete surprise did not lessen the weight of the blow. As early as February of that year Joseph Sherwood wrote to the colony that the bill had been read a third time in the Commons and would very soon pass into law.[12] What added to the shock was the manner in which the new tax was to be enforced.

No document requiring stamps was valid unless the proper stamps were affixed to it. The colonists, in order to do business legally, had to use stamped paper which they could buy only with sterling money from Stamp Masters whom the British Government would appoint. But the Stamp Act very explicitly directed that all forfeitures and penalties collectible in violation of the act could be sued for in a court of record *or* a court of admiralty which had jurisdiction. Rhode Islanders might ask with considerable reason and justice just what did an admiralty court have to do with the enforcement of a tax law and particularly a stamp tax which in no way could be identified with trade regulation. They regarded this innovation as a more glaring violation of constitutional right than the extension of admiralty court jurisdiction under the Sugar Act. Heretofore a colonist who refused to pay his taxes eventually was subject to the jurisdiction of the colony court within the county in which he lived. Under the Stamp Act a defendant, having committed his offense within the borders of the colony, could be tried without a jury in a court of admiralty, possibly at Halifax, Nova Scotia. This was serious business. The extension of admiralty court jurisdiction, the colonists claimed, was not only unconstitutional, but it distinguished between American subjects and their British brothers within the realm, where the right of trial by jury for similar offenses was clear and unconfined.[13] Moreover, an act of Parliament which denied rights to colonists which Englishmen enjoyed at home violated the Rhode Island charter. Not only was Parliamentary taxation unconstitutional, but the means by which Parliament intended to enforce this new tax rendered the colonists' property insecure and denied them the basic right of trial by jury.

How seriously the colonists regarded the extension of admiralty court jurisdiction in 1764 and 1765 has not been sufficiently appreciated by American historians. The fact that most of the colonial assemblies included this grievance in their Stamp Act Resolves, often in the same breath with a denial of Parliament's right to tax,[14] indicates, it seems, that a fear of admiralty court justice was almost as great as a fear of taxation itself. Moreover, the four documents drafted by the delegates to the Stamp Act Congress in October, 1765, gave a very prominent place to this grievance, coupling it in the declarations and resolves with the new stamp tax as having "a manifest tendency to subvert the rights and liberties of the colonists."[15] Of the seventeen paragraphs which made up the Congress' petition to the House of Commons, two are devoted exclusively to the danger in the new and extensive powers given to the admiralty courts. Trials by their peers and freedom from "all taxes but such as they have consented to in person, or by their representatives," the delegates insisted, have ever been considered the "best birthrights" of Englishmen.[16]

The passage of the Stamp Act in the spring of 1765 must have suddenly impressed upon the colonists throughout America that the British imperial system had taken a very ominous turn. Before 1764 litigation involving the regulation of trade had found its way into the courts of common law or at least had come under the influence of these courts where the colonists had local protection. Moreover, taxation was exclusively the business of the colonial legislatures and was enforceable also in the colony courts. The extension of admiralty court jurisdiction by two acts of Parliament passed within the space of a year promised to alter substantially what colonists had been accustomed to for longer than any of them could remember. The whole colonial system, it appeared, no longer rested on the co-operation—or lack of it—of the colonists and their courts of justice, but potentially on a number of admiralty court judges appointed in England who presided alone over courts which had no juries. To the colonists this was a major change in British colonial policy.

So far we have found local and peculiar practices and habits which, when encroached upon by Parliament, were the springs of grievances not unjustifiably complained of also in constitutional terms. Rhode Islanders opposed the extension of admiralty court jurisdiction under the Sugar Act because this extension, besides depriving colonists of the rights of Englishmen, seriously interfered with their control of the colony's admiralty court. Parliamentary taxation in both the Sugar and Stamp Acts was not only taxation by a legislature in which the colonists were not represented, but it encroached upon a taxing procedure which was close to the heart of government by faction. Now, enforcement of the Stamp Act—in fact, enforcement of the whole colonial system—in the courts of admiralty instead of common law courts would not only deprive the colonists of the right of trial by jury and distinguish them from fellow subjects in England, but it would encroach upon a local judicial system which, like the rest of the government, was responsive to the faction in power.

That the courts of justice in Rhode Island were biased was a distinct possibility. The charter gave authority to the General Assembly to establish courts of law "ffor the hearinge and determininge of all actions, cases, matters and thinges . . . which shall be in dispute."[17] At the time of the Ward-Hopkins controversy there were three distinct courts within the colony whose judges were chosen yearly by the General Assembly: the Superior Court of Judicature and General Gaol Delivery with five judges; five Inferior Courts of Common Pleas—one in each county—with five judges each; and five county Courts of General Sessions presided over by the justices of the peace of each county. Exclusive of the justices of the peace already discussed above, the Assembly elected thirty judges each May for the Inferior and Superior Courts and, of course, six clerks, one for each court.[18] Important here, too, is the fact that the General Assembly upon occasion acted as a Supreme Court within the colony. It heard appeals from the other courts and established rules for petitions praying that judgments and rules of court "may be set aside, and that Execution may be stayed."[19]

Each judge and clerk received specified fees for the work he did but no salary. For example, in 1767 among a number of other fees the judges of the Superior Court received twelve shillings apiece for the "Entry of every Action for Trial" and one shilling, sixpence, for all criminal cases where a fine was set.[20] In addition it was customary to pay extraordinary expenses to the judges when the occasion called for them. In one instance, when Stephen Hopkins was Chief Justice of the Superior Court, he received eighty-five dollars and the other judges seventy-five each "for their extraordinary time and trouble" in trying criminals in Kings County for counterfeiting gold and silver coins.[21] The General Treasurer's Accounts indicate that other sums were paid out by the colony to the judges for specific trials.[22] Critics of the courts argued that the judges ought to receive fixed salaries to make them more independent. But a defender of the Rhode Island system charged that salaries for judges would lead only to mischief and render the office more subject to party strife. After all, he concluded, the fees helped considerably; in fact, he said, they were good compensation.[23] That the judges depended upon their fees is partially indicated by the fact that in 1767 the Superior Court justices petitioned the Assembly to raise them, because those which then existed were "altogether inadequate to the Charge Time Trouble Fatigue & Expence necessarily attending the Business of the said Court."[24] The Assembly failed to sympathize and fees stayed where they were.

From 1753 through 1760 the Superior Court of Rhode Island remained steady and serene. With the exception of 1757 Stephen Hopkins was either Governor or Chief Justice of that court throughout the period. The only changes occurred when Hopkins jumped from the bench to the Governor's chair and was replaced as Chief Justice.[25] In 1761, although Hopkins remained as Governor, the Ward faction captured the Assembly, fired the whole Hopkins court, and elected Samuel Ward Chief Justice. Ward's majority for the job was impressive, forty to twenty-six.[26] Every year thereafter as long as the controversy lasted a majority of the court shifted when one faction replaced another. When either party was re-elected the court remained substantially the same.

Election of the justices of the Inferior Courts was no different. Between 1763 and 1769 each shift in faction resulted in a shift in a majority of the judges. In 1763, when Ward lost to Hopkins, the Assembly replaced *twenty-two* of the *twenty-five* officers. The next year with Hopkins' re-election, *twenty-two* judges remained for another year. The same pattern followed for clerks of the two courts; all but one lost their jobs in 1763, but all stayed on when the freemen re-elected Hopkins the next year.

Criticism of the Rhode Island courts was frequent and severe. Most of it centered around the opinion that, like the rest of the government, the judicial system was loaded with politics. It was a colony where the law had scarcely dawned, wrote one arch critic, "where all legal rights are decided by the strength of that faction which happens to be uppermost."[27] The courts of judicature, complained another, which should be the "sacred fountains of law and justice, are often but mere instruments to execute the particular designs of party." Was it not true, he asked, that particular people, in suing for their just rights, "are frequently sacrificed by the despotism of a party" and meet with "injurious delays and impositions, both from those who ought to decree, and those who ought to execute? In a word," he concluded, "are not all concerns, civil and religious, incorporated with, or tainted by this accursed thing?"[28] This is rough talk for description of a judicial system, but it is only a sample. One writer pulled no punches and asked outright if the King were not more fit to select judges "than an ignorant and corrupt Deputy of a Town, a *Party-Jobber,* who dubs a Man a Judge for his Vote, and gets him confirmed by his Party, if it happens to be a Majority?" What is more, this same writer scoffed, the "Manufactory of Judges" was practiced alike by both parties.[29]

Others complained that the fault lay in the lack of sufficient compensation which deterred good and learned men from becoming judges. The system as it existed did not guard against bribery and corruption, they argued; a one year term was too short when experience counted in the job. For after all, judges had to support themselves and their families, and all too often the temptation was great to "Make hay while the sun shines." Who can say that the judges were not affected when the spirit of party raged in the colony? In fact, the *Newport Mercury* reported, the judges were as partial as the legislators. With two parties or factions in the government, the courts were bound to be the creatures of one or the other. The public records in this colony, the newspaper declared, "will loudly testify the depravity of courts, annually elected, without honorable support."[30]

General reports of political bias in the colony's judicial system are more easily found than specific instances when party influence directly affected justice. A few examples, however, suggest very strongly that such instances did occur. First of all, an incident in the Ward-Hopkins controversy itself indicated that even the protagonists did not trust the colony's courts. When Hopkins sued Ward for libel in 1757 over a severely critical pamphlet the latter had published, the case was heard outside the colony in Worcester, Massachusetts, for it was generally agreed that the case could not be fairly tried in Rhode Island.[31]

In 1761 Simeon Potter of Bristol, a Hopkins man, allegedly assaulted the Reverend John Usher, an Anglican priest, of the same

town. In November of that year the case went to the Superior Court
which was in the Ward faction's control—in fact, Samuel Ward was
Chief Justice. Promptly the Ward Assembly deliberately appointed a
special Attorney General to prosecute the case, replacing the incumbent who was sympathetic to the opposing party. The court found
for the plaintiff; Potter immediately appealed to the General Assembly and complained bitterly not only of the bad treatment by the
special Attorney General, but also about the Sheriff of Bristol County
—a Ward appointee in the May election—who "took up Talesmen,
whose Minds were prejudiced by Clamor. . . ." Most loudly Potter
complained of the "excessive Mulct" of £500 the court had levied on
him. When the Ward Assembly finally got around to his petition in
June, 1762, Potter refused to appear, doubtless despairing of justice
from his political opponents. But Hopkins' people returned to power
the next year, and in the first session after the general election the Assembly rendered void the conviction, sentence, and records of the
court. Simeon Potter's patience and faith in his party were well rewarded.[32]

In 1762 Joseph Tillinghast, a Ward crony from Newport, sued
Stephen Hopkins, Nicholas, John, and Moses Brown, and others in
several actions in connection with a policy of assurance. The cases
went to the Inferior Court of Common Pleas in Newport County
whose judges the Ward faction had appointed six months before at the
spring election. Hopkins and the Browns were a day late in filing
their respective pleas, and Joseph Tillinghast objected to the court's
receiving them. So the court rejected the pleas and made up judgment
against the Providence group. After Hopkins' political victory in
1763, he and his friends petitioned the Assembly for a new trial.
That body not only granted their request, but it voted that no cost be
taxed on the petition of the Governor and his friends.[33]

Politics affected litigation even before it got to court. Zebedee
Hopkins of Glocester once entered a writ against Moses Brown for
about twenty-four pounds, old tenor, supposedly owed to Robert
Sanders. Actually Brown owed Sanders nothing, but to humor the old
man Zebedee Hopkins went ahead with the writ. He wrote to Moses
Brown and apologized profusely for his conduct. But you see, said
Hopkins, "I was informed that one of Mr. Wards party offered to

wage a Considerable that I would not fill a Writt against you by Reason we was both of a party."[34] Obviously Z. Hopkins was obliged to pursue the law. This was party loyalty with a vengeance.

Once Elisha Brown had given up any further pretensions of holding high office again, he went to court to get what was owed him. He did very well against a Captain Manchester and expected final judgment for three thousand dollars in the September court of 1769. But Brown was well schooled in the vagaries of the colony's judicial system and was reluctant to let justice take its natural course alone. A court decision in his favor was hardly sufficient for this veteran of Rhode Island politics. "I have Goot Judgement against Cp[t] manchester," he wrote to Samuel Ward, "and in order to keep My self safe from thare Stopn it at the asembly, I Entend to goo a debety this faule."[35] Elisha Brown would be on the spot if any trouble occurred. Justice, it seems, was elusive in Rhode Island. "You may be sensible," wrote the Browns of Providence to a friend not as well acquainted with the system as they were, "how Difficult it is In Such a Government as this for a person to obtain these deserves."[36]

The newspapers reported that some Rhode Islanders were embarrassed by the party spirit which mocked their judicial system. But no doubt these same people willingly accepted tainted justice when it was on their side. Admiralty court justice, in any event, was not the cure they were looking for, and when it appeared that admiralty court justice was what they were going to get in large doses, Rhode Islanders as a whole bitterly objected.

The people of Providence were well aware of the danger of admiralty court enforcement of the new stamp tax and specifically complained about it in town meeting on August 15. They freely declared to the "whole world" that their natural rights were "diminished in the same Proportion as the Powers of that Court are extended." But general statements about the new danger were not enough. The Providence freemen drafted several pointed resolves objecting to the Stamp Act and carefully instructed their deputies in the Assembly respecting the authority of admiralty courts in Rhode Island. Since it had lately been drawn into question, they said, "how far the People of this His Majesty's Dominion of *Rhode-Island* have a Right of being tried by Juries," the people of Providence earnestly recommended that their deputies procure a law declaring that the courts of common law and they alone have jurisdiction in all issues and disputes growing out of the levying and collecting of any internal taxes "or any Matters relating thereto." The freemen desired the legislature in this proposed law to declare firmly that "such Process and Way of Trial" be continued "as have been usual and accustomed Time out of Mind"; and to top it off, the meeting resolved, the Assembly ought to determine "that no Decree of any Court of Admiralty respecting these Matters shall be executed in this Colony."[37]

Granted the constitutional objections were sincere, admiralty court decrees would play havoc with courts of justice which were "mere instruments to execute the particular designs of party."[38] What good were such courts to the colony that controlled them if Parliament could by-pass them in its attempt to remodel the colonial policy? A very useful judicial system would wither on the vine while colonists who violated the laws of trade or the new tax laws were yanked before a single judge who could take their property without their consent or even without a jury. To be sure, Rhode Islanders had for some time depended upon the friendly offices of Judge John Andrews who so far had prevented the admiralty court from seriously disturbing the colonists' property. But who could tell how much longer Judge Andrews would be able to close his eyes, stuff his ears, and thumb his nose at the Crown officers who brought cases to his court for prosecution?

The means of enforcement of the new revenue laws were equally as menacing as taxation itself, and during the spring and summer of 1765 Rhode Islanders debated what could be done to resist. The colony's reaction to Parliamentary taxation and increased power of the admiralty courts in America demonstrates clearly how local political issues and concerns helped to determine the course of action. If reaction to the Sugar and Stamp Acts was particularly severe, it was not only because these acts encroached upon what was believed to be constitutional right, but because they encroached also upon the advantages the colonists derived from a factional system of government. In defending these advantages the colonists were also defending their property. Again constitutional right and economic interest lay side by side, and an appeal to one sprang from a fear of attack on the other.

Although Ward replaced Hopkins in the spring of 1765, his administration was no more receptive to Great Britain's colonial designs than its predecessor. A change in leaders was but a change in faction; the factions in Rhode Island were unalterably opposed to any encroachment from Parliament, and it was truly in their interest to be so. The colony's resistance to taxes levied in England was not confined to petitions and pamphlets, controversy and political theory. Rhode Islanders found more realistic methods to impress the mother country with their attachment both to constitutional principle and to the political perquisites of government by faction.

CHAPTER VI

RIOTS, RESOLVES, AND REPEAL

I

SO FAR in Rhode Island personal resentment against Parliamentary taxation had been focused on Martin Howard, Jr., Dr. Thomas Moffat, and other members of the Tory Junto who had vigorously defended Parliament's right to tax Americans. It was not until a Stamp Master appeared on the scene that resentment developed into resistance and resistance into violence. Accompanying the news of the Stamp Act was an announcement that the ministry intended to appoint American stamp distributors, called Stamp Masters, for each colony.[1] Probably the home government assumed that the colonists would accept native Stamp Masters to execute the tax more willingly than English officers. The Lords of the Treasury appointed Attorney General Augustus Johnston, Stamp Master of Rhode Island, and the *Newport Mercury* announced the appointment on June 3, 1765. Curiously neither the Governor nor the Assembly ever received official notification of Johnston's appointment. But there in Newport as big as life was the man who claimed the position. Johnston's new office must have come as a shock to Rhode Islanders. Had the Lords selected Martin Howard, Jr., Thomas Moffat, or any of the Newport Junto who earnestly supported Parliament, the appointment would have been more understandable. But Augustus Johnston was one of their own kind; he was a Hopkins party stalwart who enjoyed considerable popularity throughout the colony. The freemen had elected him Attorney General since 1758, and for several years he had been unopposed in the spring elections, his name appearing on both Hopkins' and Ward's proxes. It was well known that he had not solicited the Stamp Master's job; that was in his favor. What greatly incensed the inhabitants was that he intended to accept it and made no secret of the fact that he would execute it.[2] This was hardly the conduct expected of the man whom the freemen had supported as their Attorney General for more than seven years and who actively participated in a judicial system which enforcement of the Stamp Act would ignore.

On August 20 Martin Howard, Jr., and Dr. Thomas Moffat learned that something was brewing in Newport. A plan was astir to hang in effigy the stamp distributor, Howard, and Moffat on August 27, town meeting day in Newport. Moffat could not believe his ears; it was understandable, he thought, that the people, in imitation of what had already occurred in Boston, might want to burn an effigy of the Stamp Master, but why the rest of them? Howard and Moffat wracked their brains for a scheme to defeat or divert the impending spectacle. They gathered with their friends of the Junto—who were adept at discovering what was going on in Newport—and learned only more startling news about the bold plan. Both men separately called upon Governor Ward who admitted he knew all about the affair, but that he did not expect the people to do more than harmlessly expose the effigies. This hardly satisfied Howard and Moffat who reported that the Governor's close friends and relatives were the chief abettors of this "unwarrantable and very daring undertaking." Moffat frankly represented the affair as an insult to the Governor and the authority of the colony, and if it came off, he admonished Ward, it would be very easy to suspect that those in power were "accessory privy to or silently approving of this detestable enterprize." Ward became uneasy and promised to summon his friends and attempt to persuade them to suppress the exhibition. That night Ward sent for two of the ringleaders, Samuel Vernon and William Ellery, both prominent Newport merchants, and entreated them to intercede with their accomplices to give up the pageant.[3]

While Howard, Moffat, and Johnston worried about the hanging of effigies in Newport, an incident occurred in Providence which indicated further the temper of Rhode Island resistance to the Stamp Act. William Goddard had suspended the *Providence Gazette* on May 11, 1765, for want of subscribers. Hoping to revive the newspaper in six months' time, he left for New York and a better opportunity.[4] Contrary to expectation he returned to Providence in August and ground out on Saturday, August 24, a single issue entitled *A Providence Gazette Extraordinary*. The heading bore two mottoes: "Vox Populi, Vox Dei" and "Where the Spirit of the LORD is, there is LIBERTY." This issue was a compendium of a "Number of very interesting Matters"; an examination of the contents reveals an effort calculated to incite the populace to some act of resistance.

First there was a letter by "Colonus" which criticized with temerity the late British regulations. The writer congratulated Americans for the noble opposition already shown and praised specifically the zeal of the Boston patriots. He excoriated Stamp Masters in general and Jared Ingersoll of Connecticut in particular. The next item of importance was the Providence Town Meeting's resolves which, besides denying Parliament's right to tax the colonies, demanded indemnification for all the colony's officers who refused obedience to the Stamp Act and recommended to the Assembly that it enact legislation outlawing enforcement of internal taxation by admiralty courts. Colonel Barré's speech in Parliament defending the colonies against the new tax—which was so roundly applauded in America, catapulting him into the role of a national hero—was followed by a small chart which meticulously tabulated the cost of stamped paper for indispensable daily activities. Then came two essays describing resistance in Connecticut and an account of the hanging and burning of effigies in Boston. In order to show that discontent was not confined to the colonies, the *Gazette* printed an account of the rough demonstrations of the manufacturers in London who suffered unemployment because of the lack of American orders for manufactured goods.

The most surprising piece of news was the announcement that Augustus Johnston, the Stamp Master, had openly declared that he would not "attempt to execute his Office against the *Will of our Sovereign Lord the People*." Johnston had made no such announcement.[5] Doubtless the printer believed that the best way to encourage the Stamp Master to give up his office was to broadcast that he had already resigned. There was three days' time for copies of the *Gazette Extraordinary* to reach Newport before the effigial hangings; parts of it were reprinted later in the *Newport Mercury*. It was a handy reminder of acute colonial grievances and must have stimulated the ringleaders who soon were to manifest their hatred for a Stamp Master and two members of the Newport Junto.

On Monday, August 26, Samuel Hall published his regular issue of the *Newport Mercury*. It related like the *Providence Gazette Extraordinary* an account of disturbances in England over unemployment caused by a slack in American orders. The weavers, glovemakers, and other manufacturers who marched on London had surrounded the House of Parliament and the Royal Palace; they insulted several unpopular noblemen, one of whom was drawn from his carriage and barely escaped with a whole skin. And, the *Mercury* reported, "some houses had been almost levelled with the ground" by the mob. In the colonies, the account continued, the whole continent is almost lost in hopelessness; the people's liberty, dearer to them than their lives, is threatened. "All America is in commotion, *and the people very exactly copy the example set them by their brethren at home.*"[6] The *Newport Mercury* printed two accounts describing specifically the Boston riots of August 14 and 15. An effigy of Andrew Oliver, Stamp Master, the mob hanged alongside one of the imp of Satan. After demolishing a new building said to be a stamp office, the crowd carried the effigies and parts of the destroyed building to Fort Hill where they burned them both. Soon they invaded Oliver's property which adjoined Fort Hill, burned one of his coaches, stripped his garden of fruit, drank his cellar full of liquors, and smashed some of his furniture. (Andrew Oliver took the hint and resigned his office the following day; his letter of resignation was read publicly in Boston.) The crowd, exulting in its success, went to have a talk with the Lieutenant Governor, Thomas Hutchinson, but he not being at home, they peacefully dispersed. The *Mercury* also acquainted Rhode Islanders with the demonstrations and effigial hangings in New London and Norwich, Connecticut.

In a last minute attempt to stave off the insulting show of effigies, Martin Howard, Jr., author of the *Halifax Letter,* in this same issue of the *Mercury* delivered a thoughtful message to his fellow townspeople. Howard announced his utter astonishment at the erroneous notions of people,

who, under a Pretence of serving the Cause of Liberty, would take away the Rights of private Judgement, and stop the Avenues of Truth, by instigating the Populace, and endeavoring to point their Fury against the Person and Interest of a Man, meerly because he happens to differ in Opinion from his

Countrymen: and in that Instance, only exercise the same Privilege which they claim and enjoy.

Howard retracted nothing he had written in the *Halifax Letter*. He solicited no "Favour or Exemption from the Abuse intended him," and, he remarked, although he became the object of the people's revenge because of his beliefs, he would never regret the cause whatever the consequences. These were bold words at the time they were written and printed. Because there were few Rhode Islanders who wanted to believe them and judge calmly their truth, their effect was to incense further the inhabitants against the writer. In the last week of August it was not a question of who was right but a question of whether the Newport Junto or Vernon and Ellery had the support of the people. In another effort to quash the next day's proceedings, two officers of the government visited Augustus Johnston and after acquainting him with the mob's plans, asked him to resign his post. Following his blunt refusal the two visitors advised him to get as far from Newport as possible—advice which he also refused. Having done their duty, the two well-wishers left him and marked him a stubborn man.[7]

Early on Tuesday morning, August 27, the promised effigies of Johnston, Howard, and Moffat, each with a halter hung round its neck, were paraded through the main street of Newport, attended by a hangman, to a spot on Queen Street about forty paces from the Court House. A few persons hastily constructed a gallows and suspended the figures from it. Each effigy bore various labels needlessly explaining to the inhabitants the cause of the pretended execution. Meanwhile, Johnston attempted to rally some of his friends in an effort to break up the demonstration, but they soon convinced him that without the authority of the government they could do nothing. Hardly a minute went by without Johnston's receiving a warning that the mob was after his skin. Reluctantly he slipped out of Newport until the party was over.

The effigies hung from the gibbet all day. At eleven o'clock in the forenoon the Governor and the freemen gathered at the Court House for the quarterly town meeting. While they elected new deputies to the Assembly and conducted the business of the town, three men outside, Samuel Vernon, William Ellery, and Robert Crook, another merchant, carefully guarded the gallows and "walked under and before it in muffled big coats flapped hats and bludgeons." Throughout the day, Newport's approving citizens appeared in small groups on tours of inspection. But late in the afternoon the three principal contrivers became uneasy lest the expected crowd should not appear. To overcome the delay and hasten the appropriate end of the day's work, "they sent into the streets strong Drink in plenty with Cheshire cheese and other provocatives to intemperance and riot." The spirituous catalyst turned the trick and broke down the townspeople's reserve. Shortly after sunset a willing mob collected around Ellery, Vernon, and Crook, cut down the stuffed figures, and tossed them into a bonfire "amidst the Acclamations of the People." The mob dispersed. The *Newport Mercury* was pleased to announce that the day's events were carried out with moderation; no one's person or property suffered any hurt.[8]

One reason for the mob's retiring so quietly after the burning of the effigies was because it was known throughout Newport that Johnston, Howard, and Moffat had left town. Even John Robinson, Collector of the Customs, took no chances with the crowd and spent that day and night under Captain Leslie's wing aboard the *Cygnet*, man-of-war, anchored in the harbor. If the mob intended violence it put it off until the objects of its hatred should be at hand. The next day all four of the exiles returned to town believing the people had satisfied their anger and resumed their good sense. Although there was not another issue of the *Newport Mercury* until September 2, doubtless the news of the second Boston riot which occurred on Monday, August 26, had reached Newport on Wednesday. The Boston mob on Monday evening had violently assaulted the houses of William Story of the admiralty court, Benjamin Hallowell, Comptroller of the Customs, and Lieutenant Governor Thomas Hutchinson.[9] The arrival of the stimulating Boston news at the same time as the return to Newport of the men marked for sacrifice brought the simmering mob—only half satisfied by the tame hangings of the day before—to an uncontrollable boil.

On Wednesday afternoon John Robinson, walking with friends on Queen Street—one being Martin Howard, Jr.—was collared by Samuel Crandal, the leader of a small hostile group. Howard and his friends offered help, and after bitter words on both sides Robinson disengaged himself. This was sufficient to alert the mob. The chief ringleaders of the day before "rushed into the streets with a chosen band of Ruffians at their heels"; their faces ludicrously painted, carrying broad axes and other tools of destruction, they flowed through the narrow streets to Martin Howard's house. There they broke in and in a short space of time destroyed all the furniture and china, plundered every room, demolished everything they could not comfortably carry off including the contents of a well-stocked wine cellar. From there they proceeded to Moffat's house where they repeated the pillage. Before three o'clock the next morning they had visited Howard's home three times and Moffat's twice; having gutted the interiors, they left only the shell-like frames standing. Howard and Moffat in the meantime had fled Newport for their lives.[10]

The apostate Attorney General turned Stamp Master, Augustus Johnston, bravely sat at home with his family during the rampage; countless messages arrived warning him that his home was in danger. He summoned a few of his friends to defend his property, but they refused and tried to impress him with the fact that these ungoverned fanatics meant business and would as soon kill as curse if they met resistance. After removing his wife and "small sick children" from their beds to a place of safety, his friends took Johnston by persuasion and force to the home of Nicholas Lechmere, Searcher of the port. Other friends began removing his furniture and belongings to a safer place. About eleven o'clock in the evening Johnston learned that the main force of the mob—in between assaults on the other victims' houses—was on its way to confront him. Johnston left Lechmere's house and set out straightway to meet them. One cannot help admiring Johnston's courage. Believing that he had always enjoyed a measure of popularity in the town, he hoped to prevail upon the mob to give up its violence. Luckily, he met first a friendly group which assured him that the mob intended to extort a resignation of his office or string him up on the spot. Rather than resign to an "infamous Banditti" or risk death at the hands of a rampaging mob, Johnston about midnight escaped to the *Cygnet*. The rabble soon reached and surrounded his house with the idea of treating it in the same manner they had Howard's and Moffat's. They found the furniture removed and the Stamp Master gone. After a few friends promised them that Johnston would resign his office the next day—the mob threatened vengeance if he failed to do so—the rioters returned for a final fling at what was left of Howard's house.

Collector Robinson along with Benjamin Wickham, a retired army officer, with whom he lived in rooms adjoining the Customs House, did not wait for the mob but took refuge aboard the *Cygnet*. Before leaving town Robinson considered applying to the government for protection but soon realized the folly of the idea. The tumultuous mob, fresh from its plunder, surrounded his house, entered it through the windows they shattered, and demanded his surrender. They gave up after learning that he had been for some time aboard the man-of-war. From the Customs House the crowd hastened to John Nicoll's house, but he too had quickly got aboard His Majesty's vessel. The next morning on board the *Cygnet* Captain Leslie entertained at breakfast Johnston, Howard, Moffat, Robinson, Lechmere, Wickham, and Nicoll.

On Thursday, August 29, Johnston's friends sent a message informing him that if he should come ashore they believed a peaceable settlement might be reached. The Stamp Master agreed, and once in town his friends told him of their promise the night before. Johnston learned, too, that not only his friends, who were involved for interceding in his behalf, but his family also were threatened with destruction. Faced with these facts and the knowledge that the colony's government intended no support—Governor Ward having conveniently left for his farm in Westerly the day after the hanging of the effigies—Johnston signed and presented to the ringleaders a paper indicating that he would not accept the office without the consent of the townspeople. His note was extracted from him on pain of consequences injurious to himself, his family, and friends. Nevertheless, his signing and delivering the note to the leaders of the riot was a disingenuous gesture on his part; he reported later to his friends aboard the *Cygnet* that he had no intention of abiding by it. Since the note was not attested several of the rioters became suspicious. They sought out Johnston and made him swear to the note he had written, which when done, appeased the ringleaders and allayed the suspicions of the mob.[11]

Thursday afternoon, August 29, was a turning point of the riot. The town had been in the hands of the mob for three days, but men like Samuel Vernon, William Ellery, and Robert Crook had succeeded in directing the enthusiasm toward ends in some way related to resistance to the Stamp Act. But on Thursday afternoon the riot lost direction, and there emerged from its ranks one John Webber, about twenty-one years old, who had been in the colony only three or four days. It appeared that Webber, first identified as an Irishman but later as English, had been induced by the native ringleaders to assist with the dirty work. He had played a conspicuous part in the demolition the night before. Dissatisfied with the momentary lapse in the fun, Webber strutted around Newport on Thursday boasting that he had been the leader of the mob. He managed to insult a number of people including the very men—doubtless Vernon and Ellery—who had set him to work. This turn of affairs split the mob in two; the group which adhered to Ellery and Vernon had tired of the proceedings and were content to let matters rest. The second group with Webber as its leader saw no reason why they should halt their revelry and looked around for more mischief. The original leaders became apprehensive, in fact, frightened of the boisterous Webber, and in an attempt to atone in some measure for their own contribution to the riot seized Webber with the help of sheriff Wanton and carried him aboard the *Cygnet.*

When Webber's followers learned that he had been betrayed by the men who had hired him, they gathered quickly, turned on their former friends, and threatened immediate destruction to the houses of the original leaders and the sheriff unless Webber was brought ashore and released. Ellery, Vernon, and their supporters decided that their property was safer with Webber in Newport than with Webber imprisoned aboard the man-of-war. Some of them rowed out to the vessel and by a "scandalous lie as to the man's innocence" procured his release from Captain Leslie whom they told that the authorities in town were in pursuit of the real ringleader. Once ashore and joined by his fellow rioters, Webber assumed his earlier bravado, insulted the whole lot of former accomplices, and threatened anew to pull down their houses.[12]

The riot which had begun with the express purpose of manifesting revenge against men who defended Parliamentary supremacy and execution of the Stamp Act had developed into an aimless and half-ludicrous brawl between two factions of the rioters. The original leaders were scared out of their wits. They begged and entreated Webber to give up, bribed him with money and a new suit of clothes, in fact, promised him anything he pleased. Sheriff Joseph G. Wanton groveled and cringed before the rabble-rouser. "What would you have of me?" the sheriff supplicated; "I will do every thing to satisfy you; I will lay myself down, and let you tread on my neck, if that will satisfy you." As tension mounted, several Newport gentlemen decided that the whole business had gone far enough. Godfrey Malbone, Jr., and a number of his friends threatened to take matters into their own hands and fight fire with fire. If the mob would not disperse by persuasion they would force it to do so. Both factions decided to do as they were told; the once proud insurgents moved slowly homeward. The inhabitants of Newport spent a quiet night in their homes.[13]

Bright and early Friday morning John Webber again paraded about the town declaring that the business was far from complete and bragging that he was the leader of the mob. He threatened the whole town with destruction and in particular the homes of the traitors who had turned him in the day before unless they met his demands and made good their promises. The people of Newport anticipated another day of riot and plunder. Webber swaggered through the streets continuing his threats, when he met quite by accident, Johnston. Webber treated him with great insolence. Augustus Johnston, the Stamp Master, the most hated man in Newport and the principal cause of the extended riot, "heroically seized upon him" and with the help of a few others carried and clapped him into jail. The peace of Newport was finally restored.[14]

Martin Howard, Jr., and Thomas Moffat were thankful only for their whole skins. They had been publicly and shamefully exposed in effigy, they were "stript pillagd and plundered" of their worldly goods, and they had been hunted like wolves in the streets of the town. And all this they knew to be only because they had asserted and maintained the authority and jurisdiction of Parliament in America. Their presence in the colony was intolerable to a great number of the inhabitants. The government had not made the slightest effort to protect them; and so without even coming ashore they embarked on Saturday, August 31, aboard the *Friendship* for Bristol, England.[15]

On Saturday afternoon Governor Ward returned to Newport from his farm in Westerly.[16] Samuel Ward was a great believer in Pope's maxim, "Whatever is IS RIGHT."[17] If the people wanted harmlessly to hang and burn in effigy several townspeople, it was all right with him. He saw to it, however, that his private duties called him away from Newport the next day. How could he foresee that the town would be turned upside down in his absence? When he returned Newport had resumed its tranquil state. The only changes that he might have seen were that two of the local residences were lacking their insides, several of the prominent citizens were missing, and the lodgers at the county jail were augmented by one. It might also have been apparent to Ward that the Customs House was shut tight and would not open for business until several days later when the Governor succeeded in convincing Robinson that it was safe for him to come ashore.[18]

Not until the Assembly met in its regular September session was any action taken in regard to the riot. The members requested Governor Ward to issue a proclamation for apprehending the participants and for preventing "such Riots in the future." The calm of Newport had been undisturbed for almost two weeks when the proclamation appeared.[19] The government seized none of the offenders. Only John Webber, whom Augustus Johnston had put in jail, was in the colony's custody.

Once in England Howard and Moffat told the whole story, naming several significant persons as instigators of the riots. When the Assembly learned of this it promptly directed the Governor to assure the agent that the mob which committed the depredations was neither encouraged nor animated by "any Person of Consequence (as far as the General Assembly have any Knowledge in any such Matter)." The Assembly hoped that this assurance of its members would "have as great Weight, as the Suggestions of any evil minded Persons on the other side of the Water."[20] Howard and Moffat, however, did achieve a small measure of satisfaction; their very presence in London kept alive the threat against the colony's charter. Too, the

British Treasury refused to pay a grant of money long due to the colony for its efforts in the Crown Point campaign of 1756 until the colony made a reasonable compensation to the sufferers in the riot.[21] The Assembly could see no possible connection between the money owed them and the sufferings of Howard, Moffat, and Johnston and so refused any compensation until the colony had been paid what it believed was due from the British government. The affair stretched over the years in a stalemate; the colony never received the grant, nor did the victims of the riot pocket a penny for their sufferings.[22]

There was no violence at this time in Providence. The *Newport Mercury* printed an account carrying a Boston dateline that some of the Providence people, "struck with the patriotic behavior of their brethren at Newport," hanged an effigy of the colony's Stamp Master from the Great Bridge on August 29. It remained all that day and the next and then was cut down and burned by the populace.[23] In contrast to the proceedings at Newport this was a tame affair. There was no provocation for violence at Providence because there was no publicly expressed opposition to the convictions of the people. There was no one in Providence against whom a mob could conscientiously manifest its hatred for a stamp duty. The people satisfied themselves by meekly hanging and burning an effigy of Johnston who was twenty-five miles away.

How different were the circumstances in Newport. Martin Howard, Jr., and Dr. Thomas Moffat had officiously thrown their unpopular ideas about Parliament in the faces of Rhode Islanders through the *Halifax Letter* and the numerous essays and letters in the *Newport Mercury*. But their most heinous crime was their petitioning the King to revoke the colony's charter. These were the people who begged the King to destroy the government which Rhode Islanders, through their factions, had so far successfully manipulated to their own interests. Martin Howard, Jr., and Thomas Moffat had attempted to demolish a system of politics which supported directly and indirectly hundreds of the inhabitants. In addition they tried to undermine a government which countenanced the violent measures used by the people to thwart the power of Parliament in Rhode Island. Probably there were very few Rhode Islanders who did not believe that the offenders got what they deserved. John Robinson and his assistants as customs officials executed the unfair Sugar Act. They represented the burdensome regulations which encroached upon the colony's trade. More concretely, it was they who prosecuted when a merchant brought home undeclared molasses, and so they suffered at the hands of the mob.

But the people of Rhode Island reserved a special resentment for Augustus Johnston who had willingly accepted the office of Stamp Master. The Stamp Tax levied by Parliament was a particularly onerous encroachment on a self-governing colony which suffered its freemen to shift the burden of taxes from one town to another or to pay no taxes at all when the apportionment displeased them. Not only was this tax to be levied by a legislature over which the freemen had no control and be enforced in the courts of admiralty, but it was to be executed in the colony by a man whom the freemen had supported for a number of years as a part of their system of politics. Johnston's crime was that he betrayed the freemen of Rhode Island and their political system which maintained him.

Rhode Islanders' intense dislike for defenders of Parliamentary supremacy, royal officials, and an apostate Attorney General would probably have been sufficient in itself to provoke rebellion. But in addition the freemen had discovered that relief from the King and ministry or disavowal by Parliament of its right to tax was not forthcoming. They had remonstrated against the Sugar Act; they had petitioned the King to relieve them from an impending Stamp Tax. Their Assembly had sanctioned Hopkins' pamphlet which protested against both of these measures. The colony had tried to represent its case in Great Britain by the only means it knew. Other colonies had petitioned Parliament against the same grievances. But the British government would not listen; King, Parliament, and ministry turned a deaf ear. Rhode Islanders were balked overseas by an arbitrary refusal to listen to reason; they were antagonized daily at home by men who wholeheartedly supported this peremptory treatment. Many saw the futility of future protest but at the same time absolutely refused to surrender what they knew to be a considerable advantage and believed to be a positive right. And so a number of people in Newport turned like angry children upon the nearest objects of their resentment. Their anger knew no bounds; it fairly exploded. Although it did not stave off the Stamp Act, the riot in a sense was a success. It eliminated Howard and Moffat from Newport; it forced Augustus Johnston to resign his office; and it impressed upon the world in general the colony's determination not to submit to the authority of Parliament.

## II

Rhode Islanders did more than gut houses of the friends of Parliament during the summer and fall of 1765 to manifest their conviction that the Stamp Act was unconstitutional. When the General Assembly met in East Greenwich in September, it drafted resolves in protest to the Stamp Tax closely modeled after those which Patrick Henry submitted to the Virginia House of Burgesses in May. Although the Burgesses accepted only four of Henry's resolves, six of the seven which he proposed were printed for the first time in the *Newport Mercury* on June 24. Those passed and unpassed appeared in Rhode Island as authentic and acquainted the people with the radical temper of some of their countrymen in the Old Dominion.[24] Several Rhode Island towns drafted resolves of their own and sent them to the Assembly along with instructions to their deputies indicating their sentiments about Parliament's attempt to levy stamp duties.[25] Moses Brown and Henry Ward in committee with three others had these and Patrick Henry's before them when they drafted the colony's official resolves against the Stamp Act in September, 1765.[26]

The Rhode Island Resolves declared that the General Assembly had always enjoyed the right of determining matters of "taxation and internal police"; this right had never been given up, but the King and people of Great Britain had constantly recognized it. Furthermore, the Assembly explicitly denied the right of any other power to lay taxes and imposts upon the people of Rhode Island, and any attempt to do so had "a manifest tendency to destroy the liberties of the people of this colony." If the Assembly had stopped there, its resolves would have indicated that Rhode Islanders believed in concert with most Americans that Parliamentary taxation was unconstitutional. But the Assembly went further, further than any other colony was willing to go at this time. The Assembly accepted one of Patrick

Henry's rejected resolves, modified it slightly, and asserted that Rhode Islanders were not bound to obey any law imposing an internal tax if it were levied by any body other than their own Assembly. This resolve actually encouraged disobedience to the Stamp Act, a stroke no other colony dared at this time. Furthermore, the last resolve, patterned after one from the Providence town meeting, directed all officers of the colony to proceed as if the new duties did not exist, and the Assembly would indemnify them for their conduct. As far as the General Assembly was concerned the Stamp Act, although passed by Parliament, did not bind Rhode Islanders.[27]

When the Assembly met at East Greenwich in September to draft the Stamp Act Resolves, it also acted on the Massachusetts proposal of the previous June inviting the American colonists to participate in a general congress to discuss the difficulties produced by the new acts of Parliament.[28] Other colonies had earlier considered the same proposal, and a number had agreed to send delegates to New York on the first Tuesday in October in order to consult together and send representations to King and Parliament. The Assembly quickly acceded and set to work preparing instructions for its delegates. The choice of commissioners, as they were called, created some excitement. Jabez Bowen of Providence, a strong Hopkins supporter, was "Impatient to hear" who they were;[29] he was doubtless disappointed to learn that the Ward Assembly chose two members of the southern faction, Secretary Henry Ward and Metcalf Bowler, deputy from Newport, to represent it in New York.[30] Resistance to Great Britain was usually a bi-partisan activity in the Assembly. In this case, however, it was apparent that if any fame or notoriety redounded to the colony for its participation in this first, natively inspired congress of the colonies, the Ward party wanted all the credit. The coffers of the colony were close to empty in September, 1765, owing to the difficulty the government was having over the general estimate and the collection of taxes. Before the Assembly handed over the hundred pounds it voted for the delegates' expenses, it directed the General Treasurer to hire the money.[31] He succeeded, and with fifty pounds apiece in their pockets, Bowler and Ward set out for the Stamp Act Congress in New York.

The part played by the Rhode Island delegates is obscure in this intercolonial congress which registered an official declaration of the unconstitutionality of the Stamp Act and the very great danger in extending the limits of admiralty court jurisdiction. Unfortunately the members kept no record of their debates. Neither of the colony's delegates was chosen a member of any of the three committees which drafted the addresses to the King, Lords, and Commons.[32] However, if Bowler and Ward correctly reflected in New York the opinions of the General Assembly at home, as they were manifested in 1764 and 1765, then they found themselves supporting more advanced ideas about the power of Parliament than those of the majority of the delegates which drafted the declarations. When it came time to vote they must have suppressed their more extreme views and for the sake of union agreed to the declarations and addresses. Although the colony itself had not petitioned Parliament since its protest to the old Molasses Act of 1733, its commissioners in this instance apparently did not hold out against addressing both houses of the supreme legislature. Ward and Bowler signed the documents, and four days after the commissioners wound up their affairs in New York, they sailed into Newport Harbor. On the very next day in South Kingstown they submitted a written report along with a copy of the proceedings of the congress to the General Assembly which promptly accepted them.[33] Each colonial Assembly from New Hampshire to Georgia—except the Virginia Burgesses, who had clearly declared their stand earlier through Patrick Henry's resolves—approved the proceedings and supported the congress.[34] By ratifying the declarations and addresses the Rhode Island Assembly took its place with the other colonial governments in joint opposition to Parliament's claim to tax America and subvert the right of trial by jury.

## III

About the middle of September a ship arrived in Boston from London carrying twelve tons of stamped paper for Massachusetts, New Hampshire, and Rhode Island. On October 15, Rhode Island's share arrived in Newport Harbor in His Majesty's sloop, *Viper,* and was reloaded aboard Captain Leslie's *Cygnet.* Rhode Islanders had watched the maneuvering of the stamped paper with considerable apprehension, and as November 1 drew closer the articles and essays in the *Newport Mercury* grew hotter in language against the Act and its sympathizers.[35] The fact that the stamped paper was actually in Newport, although on board a man-of-war, was a cause of great anxiety. Of course, Augustus Johnston was singled out as the villain who ordered it to be delivered.

November 1 seemed like the Day of Judgment about to dawn upon Rhode Islanders. United almost to a man against the Act, nevertheless, they could not be certain that some superior force would not descend upon them and rigorously enforce the hated duties. In other colonies and probably in Rhode Island, young couples hastened to secure marriage licenses "so as not to pay dearly for stamping,"[36] although the Act did not include taxing such licenses. Ship owners and ship captains, unwilling to take chances, rushed to clear Newport Harbor before the fateful day. The Collector was never so busy as during the week prior to the effective day of the Stamp Act when about eighty vessels were cleared or entered for departure. More than half of these were destined for Surinam or the West Indies.[37] There was an "uneasyness appearing already in the People," Joseph Wanton, Jr., reported on October 31. He had business before the General Assembly, but he did not "chuse to leave Home, not knowing what to morrow may Produce."[38]

On the first of November, "The drowsy Dawn usher'd in the gloomy-ey'd Morn with a sable Veil!—wild Horror threaten'd the wide vault of Heaven." The sun was darkened; all "Nature seemed to languish." At noon a prodigious number of melancholy mourners and spectators marched with "sullen tread" in funeral procession to the burying ground in a final farewell to departed Liberty whose bier they carried. People of all ranks attended from the highest to the "Blacks, who seem'd from a Sense of their Masters Sufferings, to join the Mourning Course." At the edge of the grave a son of liberty "emerged from the horrid gloom of Dispair" and reverently addressed the saddened multitude. But Liberty was not dead; she was snatched "from the Jaws of frozen Death" by a Guardian Angel sent by the Goddess Britannia. Old Freedom ascended "to the Orb of the rising Sun, to remain unvulnerable from the Attack of lawless Tyranny and Oppression." At this point, the writer of the account in the *Newport Mercury* was carried off in a fit of ecstasy which rendered him totally unable to describe the actual and glorious ascension of Liberty in her flight heavenward. Posterity was left to imagine the perfect beauty and otherworldliness of this rapturous moment in the history of Newport.

After the ceremonies at the grave, Newport was suddenly transformed from a city of mystical sorrow to one of worldly joy and celebration. The afternoon was spent in great rejoicing; bells were rung and the Court House decked with flags. The whole affair, the newspaper reported, was carried off with decency and showed a manly, sensible behavior. The best results, the *Mercury* counseled, would come from a "calm steady determined Opposition."[39] John Webber, the rioter who had been in jail since late August, added to the excitement by attempting to hang himself in his cell, but he was interrupted before the job was complete. Webber was back in the news on another count. Sheriff Joseph G. Wanton received two threatening letters informing him that if he did not release Webber, a mob would storm the jail and remove him. Nothing happened on November 1. The next evening a large group of men surrounded the jail but dispersed when an alarm was given—that is, all but two who were seized and spent the night with Webber.[40]

Demonstrations occurred in a number of other towns from Portsmouth, New Hampshire, to Charlestown, South Carolina.[41] A wag in Annapolis, Maryland, took the prize for his laconic report of the times which he described as *"Dreadful, Dismal, Doleful, Dolorous, and Dollar-less."*[42]

Rhode Islanders were faced with three courses of action. They could set up Augustus Johnston as Stamp Master, order the stamped paper brought ashore from the *Cygnet,* and pay the taxes on the hundreds of pieces of paper specified by the Act. This would have been entirely inconsistent with the character of their opposition up to this time. Secondly, they could shut up shop completely and refuse to do business which required stamped paper. This would have meant that the courts would close, trade would cease, newspapers would stop publication, and the inhabitants would be subjected to numerous other stoppages, some drastic to the economy of the colony. Several colonies attempted to do this but succeeded only in part with the result that here a court closed and there a printer stopped his press.[43]

Lastly, Rhode Islanders could continue in business as if the Stamp Act did not exist. This was exactly what happened.

It was generally known in the other colonies that Rhode Island was the first to set the example of disobedience which was later followed by the other governments.[44] In the first place, Governor Ward refused to take the oath for executing the Stamp Act, and, it was reported, he declared publicly "that he would sooner renounce his Office of Governor, than enter into an Engagement subversive of the Rights and Privileges of his Country."[45] The *Newport Mercury* continued publication throughout the whole period the Act was supposedly in effect without any sign of a stamp on it.[46] The Inferior Court of Common Pleas of Newport County sat as usual in its regular November session and again in January without regard for stamps. Metcalf Bowler, a delegate to the Stamp Act Congress, was a judge of this court.[47] Providence County Inferior Court "proceeded in business as usual."[48] Although the Superior Court of Judicature did not meet in regular session in Newport until spring, 1766, three of the judges transacted court business without stamps on November 27 in order to discharge two insolvent debtors.[49] When the Superior Court met at Providence in March, it appointed Silas Downer to act as Attorney General, "the King's Attorney being absent. . . ." This was a bit of irony Rhode Islanders must have thoroughly enjoyed. The King's Attorney was Augustus Johnston, the discredited Stamp Master still hanging around Newport. Silas Downer, who took his place, was a very active member of the Providence Sons of Liberty.[50]

Governor Ward won an unexpected honor when, at the request of the Assembly, he issued a proclamation calling for a day of public thanksgiving on the last Thursday of November. The patriots of Boston focused attention on Ward as the first Governor in America who dared to direct "the ministers and people within his jurisdiction publickly to implore Almighty God, 'That our RIGHTS, Liberties and Privileges may be precious in His Sight,' and that 'He will be pleased to frustrate every Attempt to deprive us of them. . . .' "[51]

Late in November Collector Robinson asked Augustus Johnston for a supply of stamped paper so that he could proceed legally with the business of the Customs House. Johnston honestly replied that if he attempted to land the papers from the *Cygnet* without the consent of the inhabitants his life would not be worth a shilling, and consequently he saw fit not to comply with the Collector's request.[52] In fact, the *Newport Mercury* reported that there was not a "Stamp Master from New Hampshire to Georgia that will execute his office."[53]

The Lords of the Treasury instructed Governor Ward to assist and support the Stamp Master in his colony and to see to it that under-distributors were well supplied with stamps. The Lords also specifically required the Governor to superintend the Stamp Master's bond if he had not already executed it.[54] These instructions, which he felt bound to answer, embarrassed Ward since he had no intention of executing any of the orders that the Lords of the Treasury had given him. It occurred to him, however, that if Johnston officially resigned his office before the Governor and council, Ward could honestly answer the Lords that the Stamp Act could not be executed in Rhode Island because there was no Stamp Master.

Governor Ward immediately called a council meeting and sent for Johnston whom he asked point-blank whether he would accept the office of Distributor of Stamps. Johnston, under the steady glare of three Assistants and six deputies whom Ward had rounded up, requested a day to answer, and when the council received his note the members found it equivocal and put the question to him again. A second time he asked for a delay, and again his answer was neither an acceptance nor a refusal.[55] That night a number of Sons of Liberty visited his home for the purpose of helping him make up his mind. Johnston was not to be found, for he had slipped aboard the man-of-war in the harbor. After a night's reflection he came ashore on Christmas Day and officially and for all time renounced the office of Stamp Master. The resignation, which was sworn to and attested this time by a justice of the peace, was announced to a large assembly before the Court House amid plaudits and several huzzas. The *Newport Mercury* published Johnston's resignation in its next issue.[56]

On the day following Johnston's resignation Governor Ward blandly wrote to the Lords Commissioners of the Treasury and informed them of the Stamp Master's action. Ward added that he was sure that no one could be found who would accept the position since the inhabitants, regardless of rank, considered the Stamp Tax to be "inconsistent with their natural and just rights and privileges." In fact, he said, they believe that Act to be "incompatible with the very being of the colony."[57] Only a man in Ward's political position could appreciate the truth of this last statement. For if the power of Parliament were admitted to tax Rhode Island, then the political system on which Samuel Ward had risen to the Governor's chair would crumble beneath him. Later Ward's government occasionally issued certificates signifying that there was no stamped paper available, a practice which Captain Leslie considered to be a direct evasion of the Act since the stamps were stuffed in his ship's hold. Ward explained that the colony had no authority whatsoever to appoint Johnston's successor.[58]

Augustus Johnston's political career in Rhode Island was finished. The colony had elected him Attorney General for a number of years. The freemen did not formally remove him until the next election when they chose Oliver Arnold in his place.[59] It took considerable courage for him to remain in Newport which he did for a couple of years. However, like several other good friends of Parliament in America, he was rewarded with a lucrative position. He took up his post as Judge of the new Superior Court of Vice Admiralty for the Southern District at Charlestown, South Carolina, in 1768 with a reported salary of £500, sterling, per year.[60] It was doubtless a larger income than he received from fees as Attorney General of Rhode Island.

It is difficult to determine when Rhode Island haters of the Stamp Act began calling themselves Sons of Liberty. But the name became increasingly popular among the patriots in Rhode Island, as in other colonies, during the fall and winter of 1765-1766. It was not until the next spring, however, that any real organization took place; at that time both Providence and Newport Sons of Liberty appointed Committees of Correspondence and drafted radical resolves which pointedly admitted allegiance to the King but just as pointedly denied the authority of Parliament.[61] These committees in both towns contained prominent people including in Providence the County Sheriff, the printer of the *Gazette*, and influential John Brown. The Newport committee bristled with respectability and colonial officials. On it were William Ellery and Robert Crook, busy merchants who engineered the effigial hangings and riots the previous summer; Secretary Henry

Ward; deputy Metcalf Bowler; Josias Lyndon, clerk of the lower house and later Governor; and, of course, to keep the channels of communication clear, Samuel Hall, printer of the *Mercury*.[62]

These committees corresponded with each other, with the Boston and New York Sons, with Connecticut committees, and those in several other colonies. At the suggestion of Boston the Providence Sons agreed, should the Stamp Act be repealed, to continue as a "Union of Writers" if "insidious Ministers" or any "Denomination of Men" undertook to deprive them of the least of their liberties. As "Watchmen on the Wall," they would rouse the people at the smallest sign of danger in order to "perpetrate the Union of the Colonies for [their] mutual Safety and Comfort."[63] But the repeal of the Stamp Act blunted their operations, and the Rhode Island Committeemen, with the exception of Silas Downer, were content to accept Parliament's apparent reversal as a clear-cut victory for colonial liberty. The Sons of Liberty in Rhode Island for several years relaxed into a fraternal order which gathered each spring with storm and bluster to celebrate the repeal of the Stamp Act.

## IV

Although the Stamp Act was not officially repealed until March 18, 1766,[64] Rhode Islanders were fairly well assured of it by the time their election rolled around in April of that year. Joseph Sherwood in England had reported to the Governor that the Commons sat all night on February 22 and voted for repeal by 108 votes.[65] Whether the repeal of the tax had any effect upon the colony's election would be hard to determine. During the campaign, however, Ward was praised for his "steady Opposition" to it which had "merited the Approbation & Thanks" of the whole country.[66] (From the knowledge we have of Ward's activities during the Stamp Act crisis, it is a little difficult to discover just what he had done to deserve this universal praise, except to give the inhabitants a free rein to resist as violently as they saw fit—an opportunity which was probably fully appreciated by a majority of the people.) Ward entertained some thoughts of retiring early in the campaign and informed his wife that he would do so as soon as he could accomplish it with propriety. But no man likes to quit when he is ahead; he consoled her in her loneliness with the fact that "however perplexed the Scene may appear the Stage is under Direction of infinite Wisdom and Goodness and may the Almighty assist Us to act our Parts in a Manner acceptable to Him."[67] God's "infinite Wisdom" persuaded Ward to remain in the race, and early in March he submitted the usual peace proposals to the opposing faction in an attempt to quiet the "intestine broils."

Ward's truce plans were as unwelcome in Providence as Ward himself, and once they were heard and dismissed, both sides attacked the more serious problems of the annual campaign. The Browns of Providence were sure that nothing this year could save Samuel Ward, "Butt a Large Sum of Money," which, they gleefully added, "we are advised by M^r Wanton, they Cant Git."[68] Mr. Wanton's report on the campaign fund of his opponents may have comforted his friends, but it was not accurate, at least not in Providence County under the Browns' very noses. John Dexter, a Hopkins party lieutenant in Cumberland, reported that after riding a whole day in the rain to secure but twenty votes, he learned that one of the party faithful had fallen off, had gone to Providence, and "Returned Back well Lined with the Last Bank" in the interest of Samuel Ward. But Dexter remembered that the distributor of Ward funds in that area had "fingers like fish hooks" and was "not very Politick" and would probably pocket the money himself after voting for Ward and his friends.[69] Anyway, God's "infinite Wisdom," or the repeal of the Stamp Act, or a judicious distribution of the "Last Bank," convinced sufficient freemen to go along with Ward for another year, and he settled down at the head of the government with a comfortable majority of 235 votes. Curiously silent, but apparently willing, Elisha Brown shared the prize and took his seat in the council as Deputy Governor.[70]

Rhode Islanders in general believed that the Stamp Act was repealed on their constitutional terms and that Parliament was convinced of its error in attempting to tax America. The Declaratory Act which preceded repeal announced Parliament's right "to bind the Colonies and People of America . . . in all Cases whatsoever."[71] Most Americans, however, agreed with William Pitt and distinguished between taxation and legislation. Because the power to tax was not specifically mentioned in the act, they believed Parliament had given up its claim in this matter. But the members of Parliament understood the act to include taxation, the framers having deliberately left the word out in order not to offend Pitt and those who agreed with him. This ambiguity caused considerable trouble later, but it satisfied Parliament which believed it had settled the question for all time.[72]

It was apparent to only a few that the men most responsible for the repeal were the English merchants who traded with America and who brought pressure upon Parliament to repeal the Act because the colonists' nonimportation of English goods and the Stamp Act itself hurt their business. In fact, Henry Cruger, Jr., in England, wrote to his father, *"some English Merchants are ruined by it."* It was expedient, then, to repeal the Stamp Act on economic grounds. If Rhode Islanders did not influence Parliament to change its mind by denying that body's right to tax, they contributed indirectly to repeal by withholding orders for British goods. Indeed, Parliament might have repealed the Act sooner had nonimportation been more effective, but a trickle of American orders, in Cruger's opinion, convinced Grenville that the colonists might soon submit altogether.[73] Aaron Lopez of Newport would have been a contributor to this trickle of trade had Cruger not stopped his orders until he was sure "which way this Momentous Affair wou'd turn and terminate." America's partial boycott of English manufactures was made nearer whole by British merchants who refused to give out a *"single* order for Goods, on purpose to compell all Manufacturers to engage with [them] in petitioning Parliament    ."[74]

But all this was not clear to Rhode Islanders in May and June when they celebrated the repeal of the Stamp Act. Newport burst forth into joy and illumination; bells were rung, shipping in the harbor displayed its flags, and the Liberty Tree was adorned with colors.[75] William Ellery ordered the gunner of Fort George to blast away with twenty-one rounds at noon and one at sunset, hoping the colony would allow the expense for the powder, which it did.[76] Newporters, however, were careful to avoid any riot and disorder; the Sons of Liberty controlled the whole affair, and the *Mercury* was pleased to report the lack of disturbances among the inhabitants who were extremely cautious about "giving away indiscriminately their liquor."[77]

The people of Providence contained themselves with difficulty until June 4 when they combined their celebration of the repeal with the King's birthday party. Providence far out-distanced Newport in noise, toasts, and piety. The townspeople awoke to the ringing of bells; a battery of cannon dug into the parade was discharged to the pleasure of all. The Court House was decked with flags, and the ships at anchor in the harbor ran up their colors simultaneously at a given signal. At eleven in the morning the celebrants gathered on the parade and briskly marched in order to the beating of drums and the sounding of trumpets to the Presbyterian meeting house. There the Reverend David S. Rowland delivered a patriotic sermon from Psalms, CXXVI, 3, dedicated to Henry S. Conway, who, like Colonel Barré, had warmly defended the colonists in the debates in Parliament. At the close of his discourse on the evils of the Stamp Act, that "monster horrid to the sight, heinous deformed, and void of light," they milled around the Court House and drank His Majesty's health accompanied by a royal salute of twenty-one cannon. This completed the festivities for the forenoon. At four o'clock they reassembled and drank several

of the most loyal, patriotic, and constitutional Toasts, under a Discharge of seven, five, and three Cannon, accompanied with the Sound of Drums, Trumpets, and the loudest Huzzas of the loyal Multitude, who were liberally treated by the Gentlemen of the Town.

In the evening they were entertained with skyrockets and "divers other Kinds of Fireworks" and "an elegant boil'd Collation served up to the Company." In order to include the Daughters of Liberty, a grand ball was given by several prominent citizens. At eleven o'clock, when every heart was "full fraught with Joy and Loyalty," the company retired.

The townspeople were more than pleased when they later learned that they had out-swallowed their Boston friends by twenty draughts. The people of Providence managed to put away thirty-four toasts which included the King and Queen (separately), Conway, Pitt, Barré, Franklin, Stephen Hopkins, Trade and Commerce, the Arts and Sciences, and for good measure, the Downfall of Popery. Whom they did not drink to was more indicative of their political feelings than whom they toasted. They did not tip their glasses to Parliament which had repealed the Stamp Act. Neither did they drink to the health of Samuel Ward, Governor of the Colony of Rhode Island.[78]

The Assembly sent effusive thanks to everyone in England who had anything to do with the repeal of the Stamp Act except Parliament— an omission Rhode Islanders bragged about in the newspaper.[79] A committee drafted an address to the King which thanked him for his assent to the repeal of the Act and which merely alluded to the colony's "due Regard and Submission to that August Body the British Parliament." Governor Ward wrote to Barlow Trecothick and other merchants in England expressing the Assembly's gratitude for their "Zealous exerting themselves in Favour of America."[80] The colonists learned later that Rhode Island and Quebec were the only colonies which thanked this committee in London for help in repeal, a fact which galled the English merchants since it cost them £500 to put it through.[81]

Providence ostensibly outdid Newport in demonstrating its satisfaction over the repeal of the stamp duties. But the fact that it delayed its celebration until the King's birthday, instead of filling the bowl at the arrival of the welcome news, was in itself indicative of a feeling among a few that Parliament had played a sinister role in the whole affair. It was from Providence that the warning came in the summer of 1766 that in spite of the withdrawal of the Stamp Tax, "the Principles upon which the Repealing act was passed, were not at all inconsistent with those of the act repealed." The Parliament, it occurred to the few Rhode Islanders who gave the Declaratory Act a second look, "claimed a *Right* to do all that the Stamp Act did, and more too, whenever *they* should think it expedient to assert that Right."[82]

Silas Downer, a lawyer and scrivener from Providence and a prominent member of the Sons of Liberty, probed deeply into the motives of Parliament. It was never a question, he wrote to the Sons of Liberty in New York, "whether we was able to pay the Tax; but whether the Parliament could constitutionally impose it." Because Americans were distinguished from their fellow subjects in Britain in the matter of right, there arose the violent discontent in America which he euphemistically called the *"lawful, necessary, and highly commendable Opposition. . . ."* Downer could not see why Rhode Islanders owed any thanks to the legislature of another realm for unmaking an act for taking their property which it could not execute, and which it had no more right to enact than the "Divan of the Sublime Porte." Americans ought to be extremely cautious, Downer warned, that nothing escaped them which could possibly be twisted to mean the least recognition of Parliament's authority to tax the colonies. Moreover—and here he expressed that independent attitude nourished by Rhode Islanders for a hundred years—Americans should deny in the most positive terms the authority which Parliament had taken upon itself not only in taxation but in many other matters. They should "constantly and fervently maintain that many Acts of that Senate have Validity and Operation here only by voluntary Adoption and Introduction." In fact, Downer declared, no one could demonstrate that "even the Common Law of England hath place here in any other Manner." He called for a vigilant union for the preservation of the rights of the people which would sound the alarm as danger approached. Parliament had repealed the Stamp Act, but the Declaratory Act, according to Downer, was a road ready paved for similar impositions in the future.[83] While Americans celebrated and congratulated each other on the best of Kings and were lulled by the soft music of Parliament, men like Silas Downer jarred their fellow colonists with warnings of things to come. And while Samuel Ward dreamed of long and profitable terms as Governor of Rhode Island, Charles Townshend planned a long and profitable revenue from America.

CHAPTER VII

## MORE TAXES AND MORE POLITICS, 1767-1771

THE HISTORY of Rhode Island in the late 1760's and early 1770's has meaning only when it is considered in light of a constant effort to defend the virtual independence which the colony had enjoyed for so long a time. New taxes, determined customs officials, ubiquitous naval officers, even an American nonimportation agreement, challenged self-determination and provoked in Rhode Islanders further expressions of that independent attitude which they had maintained for a century. Resistance to the encroachment of Great Britain and its Parliament was based primarily on a stubborn defense of the charter and the right to govern themselves according to their lights. Although politics continued to absorb much of their time, interest, and money, Rhode Islanders were forced again and again to turn their attention to what Parliament was doing or was about to do to them.

Despite the repeal of the Stamp Act an uneasy feeling crept over the people in the spring and summer of 1767. The year before Parliament had reduced the impost on molasses to a penny a gallon, but this very act contributed to the people's apprehension, since the duty was payable on *all* imported molasses whether it came from the foreign or British islands.[1] The duty had lost even the scent of a trade regulation and now *appeared* to be what it always had been—a tax on the molasses trade. The colonists' experience with Parliament over the Stamp Tax had left scars which would never be completely erased. There were probably very few who believed as did Ezra Stiles's friend, Benjamin Gale of Killingly, Connecticut, that the Stamp Act had "laid the foundation for Americans being an Independent State."[2] On the other hand, as one observer commented, the Stamp Tax had served a "noble Purpose" and gave Americans "Sight enough to *see Men as Trees walking*."[3] The arguments which the colonists had forged and polished were poised for further use if the occasion re-

quired. Parliament's assertion in the Declaratory Act of its power to
bind the colonies in all cases whatsoever made it quite possible that
such an occasion might arise.

I

Rhode Islanders had presented a united front against the encroachment of Parliament during the Stamp Act crisis, but their unity was
owing to a general determination to oppose taxation and the authority of Parliament, not to any agreement between the factions over the
internal politics of the colony. In 1767 politics resumed its normal
place in the lives of the people after having shared the stage for two
years with the noisy resistance to the demands of the British government.

"From what we Can Collect there will be a Violent Battle this
spring," the Browns reported, as they looked over the prospects of
the election of 1767.[4] Ward and his friends had been in office for
two years, and the northern faction was eager to close with its enemies in Newport and Kings Counties. But according to custom, the
chances of a coalition to end the fighting had to be exhausted before
each party settled down to the more exciting business of the campaign. The flag of truce, slightly soiled by this time, was first hoisted
over the Ward camp, and Elisha Brown and his warriors trotted out
to treat with the northern generals. Ward's people magnanimously
proposed that they themselves name the Governor this year, their
opponents the Deputy Governor, and each party choose alternately
the ten Assistants, that is, five from each side. The other general
officers, they suggested, should remain the same. Such a plan, they
said, would remove "the Principle Cause of the warm Contentions . . ."
and there would be need for only one prox.[5]

The Hopkins faction was quick to see that this coalition if agreed to
would eliminate *its* chief from the Governor's chair, but not Samuel
Ward, who would obviously be chosen by his party for the office.
A northern committee rephrased the proposal and demanded that
Ward also retire from the race. Hopkins' friends declared that although their party had an equal right to nominate the Governor they
would forego that right for the sake of peace.[6] But the Providence
people prefaced their counterproposal with such "lavish encomiums"

upon Hopkins and with such severe criticism of the incumbent's administration—"Anarchy growing more visible every Day"—that the Ward people gave up in disgust and replied that they "must forever be justified in refusing to comply with proposals made in such Terms."[7] In order to set the record straight and to convince the freemen on whose head the blame rested for the defeat of the coalition and the resumption of hostilities, Samuel Ward collected the correspondence which had passed between the factions, printed it in a broadside, and distributed it throughout the colony.[8] By this time the campaign was in high gear.

Electioneering in the spring of 1767 was distinguished for its intensity and expense. Sums of money from Providence were sent at the opportune moment to several towns in order to secure deputies and numerous votes for the candidates. Campaign orders to a Hopkins agent in East Greenwich reminded him not to forget the "many persons that is Stranious for M.ʳ Ward who may be agreed with for a small Sum to Lay Still."[9] Instructions for the financial arrangements in West Greenwich were explicit. The Browns wrote to Richard Greene: we have

Concluded to Send a Man from this Town who is to be in West Greenwich Next Munday with the Money allotted for that Town who is to stay their till town meeting is over, and to take a Room to him Self in order for pay.ᵍ off all those who may be agreed with by our Friends. We Lave it wholly to you & other Subscribers with you to put the Money you Rase in to aney of the Towns in Your County wair you think it will be most wanted to obtain the Deputys, we shall take care that the Money to go from here to Coventry is Sent Timely.[10]

The sanguine Browns had the "Gratest Expectation" of giving their "Inemeys a Good Drubbing,"[11] and their efforts, according to Elisha Brown, were "beyond Every thing for Expence."[12] The Reverend David Rowland wrote to Ezra Stiles that the Providence people were determined the southerners should have the Governor no longer and were "using the most unmerited endeavors" to turn the trick. "Too many," he lamented, "don't stick to perjure, or be perjured, and I begin to suspect they will succeed."[13] Ward and his friends fought equally hard, and as election day approached excitement mounted and tension increased.

The election of 1767 marked the tenth year of the struggle between the two parties; when the votes were counted Hopkins had recaptured the government by a majority of 414 votes, the largest ever obtained by either candidate. The colony was split through the middle from Bristol Ferry due west, with majorities for Hopkins and Ward in towns on the north and south of that line respectively. Neither Samuel Ward nor Elisha Brown received a single prox in the town of Providence.[14] Fifty-nine per cent of the deputies were replaced; ten new Assistants sat in the council. A new slate of sheriffs was commissioned, and five new judges took over the Superior Court.[15] And then to complete the revolution the Hopkins Assembly at its first session repealed an act of 1746 which required all new freemen to take an oath against bribery and corruption. And, what is more, it promptly thereafter resolved "that every Person who hath taken the aforesaid Oath be wholly absolved therefrom, as fully, amply, and effectually, as though he had never taken the same."[16] It is doubtful that either party had ever made a more barefaced move to keep itself in power.

Elisha Brown was humiliated. He was shamefully defeated for Deputy Governor by Joseph Wanton, Jr., who smothered him with a majority of more than six hundred votes.[17] He returned to North Providence to lick his wounds and reflect deeply upon his misfortune. Something happened to Elisha Brown at the election of 1767; he never recovered the spirit which was so evident in his earlier political operations. "After being beet and Oblig'd to Quet the feeld as wee was this spring," he confessed to Samuel Ward, his running mate, "I Seem to be Entirely seteld in My Mind not to Engage aney more in So hi A post of trust in goverment afars. . . ." It was possible, he admitted, that he "mite be of Serves in the Lore hous."[18] Uncle Brown did "goo a debety" another year, but he never set foot again in the council chamber.

## II

Not long after Hopkins and his friends took over the offices of government in 1767, Rhode Islanders learned that Parliament had given them new cause for uneasiness. For under the guidance of Charles Townshend that body was seeking new ways to tax the colonists. According to the newspapers Townshend admitted that he

did "not expect to have his statue erected in America" for his activities in the House of Commons that year.[19] Three days after he had
impressed the galleries with the claim that he would sooner cut off
his hand than tax the colonies, he moved for leave to bring in a bill
for taxing several articles imported into America. His new plans included an act for settling fixed salaries on colonial governors and
judges, to be paid out of the revenue, and a design for establishing
an American Board of Customs to enforce all the acts of trade in
addition to the new taxes.[20] Sherwood later confirmed the bad news
in a letter to Hopkins and added that the articles to be taxed were
glass, lead, painters' colors, tea, and paper.[21] By the middle of October
Rhode Islanders learned that the Townshend duties, as they were
dubbed, would become effective on November 20, but that the pro-
vision for changing the administration of government by paying the
governors and judges from the revenue would only apply to colonies
"where it shall be found necessary."[22] After all the reports that had
gone home it was curious that Parliament did not find it necessary to
meddle with the judges and Governor of Rhode Island. Certainly the
introduction of a Civil List would have altered greatly the complexion of politics in the colony and particularly the Assembly's control of the courts. Rhode Islanders at least were spared that blow.

In a separate act Parliament established American Commissioners
of Customs to reside in Boston.[23] As far as Rhode Islanders were
concerned the only bright spot in this ominous change, which settled
the machinery for enforcement of the acts of trade in the midst of
the trade itself, was that John Robinson, Collector at Newport, was
appointed one of the Commissioners. Robinson washed the molasses
of Rhode Island off his hands on November 25 and set off for Boston
to take his seat at the Board.[24] It was not long before he wished he
were back in Newport.[25]

Omission of a Civil List was hardly anything to crow about when
the colonists realized that the Townshend taxes and any act of
Parliament relating to trade or revenues were of course enforceable
in the admiralty courts. What is more, hard on the tail of the new
taxes came an Order in Council establishing four new courts of Vice
Admiralty in America at Halifax (replacing the old one there), Boston, Philadelphia, and Charlestown. Supposedly the establishment of

new courts liberalized admiralty court procedure, since it was generally agreed that the over-all court in Halifax was too far removed
from the centers of activity to be convenient for either defendant or
prosecutor. The new plan divided the thirteen colonies into three
districts with a court in each which had appellate and original jurisdiction over violations occurring within its area.[26] Again it appeared
to Rhode Islanders that not only were they to be taxed without their
consent, but if they violated the new tax laws, their cases were cognizable in courts of admiralty without juries. If a customs collector
had earlier been reluctant to appeal to the court at Halifax because of
the inconvenience in carrying a case to Nova Scotia, he probably
would not find it difficult to appeal to, or even request original jurisdiction in, the new court at Boston in full view of the Commissioners
of Customs. Not only were the local courts of law by-passed again in
this new scheme of things, but a court so close as Boston would probably put friendly Judge Andrews out of business, or so it seemed in
1768. Despite the fact that the Order in Council forbade an admiralty
court judge to accept fees and gratuities "for any judgment given, or
business done,"[27] he was still, according to Rhode Islanders, a "base,
and infamous tool of a violent, corrupt, and wicked administration."[28]

But the new procedure did not seem to help the Crown's cause in
Rhode Island. Despite the proximity of the Boston court, the common
law courts as late as 1773 were still dictating terms to the local
admiralty court and usurping the latter's authority, much to the disgust
of the loyal register, Thomas Vernon, who constantly complained and
wrote home about the misdemeanors and irregularities in court administration. He hoped the King and ministers could have a true
picture of the state of the colony which, he said, would be the means
of "changing the constitution"; otherwise, he lamented, "no person
that is a friend to Gov.ᵗ & good order can exist in this Colony."[29]

Moreover, Rhode Islanders continued to believe that treatment in
an admiralty court distinguished them from their brothers in England
respecting the rights of Englishmen. Attorney General Henry Marchant, home on business for the colony in 1771-1772, attended a
court trial in Edinburgh where he heard justice so fairly meted
out in a tea case that his "blood boiled with Indignation at the
amazing arbitrary Regulations" forced upon Americans. A colonist's

property, he complained, was subject to the sole determination of a single judge, and the colonist himself was "totally deprived of the Benefit of his Peers—Oh Britons," Marchant warned, "think of this & if not blush,—Tremble."[30]

Rhode Island's official reaction to the Townshend duties had little to distinguish it except that its protest as usual was a petition to the King and not Parliament. The Assembly was content to deny Parliament's right to tax the colonies, calling the new acts an infringement of those rights and privileges derived from nature, the British constitution, and the colony's charter.[31] Distinguished or not, the petition was rejected, since, wrote Lord Hillsborough, the King found it based on claims and pretensions "inconsistent with the authority of the supreme legislature over all the empire." Their petition stopped, Rhode Islanders took solace in roundly applauding the Circular Letter which the Bay Colony sent to her sister governments objecting to the new taxes and suggesting harmony in the protests sent home. The King and the ministry branded the scheme an "unwarrantable combination" and ordered the Massachusetts house to rescind the Letter. When the members refused by an overwhelming majority, the "Glorious 92" anti-rescinders were convivially toasted in the taverns of Newport and Providence. Moreover, the Rhode Island Assembly came to the Bay Colony's support and, in what looked like spite for the King's rejection of the petition, reported to the ministry that it agreed wholeheartedly with the sentiments of its Massachusetts neighbors.[32]

Unofficial response to the Townshend taxes had more color. Moderation was balanced by a resurgence of that independent attitude toward Parliament which had punctuated the thoughts and activities of Rhode Islanders for some time. After news of the new taxes arrived but before they became effective, the *Providence Gazette* printed an eloquent essay on the natural rights of mankind which declared it a self-evident truth that all men were by nature equal. Men were free from subjection to all laws until they entered into a civil society by their own consent. On this consent, the writer insisted, depended the obligation of all human laws. By this reasoning, he wrote, the Parliament of England could not extend its jurisdiction beyond its constituents, and its statutes, made in England, should not bind America. Others followed this writer's lead and shifted their argument from a denial of Parliament's right to tax to a bolder denial of Parliament's legislative authority over the colonies.[33]

It was left to Silas Downer to express these ideas in their extreme when he addressed the Sons of Liberty in Providence at the dedication of the town's Liberty Tree in July, 1768.[34] Downer cheerfully admitted allegiance to George III but denied in explicit terms "any other dependence on the inhabitants of that island, than what is mutual and reciprocal between all mankind." In fact, he insisted, "I cannot be persuaded that the parliament of *Great Britain* have any lawful right to make *any laws whatsoever* to bind us. . . ." But Downer did not stop here. He reviewed colonial grievances commencing with the Post Office Act (passed in the ninth year of the reign of Queen Anne) which, although convenient, was a tax and therefore outside Parliament's authority. He damned the acts of trade and called them an open violation of the laws of nature. The Woolens Act of 1699 and the Iron Act of 1750 deprived the colonists of God's blessings. These prohibitions, Downer charged, were "infractions on the natural rights of men, and are utterly void." Such an attack was unusual in the 1760's. No matter how bitterly the colonists opposed the authority of Parliament, they seldom, if ever, complained of its right to regulate trade and only infrequently objected to its laws restraining manufactures. Among several other charges Downer claimed that the change in administration of justice, which accompanied the Townshend duties in some of the colonies, polluted the courts of justice in America, hitherto undefiled by the corrupt methods practiced in Great Britain. (This charge came with ill grace from a Providence lawyer trained in the judicial system of Rhode Island.) Silas Downer expressed the most advanced theory of the British Empire so far offered by a Rhode Islander. He outdistanced Stephen Hopkins whose *Rights of Colonies Examined* admitted Parliament's power to regulate trade and superintend other general matters of the Empire. According to Downer the American colonies were self-governing states within the British Empire owing allegiance only to the King.

Discussion of natural equality provoked one Rhode Island critic to question the sincerity of the colonists' attack on the "distant prospect" of enslavement by Parliament when Americans themselves were guilty of enslaving *"thousands of tens of thousands of their fellow creatures! ! !"* A plea for human equality was unique in Rhode Island at the time of the Townshend duties, but this writer pulled no punches and argued pointedly that the only way to prevent slavery from abroad was to put a stop "to that hellish practice of deluding and enslaving another part of the human species, I mean Negroes." If liberty meant anything, it was applicable to all, for Negroes, he trumpeted, were Sons of Liberty, too.[35] Here in 1768, it seems, is a worthy example of the anti-slavery impulse which some Rhode Islanders encouraged and nourished so admirably during the Revolution and in the early days of the Republic.

## III

Although all previous attempts to end the bitter factional struggle seemed disingenuous, doubtless there were a number of conscientious Rhode Islanders who regarded the annual contest as expensive, dishonest, harmful, and ridiculous. For over ten years now the parties had fought one another, and although individuals obviously gained from the practices, the public welfare had suffered. Moreover, with new threats from Parliament staring them in the face, some Rhode Islanders argued that the colony's first line of defense against further encroachment was a cessation of "intestine broils" and establishment of some kind of political unity.

No doubt the proposals offered by the northern faction in 1767 would have been accepted had they not been couched in terms which offended the Wardites. In the spring of 1768 both sides—possibly in a moment of weakness—withheld their bitter words long enough at least for the leaders to arrive at what looked like an agreement between factions. After several letters between Newport and Providence and a meeting of representatives in both towns, the opposing generals agreed on a coalition government in which both party bosses consented to resign their pretensions to the chief office. Hopkins and his friends would name the Governor from Ward's people; Ward and his cohorts would name the Deputy Governor from Hopkins' adherents, and each party would nominate five Assistants alternately. The other general officers, that is, the Secretary, General Treasurer, and Attorney General, would remain as they were. A late addition to the agreement directed that in order to eliminate the evils of party from the courts of law, the thirty judges of the Superior and Inferior Courts would also be named alternately by each side. The General Assembly, however, would elect the clerks, sheriffs, justices of the peace, and miscellaneous officers in the usual way. And so an agreement was reached for the sake of harmony at this "Crittical Juncture," and to "accommodate the unhappy Differences which have so long distracted the Colony."[36]

The details of the coalition were not as easily worked out as the leaders had hoped. According to Elisha Brown, it took Hopkins, Ward, and their committees five days in conference at Newport to agree on Josias Lyndon as the new Governor.[37] This delay was only the beginning of the difficulties which surrounded the coalition from the outset. Josias Lyndon, a Baptist from Newport, was the unpretentious clerk of the lower house, and probably there was no less controversial figure or more neutral character in the government of the colony—doubtless why Hopkins and his friends chose him. The deputies had elected him clerk for a number of years regardless of which party was in power. Against his "Judgement Inclination and Disposition,"[38] Lyndon set up for Governor at the request of the party leaders. Large elements of both Ward's and Hopkins' parties promised him unflagging support. Hopkins, Moses Brown, and more than seventy of their friends in the northern town signed and sent a letter to the erstwhile clerk pledging to do all in their power "by every lawful means" to elect him. We desire, they wrote, that "the blessing due to the peace maker may rest on you."[39] Ward's people named Nicholas Cooke of Providence, Deputy Governor; he had not been in politics since the French War when he sat in the upper house. (Elisha Brown disliked him intensely.)[40] After each party nominated its five Assistants the prox was printed.

Support in other parts of the colony was not so solid. The people of East Greenwich were far from unanimous in their backing of Lyndon. On April 11 a group of insurgents met and firmly determined to destroy the coalition and, the Browns reported, keep this "unhappy Colony Inraged with party Disputes."[41] Only a week after Lyndon consented to preside over the government in the interests of peace, another outburst occurred in South Kingstown, an occurrence which momentarily shook the neutral candidate from his desire to heal the wounds of contention. But pledges of support like Hopkins' letter from Providence persuaded him to resume the role of peace-maker.[42] In Newport some of the Hopkins people bolted and rallied around Joseph Wanton, father of Colonel Wanton, several times Deputy Governor under Hopkins. Wanton set up for Governor and distributed a prox, a political scheme which Ezra Stiles described as an Episcopalian attempt to take over the government. The apothegm in one town, according to Stiles, was no "Chh Governor, no Bishop," which considerably pleased the Newport Congregationalist.[43] Wanton was unable to command in this instance a very sizable following.

Elisha Brown was irked at the whole proceeding. He was not a member of the Ward committee which agreed with Hopkins on the nomination of the officers. Ward had asked his advice by letter about the choice of Deputy Governor, but Brown sharply replied that he could hardly choose a man for the job before he was "Sensable who would be hit on for Governor." Uncle Brown was particularly vexed over the choice of "Squiar Cuck" [Nicholas Cooke], and he told Ward that it was "Enposoble to make [their] frinds in this Countey" easy under him. It is probable that the later collapse of the Ward party was owing in part to its failure to include the cantankerous politician from North Providence in its plans in 1768. His enemies, he told Ward, made sport of him for being left out of his party's schemes when everyone knew he had been the principal spokesman of the "Suthern Entrust" in the northern county. This was particularly hard, he said, when at any time he could have given up to the Hopkins people and "had aney thing askt for."[44]

In spite of these defections the agreement to support the coalition stuck, and when the freemen went to their town meetings on the third Wednesday in April they gave Josias Lyndon a tremendous majority over Joseph Wanton, Sr. (2278-760). One report claimed that Wanton carried five towns, while another said it was only three. Anyway, Lyndon won in both Newport and Providence by large majorities.[45] The *Providence Gazette* crowed over the victory and took pleasure in listing for the public the "happy Instruments" who were selected to "unite the two late contending Interests" and restore peace and harmony to the colony.[46]

But Josias Lyndon's troubles had just begun. Despite his efforts to carry out the details of the coalition, it appeared that he was obstructed from the very beginning.[47] The freemen, of course, chose the deputies to the Assembly, and their election had nothing to do with the coalition. Thirty-five changes (more than half the total number) occurred when the lower house met in May, 1768. This seems to imply that there was a swing away from the Hopkins government which had controlled the colony the previous year. Only one other election in the 1760's up to this time had produced a larger alteration in the lower house, and that was in 1767 when Hopkins took over the reins after two years of Ward. In spite of Lyndon's efforts to prevent it, when both houses met in grand committee to elect the remaining colony officers for the year, the government took a turn toward the Ward side of the field. Three of the five sheriffs were definitely in the southern interest. There were several changes in the number of justices of peace. The total figure is not known, but without counting those of Providence and North Providence, fifty-four new ones were commissioned by vote of the Assembly. Caleb Carr, who had served as Captain of Fort George under Ward in 1765 and 1766, was again elected to that office. The deputies chose William Ellery, a Ward crony from Newport, for Lyndon's old post as clerk of the lower house.[48] When the Assembly met again in June it found the general estimate of ratable estates, which the Hopkins administration had labored to produce the year before, "defective in many Respects" and ordered it promptly corrected. Moreover, it refused to levy a new tax until the corrected estimate was accepted and passed into law.[49] There is no doubt that in spite of Lyndon's efforts to keep a balance of power between the parties the coalition government of 1768 was slanted in favor of the Ward faction.

This became even more apparent the next year when the question arose of continuing the coalition; most of the Hopkins faction in 1769 shunned it like the plague. Josias Lyndon wished he had never left his clerk's desk, for he found himself caught between the opposing factions. The Wanton element of the Hopkins party had already defected the year before when its members turned their backs on the coalition and set up Joseph Wanton, Sr., against Lyndon. Colonel Wanton, his son, who was really boss of the northern party's Newport wing, had run hot and cold all winter and Lyndon could expect little support from him.[50] Samuel Ward hedged, not wanting to commit himself until he saw which way the northern powers would turn, that is, for or against the coalition. Fearing for a time that Lyndon could not command the strength to win the election, Ward toyed with the idea of running himself, promising his wife, however, that he would not subscribe a shilling and "that no great Inconvenience would arise. . . ."[51] But he thought better of the plan and about the middle of April belatedly assured Lyndon that he would use his interest for him. The peacemaker printed his prox and hoped for the best.[52]

For additional assistance Lyndon turned his eyes northward where he had won considerable support the year before. Political affairs in the north were in a state of turmoil. The people of Providence, Elisha Brown reported, seemed to be in great confusion; "there is no Sertenty how it will goo in this Countey. . . ." Brown himself was disgusted with the whole situation. A thorough party man, he had never approved of the coalition, and when in 1769 Ward asked him to support the Lyndon prox, he replied that the disagreeable proceedings in his own party had made him "allmost Redey to a peare in the other Entrust." Nothing but "Raial frendship and a sensear Regard" for Ward kept him from joining Hopkins. He promised, however, that he would support Lyndon and Henry Ward individually, but "as to my Riten Leters" throughout the county in favor of the whole prox, he wrote to Ward, "I Cant, for My one brest Denis me [for my own breast denies me]."[53]

Hopkins' people in Providence were divided among themselves. Expecting the support they had promised him, Lyndon listed Judge Daniel Jenckes on his prox. But the Judge promptly announced in the newspaper that the Governor had made use of his name without his leave.[54] Lyndon turned to the Browns and found them split in their opinions. John and Joseph were still strong for coalition, but Moses refused Lyndon any support whatever. Even Stephen Hopkins pussy-footed behind the scenes debating where to throw his strength. Lyndon, who was provoked at every turn, suspected collusion. In his mild-mannered way he suggested that Joseph Wanton, Jr.—who had made a hurried trip to Providence to consult with Hopkins—had spread stories to his disadvantage, which, he lamented, was a "common Thing in Party." Nevertheless, poor Josias Lyndon swallowed his embarrassment and decided to carry on.

The Hopkins faction repudiated Lyndon, Moses Brown explained, because he had knuckled under to the Wards instead of upholding the balance of power in the government—a condition, said Brown, "Essentially Necessary to presarve the Freedom of the Constitution."[55] The upshot of it was that Hopkins and his friends, except John and Joseph Brown, were persuaded—probably by Wanton, Jr.—to support Joseph Wanton, Sr., for Governor in opposition to Lyndon. So Wanton printed a prox (motto: "American Liberty") with Darius Sessions of Providence for Deputy Governor and Nicholas Tillinghast of Providence for Secretary against Henry Ward.[56] The Ward-Hopkins controversy, which had never really ceased, continued in 1769 as Lyndon *versus* Wanton. All schemes of coalition were forgotten, and both sides sharpened their weapons for the battle. The Wantons were sanguine yet worried for fear that the "Expectations from the North are vain." Samuel Ward, it was reported, took "more pains tha[n] ever he did—" but this time for Lyndon.[57] The peacemaker who had hoped to soothe the "intestine broils" was embarrassed to find himself the protagonist of the southern faction. Elisha Brown forecast the outcome when he wrote Ward: "I beleve Wonton will Goo ahed as Hopkins is yousing his Entrust for him."[58]

When the votes were counted Wanton had overwhelmingly beaten the clerk from Newport. In fact, Lyndon won in only eight of the twenty-eight towns. One of these was North Providence, which seemed to indicate that Elisha Brown had managed to take some interest in the "Lindal procks." Eight of the ten Assistants listed on Wanton's prox took their seats in the new council. Henry Ward claimed his job as Secretary against Tillinghast, and although outvoted in most of the towns of the north, he, too, carried North Providence.[59] There was some life in Uncle Brown yet.

Meanwhile, the battle between parties was being fought on another level. The alleged truce between factions in 1768 had concerned only the general officers and judges. The fight for deputies and the control of the Assembly continued apace. The next year as early as February 4 William Ellery busied himself with plans to secure for his side a large majority in the lower house. Once the new Assembly met, Ellery wrote to Ward, the chief bone of contention in Newport would be the office of sheriff. The Hopkins wing in that town was prepared to "strain every nerve" to elect Walter Chaloner to the office. (He had served in their administration in 1767.) Ellery and his friends were bitterly opposed to him, and in campaigning against him they introduced a new weapon into the politics of Rhode Island which had not yet been effectively used. In 1765 Hopkins had hinted that Ward and his people were not as friendly to the charter as the northern faction. The northerners worked hard to identify the Newport Junto with the Ward party, but the southerners won in spite of the accusations. In the campaign of 1769 Ellery claimed that Walter Chaloner, "who pushes so vigorously" for an office in this colony, was a "Red hot Tory" and an "enemy to Civil and Religious Liberty." What is more, he was "as great a Bigot to the Established Church as ever existed" and a half-pay officer of the Crown. This was the man their enemies supported for sheriff of Newport County.[60] This was the first but not the last time the Wanton-Hopkins regime was charged with Toryism.

The period of political finger crossing—the time between the annual town meetings and the general election in May—was spent by both sides in marshalling forces for the battle in the Assembly when the colony officers would be chosen. Joseph Wanton, Jr., whose political position was considerably enhanced since his father was in the Governor's chair, was full of plans and schemes aimed at consolidating his party's victory. Since the lower house was about equally divided, he wrote to Moses Brown, they must take every possible precaution in the "Assignment of Matters" lest they give offense to friends which might prove fatal. There was not a single man to spare, he warned, and "several Important Points to Carry. . . ." Wanton solicited Stephen Hopkins' co-operation in the campaign. His presence at the election, Wanton told Moses Brown, was "absolutely necessary as the Distinction of Hopkins & Ward is still kept up." In addition Wanton admitted the party's "sole Reliance" on Moses Brown "to Steer the Lower House," and in particular, to attend to their "good Friend Chaloner who has a powerful antagonist that threatens w^th Money &c."[61]

Despite the fact that William Ellery, a Ward supporter, was re-elected clerk of the lower house, the other officers chosen by the Assembly indicated a turnover in the government strikingly similar to pre-coalition days when one faction replaced the other. The freemen sent forty new deputies to the lower house which was a replacement of almost two-thirds the total number and the largest change which had occurred for a dozen years. Of the ten Assistants, eight were new. None had ever sat in the council during a Ward administration. The General Assembly turned out four of the five judges of the Superior Court. Joseph Wanton, Jr., and Moses Brown were successful in their efforts to put Walter Chaloner back into the sheriff's office in Newport County; he remained there until 1775. Two other sheriffs, Beriah Brown and Henry Rice, were inveterate Hopkins appointees. The Captaincy of Fort George returned to Thomas George whom the Assembly had appointed in 1767 under Hopkins. The Governor's plum, the Naval Office, Wanton awarded to his son, William.[62]

Although the experiment in coalition was renounced in 1769, the parties had never really succeeded in coalescing in 1768. Indeed, they had agreed not to wrangle over the general officers and the judges in that year, but this was a far cry from establishing a neutral administration. The freemen's choice of deputies followed the familiar political patterns of the previous ten years, and the new lower house was bound as usual to reflect one faction or the other. The coalition failed because the Governor and council could not stifle the Ward bias of the lower house, and the administration which followed smacked of the southern faction. According to Moses Brown, the Hopkins party refused to support Lyndon and the coalition a second time because they did not maintain a neutral government. Hopkins and his friends reacted strongly to the Lyndon-Ward regime. The next year they set up Joseph Wanton and took over the government.

IV

Petitions and protests, constitutional arguments and debates may have satisfied the colonial theorists as a means of combatting the Townshend duties, but economic pressure was the only language that Parliament really understood. As in the case of the Stamp Act, most Americans soon realized that an effective nonimportation was their best bet to force the home government to listen to reason. At the very

time Rhode Islanders were halfheartedly attempting to form a coalition of parties in order to bind political wounds, they were trying also,
with similar lack of enthusiasm, to co-operate with other colonies in a
boycott of British manufactured goods.

Newport and Providence got off to voluble starts as early as 1767.
The newspapers were filled with patriotic letters and essays dissemi-
nating plans for home industry and nonconsumption of English
goods. Meetings were held and committees appointed. Letters from
merchants in Boston and New York stimulated temporary interest in
concerted action, but no formal agreements were made, and British
manufactures continued to come into the colony. Long after the merchants in other colonies had solemnly pledged to have no truck with
English goods, Rhode Islanders were doing business with the mother
country. In fact, by the summer of 1769, the colony was considered a
receptacle for British wares. Ships which were discouraged elsewhere
came to Newport where they could be reasonably certain of selling
their cargoes.[63] The Boston merchants proposed that if Rhode Islanders did not come into the agreement soon they would cease business
with the colony immediately. New Yorkers reported that already their
intercourse with Rhode Island was "nearly shut up, as if the Plague
was there."[64]

Toward the end of October Rhode Islanders decided that if they
wanted any trade at all they had better get along with their business
friends in the other colonies. Forty-seven Newport merchants volun-
tarily signed a nonimportation agreement which they believed would
satisfy the colony's critics and allow them to resume their intercolonial
trade.[65] Instead of assuaging the bitterness between the other governments and Rhode Island, the agreement succeeded only in increasing
it. The Philadelphians charged that the compact outlawed only British
and East India goods but permitted those from Germany and Russia
and other parts of Europe through Great Britain. This, they claimed,
would leave the door open for a general importation and hurt the
total effect of the colonies' design. Moreover, Rhode Islanders permitted the sale of all goods imported before January first, and, it appeared, some of them had taken advantage of this long interim,
having already ordered large quantities of manufactures which were
sure to arrive before that date.[66] The Providence agreement also failed

to give universal satisfaction to other colonial merchants. A series of meetings which began in July, 1769, culminated on October 24 with a plan not to import goods listed as superfluities almost two years before. The agreement which seemed drastically patriotic in 1767 was a timid step in 1769 in comparison to the more radical pledges of merchants in the other ports.[67] Owing to this pusillanimous attempt at cooperation, an increasing number of people in other colonies became incensed at Rhode Island. New York launched a general boycott of the colony's trade—"save only what shall relate to Debts already contracted." It was whispered "and credited by many" that South Carolina's commerce with Rhode Island would "soon, in great measure be discontinued."[68]

Early in 1770 Parliament repealed the duties on all imports lately taxed except tea. After severe soul searching American merchants decided to remain steadfast in their determination not to import from England until all the taxes were taken off. Repeal was a signal for some Newporters to renounce their agreement and import freely. Resentment in other colonies turned into rage when it was reported in several places that the nonimportation agreement had broken down completely in Newport. New York merchants told their friends in Philadelphia that three vessels from London freighted with dry goods and tea had unloaded in Newport and promptly sold their wares. Boston merchants gathered in Faneuil Hall and renounced all commerce with the Rhode Island town hoping that other ports would follow the example.[69] The *Providence Gazette* claimed that Newporters had resolved to import British goods freely and were actually advertising them for sale.[70]

Criticism of Newport did not become some of the Providence merchants who were just as eager as their southern rivals to resume importation of all goods but tea. They met and decided to do just that. The townspeople, however, got wind of their plan and called a general town meeting in which they argued with great energy about the necessity of "Harmonizing with the other Trading Towns in America."[71] They regarded the merchants' decision as "too precipitate" and voted unanimously to keep out English goods until Parliament repealed all the taxes or the other colonies generally ended their agreements. Moses Brown told the agent in London that they considered the tea tax to be a ministerial design to test Parliament's right of taxing the colonies. Although the Americans were "Sinsable that Article Comes Cheaper now than before," they were not "thereby to be Induced to Receive the Bate."[72] Early in June, 1770, the merchants tried again to undermine the town's stand on nonimportation and offered to the town meeting a substitute list of acceptable goods for importation. This was a sly move; the new list of thirty-four items included lead, glass, and paper which were lately taxed. But the town meeting voted down the scheme (39-19) in favor of its former agreement of the previous October.[73]

The boycott of Rhode Island continued.[74] Ships returned from the coasting trade without cargoes and sometimes without having broken bulk.[75] Ports in Massachusetts, Connecticut, and New Jersey joined Boston and New York in refusing any business with Newport.[76] Baltimore, New Castle, Wilmington, and Chester followed Philadelphia and determined to have no dealings with the people there "until they made atonement for their defection."[77] This treatment alarmed the Newporters and provoked them into renewing their agreement. The town meeting appointed a committee of inspection to oversee the storing of all goods imported contrary to the pact. But Newport had cried wolf too often, and in spite of the resumption of nonimportation, the town suffered at the hands of the other governments. "We are in a miserable Condition," Joseph Wanton, Jr., exclaimed, "even unable to pay the duties of our Cargoes nor can we sell a Quantity of Rum Sugar or mollasses at any price in this Town for Cash."[78]

The blame for breaking the nonimportation agreement was primarily laid at the feet of the Jews. The irate merchants of Boston claimed that the Newport culprits were "chiefly Jews," while Ezra Stiles reported that "five or six Jews & three or 4 Tories" had drawn "down Vengeance upon" a whole country.[79] Thomas Vernon, register of the admiralty court in Newport, repeated the charge but added that the goods imported were trifling in amount.[80] Ezra Stiles singled out Aaron Lopez as the chief violator. Because he refused to come into the agreement the customs officials showed him great lenity and favor. The captains of his twenty-five vessels were exempted from swearing their cargoes at the Customs House while oaths were strictly exacted from all those who had agreed not to import English goods. Once by mistake a man-of-war in the harbor seized one of Lopez' vessels with a cargo of wine which was being taken off at night by five small boats. For appearance's sake the officers condemned the ship and wine, but it was well-known that both vessel and cargo would "be set up at a Trifle and Lopez will bid them off at far less than Duties; so that he shall make his Voyage good."[81] Stiles was no bigot; he had great admiration for the Jews of Newport, often attended their services in Touro Synagogue, and read Hebrew with the rabbis. When he blamed them for violating the nonimportation agreement, he probably knew what he was talking about.

Although Providence's bad faith was not as notorious as Newport's, the northern town suffered similar treatment from the other governments. Many ports failed to distinguish between the two towns in their boycotts. Captain Abraham Smith returned from Philadelphia early in July with his original cargo. He was not allowed to sell his goods in spite of an explanatory letter he bore to the merchants there. It was read in the coffee house where, the Philadelphians charged, the "THIN colouring was seen through." The distinct parts of the colony, the *Providence Gazette* reported, "have been unhappily blended together, whereby we have suffered for the Crime of our Neighbors."[82] Since Newport's name was anathema, Joseph Wanton, Jr., proposed that the Browns carry his goods in their vessels. But the Browns, who found it almost impossible to get rid of their own cargoes, were cool to accepting Newport's burden and cordially declined the offer. The Hopkins faction, which depended upon a large number of votes from Newport each spring, was afraid that a rift might develop between the two towns which would affect their political plans. When the *Providence Gazette* reported one day that the town of Providence had passed a vote of censure against Newport for breaking the agreement, Moses Brown and Jabez Bowen rushed to the print shop, stopped the press, and had the offending article cut out of the paper. They succeeded, however, in eliminating it only from the final five hundred copies of that issue.[83]

Rhode Islanders tried desperately to convince their neighbors that they had faithfully adhered to the nonimportation agreement, and that all reports to the contrary were without foundation. Before their irresistible arguments had taken effect, the agreements began to collapse in all the ports. It was suspected sometime earlier that New York had broken the pact.[84] Sherwood wrote Moses Brown in September, 1770, that great quantities of goods were on the way to that port, and he assumed that the other colonies would be forced to import in their own defense.[85] In October the Boston merchants opened their wharves and warehouses to everything but tea. Late in November Nicholas Brown & Company and the firm of Clark and Nightingale advertised in the *Providence Gazette* assortments of English and Indian goods which must have been ordered several months earlier.[86]

Despite Rhode Island's tenuous contribution, the nonimportation agreements throughout America had some effect. Reports circulated in both colony's newspapers that the value of exports from England in 1769 and 1770 were drastically smaller than they were in previous years, resulting in a loss of employment among both English manufacturers and seamen. American nonimportation might have been more effective had the reduction in American orders not been offset by an expansion of English trade with other parts of Europe in these years. Still, a refusal on the part of many Americans to do business with British merchants helped to persuade Parliament to repeal the Townshend duties, except for the tax on tea which the legislature clung to as a symbol of its right to tax the colonies.[87] According to William Ellery, Parliament would have given up that, too, if the colonists had adhered to the agreements six months longer.[88]

Nonimportation cut deeply into one of the few means Rhode Islanders had to support themselves. The merchants shunned it as long as possible. They reluctantly co-operated when the loss of their coasting trade forced them to, and when the people in general, as in Providence, took over its enforcement. Riots were cheap; nonimportation cost them their shirts, and Rhode Islanders balked as they did at any external force which interfered with their government or economy.

## V

Interest in boycotting English goods, halfhearted or not, did nothing to lessen the intensity of party politics. After the failure of the coalition the controversy continued, rivaling in bitterness the hottest campaigns of the middle 1760's.

Probably the sharpest issue in the election of 1770 was the permanent location of Rhode Island College (later Brown University). Like other political issues it became absorbed in the controversy which obtained between the Ward and Hopkins parties and between Newport and Providence. The Assembly had chartered the college in 1764, and its incorporators included several key figures in the colony's government: Hopkins, Ward, Lyndon, Joseph Wanton, Jr., Ellery, Nicholas Easton, Darius Sessions, Daniel Jenckes, and Nicholas Brown—but not Uncle Brown.[89] The college, which was Baptist inspired, opened its doors temporarily in Warren, Bristol County, but by 1769 the permanent site of the institution became a matter of serious dispute. Newport, of course, expected the prize because of its superior size, excellent harbor and communication facilities, comparative wealth, and the Redwood Library. Providence, on the other hand, was not to be outdone and boasted similar attributes. What the northern town lacked in size and wealth its citizens believed it made up in spirit and energy. The Baptists of Bristol County were determined to keep the college where it was, and a sizable subscription in Kent County was offered to lure it across the Bay. But controversy in Rhode Island usually acquired a north-south aspect, and it was not long before the contest was between Newport and Providence.

The matter came to a head at a corporation meeting in Warren on February 7, 1770. Each town had quickened its efforts to subscribe money for building—the prize, of course, to go to the highest bidder —and considerable time was taken in the meeting in deciding which town actually showed the largest contribution. The dispute pitted the Browns of Providence against Samuel and Henry Ward and William Ellery. It was finally agreed that Newport's subscription surpassed that of Providence; but the Browns very neatly convinced the corporation that the higher cost of construction in Newport in effect lowered that town's contribution below the sum pledged in Providence. The Browns' practical insight impressed the corporation, and it promptly voted to erect the college edifice in the town of Providence to be continued there forever. Probably the corporation was impressed also by the workmanlike energy of the northern merchants and the fact that Providence was more a Baptist town than Newport.[90] Anyway, it was a clean victory for the Hopkins group which, despite Newport's larger support in pounds and shillings, had whisked the college out of the clutches of the southern faction.

Immediately the Ward people charged that party politics had put the college in Providence instead of Newport.[91] There was a great buzzing about what could be done to defeat the Providence design. By the end of February talk centered around Newport's founding its own college. William Ellery fell upon this new scheme with enthusiasm; he called upon Ezra Stiles and explained the plans for an institution which, he said, would give "equal liberty to Congregationalists, Baptists, Episcopalians, Quakers,"[92] a freedom some claimed the Providence college denied. Early in March the backers of the Newport scheme placed a charter before the General Assembly which the lower house approved. It struck a snag in the council which, according to the *Newport Mercury,* referred it to the next session for party reasons. The managers of the affair pressed the upper house to concur, fearing that any delay would kill its chances for success.[93] Despite this the upper house remained steadfast, and there the matter hung until May.

It was clear that the Newport college would be an issue in the election of 1770, and a Ward victory would probably establish a second institution of higher learning in Rhode Island. In fact, by the time the new college charter reached the upper house the campaign already had begun. Joseph Wanton, Jr., found himself in a delicate position. His party friends in the north had settled the college in Providence, but he was expected to solicit votes for his father among Newporters who wanted a college of their own. At least that was the appearance of things in early March when he began his campaign. He was pleasantly surprised to learn that many of the people who he believed resented the action of the upper house actually justified its conduct and censured Ward for his political gyrations in behalf of the new college. Wanton, Jr., was sure, he told Moses Brown, that the scheme for a southern college was dead and, in fact, was considered by many merely as a design to answer party purposes. He had hoped some of Ward's old friends would support his father, but, he happily exclaimed, "the Number greatly Exceeds my Expectations."[94]

It soon became apparent that Samuel Ward himself would lead his troops in the campaign of 1770. Elisha Brown had been after him for some time to return to the battleground,[95] and early in April it was generally known that Ward would head his party's prox another year. Reports from several towns indicated to Ward that some of his political fences needed mending. "The late Assignment of your Interest being in Some measure broke," Samuel Nightingale of Providence told him, it will require vigorous effort on the part of all our friends to insure success.[96] Edward Sands of Block Island informed Ward that their "Sheep have not had any Shephard This Towe years Past" and would be very hard to pen.[97] The role of armor-bearer fell to Henry Ward who claimed that his brother had "no other motives in entering into the Opposition than to serve the Colony and his Friends," a frank admission at least. He wrote several letters soliciting the help of old cronies and companions in what he openly termed, "this Warfare." The campaign under the Secretary's experienced hand took a new twist when he wooed the voters of Providence County by telling them that with Hopkins in mufti the struggle was no longer between Newport and Providence. He hoped that the "Current in the North County" would not be "so violent against [his] brother as formerly."[98]

The campaign grew hot in Newport. Ward stormed the town the first week of April and exhibited "fresh instances of Rancour and malice." Wanton, Jr., reported to the northern generals that by "Incessant Application" Ward had rekindled the fire "in some that before were still, and by his Servile Behavior had I doubt not Accomplish'd his Ends in the Money Way." Wanton entreated his colleagues to secure adequate campaign subscriptions and promised to raise double the amount in Newport. On April 5 Wanton reported that Henry Ward was out gunning for a Deputy Governor, and Joseph G. Wanton was "abroad also" at Warwick or Providence "fixing the Deputies for those County's as will best Answer his own Ends."[99] As election day drew nearer, Wanton, Jr.'s, letters to the northward grew frantic. The whole county was in confusion, he reported, and their enemies attacked the Governor and made political capital of his father's friendliness to Providence and the college. What votes he would lose on this account in the south, the son hoped he would gain for the same reason in the north. But Wanton, Jr., was admittedly worried over the outcome. He told Moses Brown he trusted that the suffering he and his family had undergone for a number of years for Providence's sake would be remembered on this occasion. He was well aware how politically obnoxious he had made himself in Newport by invariably supporting Hopkins' cause. "Something is due on that account surely," he exclaimed; "let it be paid at this Time. . . ."[100] In last minute appeals, Samuel Ward boldly advertised for votes in the *Providence Gazette*,[101] and Edward Sands, although "advanst in years and unfit to Act," kissed the freemen's wives on Block Island "in auder to Oblige There Husbands to Vote for " Samuel Ward. This last took good effect, he confided to a friend, but the "Portion was hard," he said, even with the help and "strength of New England Rum."[102]

Despite the ardent campaign in Ward's behalf, Wanton defeated him by more than five hundred votes. Darius Sessions of Providence shared the victory and remained in the Deputy Governor's chair. Ward's defeat was humiliating; Stephen Hopkins had never beaten him by such a large majority. Although the towns were about equally divided in number between the two men, Ward surprisingly lost Newport, Middletown, and Portsmouth, which up to this time had always been in his pocket. Providence, of course, strongly supported Wanton.[103] Ward's disappointment was great; it was reported in Newport that when he reached home he assuaged his sorrow by publicly declaring that although he had lost the election, Stephen Hopkins himself had voted for him. On hearing this, Wanton, Jr., suggested that Hopkins sue Ward for defamation.[104]

When the Assembly met for the general election in May, the members of the lower house found both Hopkins and Elisha Brown were deputies. Although the membership of the lower house still fluctuated, the number of changes was smaller than the previous year. All ten of the Assistants listed on Wanton's prox were elected, eight of whom had served the year before.[105] The Assembly replaced only one sheriff and re-elected the Captain of Fort George. A newcomer took over the Naval Office under Wanton and kept it for the next five years. Three changes occurred in the Superior Court, one of which was the election of Stephen Hopkins as Chief Justice. The court remained substantially the same until the Revolution.[106]

Samuel Ward's career as a party leader had ended. After the election of 1770 he left politics and retired to his farm in Westerly where he proceeded to sue all the people who owed him money—people he had not dared yank into court when he needed their votes.[107] The causes of his party's collapse can be fairly well determined. It is prob-

able that Ward lost friends when the freemen learned that the coalition administration of 1768 was slanted in favor of the southern
faction. Realization of this resulted in the strong attack on the coalition by the Hopkins people the next year when they placed their candidate in the chair. Secondly, and more specifically, Ward lost friends
when he campaigned so vigorously in 1770 in favor of a college in
Newport. There were a number of freemen in the southern section
who—although sorry to lose the college to Providence—were not
willing to support another for Samuel Ward's sake. Thirdly, the political effectiveness of Elisha Brown in North Providence was greatly reduced. The party had virtually ignored Brown in preparing the coalition in 1768, and from then on his interest in the southern faction
flagged. He balked at supporting the Lyndon-Ward attempt in 1769
to continue the fight. In addition, during this period he was close to a
state of bankruptcy and was forced to spend a great deal of time suing
and being sued in an attempt to keep his head above water. E. Brown
had something more on his mind in 1770 than politics, and because
of this the Ward party's influence in the north suffered. In the fall of
that year he petitioned the Assembly for relief under the law for insolvent debtors.[108]

Lastly, the combination of Hopkins, the Browns, and the Wantons
produced a political phalanx which was difficult to halt. By supporting Wanton, Sr., of Newport for Governor, the party smelled faintly
of coalition. Owing to this, or to reasons given earlier, Newport,
Portsmouth, and Middletown repudiated Ward in 1770 and gave
majorities to Wanton, indicating a definite shift in the voting habits
of the people on the island. Stephen Hopkins' and the Wantons' prestige, the Browns' and the Wantons' money, and the political acumen
of all these people produced an irresistible political force which remained in power until a greater force, a Revolution, removed it. Although Joseph Wanton, Jr., made more noise in the 1770's, Stephen
Hopkins was the guiding spirit of the party, and from his seat in the
lower house and from the bench of the Superior Court he succeeded
in keeping his finger on the pulse of politics in the colony.

The Ward-Hopkins controversy apparently ended with the Wanton-Hopkins victory over Samuel Ward in 1770. The controversy
ended not because of a coalition of opposite parties, as historians have
for so long suspected,[109] but because the enlarged and strengthened

Hopkins faction overwhelmed its opponents who were unable to muster the political backing to continue the struggle. Politics in Rhode Island took on a more stable aspect after 1770; the Wanton-Hopkins team was re-elected with monotonous regularity. "We are now very Quiet in the Colony," Moses Brown wrote to agent Sherwood in London, "with respect to General as well as our own Colony Politics."[110] The predominance of one party quenched the fire under the "intestine broils," and although politicking did not cease altogether, it lost the bitter spirit which heretofore had characterized it.

For the next five years Stephen Hopkins was elected a member of the lower house and Chief Justice of the Court.[111] There is no doubt he retained leadership of the party. Just before the election of 1771, Joseph Wanton, who had already served two years in the Governor's chair, intimated his desire to retire owing to ill health. A little talk with Hopkins, however, convinced him that he ought to head the prox a little longer. And so, his son observed, "to Avoid giving our Enemies a Chance of Recovering the Power, together with his Natural Disposition to Gratify his Friends," he remained another year; in fact, he remained for four more years.[112] The election of 1772 confirmed the command of the party in power. "There was no opposition," Ezra Stiles commented, "but one prox going out this year." Stiles visited the General Assembly in May, after which he recorded, "In the House of Deputies I saw *Stephen Hopkins,* Esq. formerly *Governor* of the Colony; and he could be so still if he pleased."[113] But there was no need for Stephen Hopkins to be Governor. The party succeeded handsomely in its present conformation. From 1770 to 1776 the freemen replaced only a handful of the members of the upper house. With surprising regularity the Assembly re-elected many of its officers to their jobs, making only three changes in the Superior Court and the same number in the slate of sheriffs until the Revolution.[114] Indeed, the freemen of Rhode Island had need for "but one prox" in the politically peaceful days of the Wanton-Hopkins regime. But Ward and his friends were not dead yet as we shall see; furthermore, a respite from political warfare gave the colonists more time to contemplate just what the British government was up to, and despite the repeal of the Townshend taxes, most Rhode Islanders decided that it was up to no good.

# CHAPTER VIII

## A FIRM AND INVIOLABLE UNION

### I

THE THREE years between the repeal of the Townshend duties and the Tea Act of 1773 have been labeled by historians a period of conservative reaction. During this time a majority of the merchants in America supposedly adapted their businesses to the regulations of Parliament and were happy to make a little money. Many colonists looked back with disgust upon the riotous mobs of the Stamp Act crisis and decided that the business of living was better when the colonies made it a point to get along with the home government. But despite Moses Brown's assurances to agent Sherwood that "Since the Non Importation is Disolvd the Colonys Seem very Easy,"[1] Rhode Island did not fit very well into the peaceful pattern set by the other governments. Several violent outbreaks in this period forcefully demonstrated that Rhode Islanders were determined to keep up a lively struggle against the British Parliament and ministry when either trespassed upon their habitual right to handle their internal affairs. While Americans in general were content to soft-pedal the dispute with Great Britain, the people of Rhode Island continued to rehearse their own effective methods for eliminating or silencing the King's officers who got in their way. One of these outbreaks, the burning of the *Gaspee,* had serious repercussions throughout the continent, and Rhode Islanders were responsible for ending the period of imperial peace and plenty.

Charles Dudley replaced John Robinson as Collector of Customs in Rhode Island. According to Ezra Stiles, Dudley was the son of an Anglican clergyman from the west of England whose command of a handful of votes procured the Collectorship for Dudley, Jr.[2] The new Collector arrived in Newport in the spring of 1768 and soon became well acquainted with the practices of Rhode Island merchants who played every trick they knew on the King's new officer. They stole molasses from under his nose; they wrested vessels from the hands of his assistants.[3] They solemnly entered into an agreement pledging not to pay Collectors' fees higher than those already set by act of the Assembly (contrary to a law of Parliament) in October, 1764. The government itself assisted the merchants and set up a special court of common pleas for prosecuting customs officials who demanded higher fees than those prescribed.[4] The merchants let it be known in Newport that the Collector had requested "an Accommodation in the . . . dispute between them and the Custom House," and then magnanimously granted Dudley an audience in order "to put an end (if possible) to all the animosity subsisting between the Custom House and Trade. . . ."[5] Dudley was furious over this last move; he quickly denied making such a request. To the Browns of Providence he wrote: the merchants "have tried my integrity and find it can't be shaken, and now they have nothing left against me but popular Clamour."[6]

Collector Dudley protested his innocence too much. Ezra Stiles claimed that he was careful to refuse gratuities from the right people who "trumpetted through Town, that the Collector received nothing but lawful Fees." On one occasion Stiles was informed by a ship captain that his crew had "wheeled home to the Collector Wines Fruits &c. and they were not rejected nor returned." I would not, Stiles exclaimed, "for 10 Thousand Worlds, administer so many Oaths to known false Accounts or be knowingly accessory to the daily Perjuries which he midwifes into the World of Error & Sin."[7]

But the merchants of Newport were not content like Ezra Stiles to criticize the Collector in their diaries. In April, 1771, Charles Dudley was barbarously abused by persons unknown; for a time it was believed his life was in danger. In July of that year the Earl of Hillsborough, an inveterate nagger and reminder of the colony's peccadilloes, complained to Wanton about Dudley's misfortune. Hillsborough informed the Governor that the home government would no longer exhort the colony to support the customs officials in their duties. He concluded with the warning that "it must remain with those, to whom the powers of government of Rhode Island are entrusted, to consider what must be the consequences, if, after such repeated admonition, the laws of this kingdom are suffered to be trampled upon, and violences and outrages of so reprehensible a nature, are committed with impunity."[8] Hillsborough was not aware that consideration of the consequences of "violences and outrages" had died an early death several years before with the cannonading of the *St. John* and the plunder of Howard's and Moffat's property.

Governor Wanton's reply to the minister was worthy of the examples set earlier by Hopkins and Ward, who were skillful in explaining away the colony's conduct. Mr. Dudley, Wanton reported, "in the dead time of the night, singly and alone," boarded a vessel in Newport where he met several persons supposedly "drunken sailors," who cruelly and scandalously attacked him. It did not "evidently appear" that any Rhode Islander was "concerned in or privy to the abuse offered to Mr. Dudley," but those guilty were a "company of lawless seamen." After clarifying the whole affair undoubtedly to the complete satisfaction of the Assembly, Governor Wanton then complained bitterly to his Lordship about the conduct of the customs officials in America who falsely accused and misrepresented His Majesty's faithful subjects in Rhode Island.[9] Nothing further was heard from officialdom across the ocean respecting the cruel and scandalous abuse of Collector Dudley, who, it is necessary to say, recovered.

An unofficial response, however, came from Henry Marchant, Attorney General of the colony, then in England on the colony's and other people's business. Marchant received a copy of Governor Wanton's letter to Hillsborough and wrote to a friend in Newport that it did the "Governor & the Col^y much Honor." Marchant added a revealing comment on the role of the Customs Collector in Rhode Island. Dudley, he observed, had "much exposed himself—He had better learn from Robinson's Fate, to know when his bread is well buttered & be content where Robinson confesses now he lived like a Prince & wishes he had been so wise as to have been contented. . . ."[10] Apparently Collector Dudley learned from experience, for his attention to duty did not in the immediate future provoke the wrath of the colonists. Jessie Saville, Dudley's deputy in Providence, fared no better than his superior. An angry mob seized him in 1769 and beat him unmercifully to the point of death. The *Providence Gazette* unsympathetically commented that Saville "was treated with more Tenderness and Lenity than is perhaps due an *Informer*."[11]

Another incident occurred in Newport which punctuated the colonists' resistance to the acts of Parliament and the royal officials. In May, 1769, John Robinson and the Board of Customs dispatched to Newport His Majesty's armed sloop, *Liberty*, Captain Reid, to aid the customs officers in the enforcement of the acts of trade and revenue. On the day following his arrival Captain Reid seized a Providence vessel fresh from the West Indies probably freighted with undeclared molasses.[12] About the middle of July the *Liberty* brought into Newport a brig and a sloop from Connecticut, both allegedly having violated the navigation laws. After an altercation between Captain Packwood of the brig and the seizing seamen, the *Liberty* opened fire with a musket upon the Captain, and a brace of balls narrowly missed him as he attempted to escape in an open boat. Not satisfied with small arms the crew of the *Liberty* leveled a swivel which luckily misfired. The affair occurred in plain view of the townspeople who lined the wharves. The next evening an angry mob—identified later as "Persons unknown" and "chiefly from Connecticut"—after obliging Captain Reid to remove his crew, cut the *Liberty* loose, drove her ashore, leveled the masts, and scuttled her. A few days later a high tide carried the hulk aground on the north end of Goat Island where it was set afire and smouldered for several days. In the meantime the *Liberty's* boats were hauled through town and burned. The seized brig and sloop took advantage of the occasion and quickly departed. Collector Dudley reported the affair to Governor Wanton who promptly issued a proclamation directing all officers of government to use their utmost endeavors to discover the persons guilty of the crime. As usual the colony made no arrests.[13]

It probably appeared to most people that this was another example of the mobbish resentment of the "licentious republic" against enforcement of the acts of Parliament. Some people believed that the affair was carried out with the advice and consent of Joseph Wanton, Governor of the colony. Thomas Vernon, register of the admiralty court, reported that Wanton's administration continuously exerted its influence to pervert justice, "a late instance whereof is the destruction of the Liberty Sloop."[14] It is possible that Vernon mistook Wanton's inability to prevent the attack for his implication in it. In either case the scuttling of His Majesty's vessel demonstrated that Rhode Island's opposition to the authority of Parliament could still be violent on occasion.

## II

Rhode Islanders were familiar with the *Gaspee* and with the reputation of her commander, Lieutenant William Dudingston, before the schooner began her cruise in Narragansett Bay. Under another command the vessel had touched at Newport in 1765 and again two years later. In the summer of 1769 the *Newport Mercury* reported Dudingston's "piratical treatment" of a defenseless fisherman whom he brutally beat up for no apparent reason near Chester, Pennsylvania.[15] The *Gaspee* sailed into Rhode Island waters in March, 1772, for an extended stay, and without waiting upon the Governor, which was an established courtesy, Dudingston began hounding the local vessels from ocean to wharf. Governor Wanton exchanged heated letters with the Lieutenant, and when Admiral Montague in Boston was applied to, he immediately took Dudingston's part, treating the Governor with considerable indignity.[16] Dudingston and his crew became even more insolent and stopped everything afloat under the pretense of enforcing the acts of trade. They boarded small boats, fired on oyster vessels, and stole livestock from neighboring farms. They made themselves as obnoxious to the inhabitants as pirates, which some of the people were convinced they were.[17] In May the Assembly directed the Governor to write home to Hillsborough about the "wanton and arbitrary manner" of the schooner's officer.[18] By all accounts, Henry Marchant wrote later to Benjamin Franklin, Dudingston "was a very dirty low fellow—He had suffered his People to commit many Outrages upon the Possessions and Property of the Inhabitants on Shore, and had so harrassed all the Woodmen that they were afraid to go up and down the shores. . . ."[19] By June of that year Lieutenant Dudingston was damned by merchants, farmers, and seamen alike, but his depredations continued unabated.

After hotly pursuing the packet, *Hannah,* up the Bay, the *Gaspee* ran aground off Namquit Point in Warwick during the afternoon of June 9, 1772. Captain Lindsey of the packet continued to Providence and informed John Brown and a few others of the schooner's predicament. Calculating that the tide would not free the vessel until after midnight, John Brown, Captain Abraham Whipple, and some friends organized a party of townspeople and after dark embarked in several long boats for the helpless *Gaspee*. After shooting and dangerously wounding Lieutenant Dudingston, they removed him and his crew and burned the vessel to the water's edge. The people of Providence resumed their activities the next day as if nothing had happened.[20] Three days later Governor Wanton issued a proclamation enjoining all civil and military officers to exert themselves to "discover and apprehend the persons guilty." The Governor posted a reward of one hundred pounds, sterling, payable on conviction of one or more of the offenders.[21]

From the time the Newporters fired on His Majesty's vessel, *St. John,* in 1764 to the burning of the *Gaspee,* Rhode Islanders had never been made accountable for the violent attacks upon the King's officers and vessels. The colony government had never punished or even apprehended anyone connected with these offenses. When George III ordered a Royal Commission to inquire into and report on the destruction of the *Gaspee,* Rhode Islanders were shocked beyond measure; for, according to the Commissioners' instructions, it was clear that the offenders would be delivered into the custody of the commander in chief of His Majesty's Navy in America and sent to England for trial. Lord Dartmouth informed the Governor that the King's law servants in England labeled the act "high treason, viz.: levying war against the King." In addition, the Commission was empowered to call upon General Gage in Boston for troops to preserve the peace if necessary.[22]

To the *Gaspee* Commission the King appointed several distinguished gentlemen: Joseph Wanton, Governor of Rhode Island, Frederick Smythe, Chief Justice of New Jersey, Daniel Horsmanden, Chief Justice of New York, Peter Oliver, Chief Justice of Massachusetts Bay, and Robert Auchmuty, Judge of the Vice Admiralty Court in Boston.[23] This formidable array of a Governor and four judges descended upon Newport during the first week of January, 1773. Later Admiral Montague of His Majesty's fleet arrived to lend his august presence to the investigation. The Bostonians poked fun at the whole affair:

Never was a more farcical piece of mock power than that now exhibiting in this American world: an English Admiral with his flag, a contemptable

Judge of Admiralty, and two or three other geniuses, setting out in the dead of winter to vanquish the loyal Rhode-Islanders![24]

After attending the ceremonious departure of the Boston contingent for Newport, an English naval officer described the scene to a friend. It was well worth the trip across the Atlantic, he said, just to see "so respectable a squadron" as Admiral Montague with his flag and "old *mother*" Oliver, the Deputy Governor, who trembled "under his rusty sword, rigged out athwartship like the mizzen yard of a north-country cat." These, with Auchmuty, and his large white wig "(in size equal to Ld. Mansfield's)" set out overland for Rhode Island in order to "send to England for trial and execution" the people who burned the *Gaspee*.[25]

Owing to winter conditions Admiral Montague traveled overland to Swanzey on the Taunton River where he boarded a vessel for the remaining part of the trip to Newport. He sailed into the harbor, his Admiral's flag flying, and was promptly saluted by His Majesty's vessels at anchor there. The cannons at Fort George were conspicuously silent, an incident which so infuriated Montague that he refused to call upon Governor Wanton and wrote home to the Lords of the Admiralty bitterly complaining about the insult he had received.[26]

According to the Commission, the King's instructions, and the interpretation of them by the five judges, the *Gaspee* Commission was not exactly what Rhode Islanders made it out to be. Granted it was an interference with the colonists' way of doing things. Granted, too, the carrying of suspected persons to England for trial would be an arbitrary violation of constitutional right which was sufficient to turn the inhabitants against the proceeding. But the people of Rhode Island understood the Commission to have more power than the King gave it. The judges met in two sessions, once for about three weeks in January and again in the latter part of May and early June. During the whole time, however, they made no bloodthirsty attempt to yank Rhode Islanders from their homes and families and sail them to London for trial. They made it plain to Darius Sessions and Stephen Hopkins at the outset that they would seize no one without full use of warrants from the proper local authority, that is, the colony's Superior Court, over which Hopkins was Chief Justice. Judge Oliver explained the purpose of the Commissioners to Ezra Stiles. They were to inquire into and get information about the mischief, not only the names of the offenders but the causes of the affair and particularly whether the burning was owing to the misbehavior of the King's officers. If they found sufficient evidence for conviction they were to apply to the civil authority of the colony for apprehending the suspected people.[27]

It is apparent that all these facts were not explained to the inhabitants who for the most part were left in ignorance of what the Commissioners were going to do. It seems, too, that Governor Wanton, who was a member of the Commission, Darius Sessions, and Stephen Hopkins, prominent officers in the colony's government, were culpable in that they neglected to inform the people correctly about the purpose of the inquiry. It may be that this was a deliberate attempt to keep the inhabitants stirred up and bitterly prejudiced against the Crown's way of handling the affair—a stratagem which might have helped to turn attention away from the culprits in Providence.[28] Anyway, Rhode Islanders expected the worst and were cognizant only of a Royal Commission then sitting in their midst with power, they believed, to condemn them unheard and hurry them off to the gallows in England. General Gage's troops were poised in Boston to move on the town when called upon. Five of His Majesty's warships, totalling over one hundred guns, rode at anchor in the harbor.

The *Gaspee* Commission posed a new threat to the virtual independence of Rhode Island whose government up to this time had been left free not to apprehend, convict, and punish those guilty of serious crimes against the Crown. Inquiry into colonial wrongdoing by Crown appointed officers and removal of suspects to England for trial were outright violations of that "darling privilege," the right of every Englishman to trial by a jury of his peers in the vicinage of the crime. But, as in the extension of admiralty court jurisdiction under the Sugar, Stamp, and Townshend Acts, behind constitutional objections lay local and peculiar habits and customs which the new treatment would annihilate. A Royal Commission would not only make useless a judicial system biased in favor of party friends, but it would prevent the colony courts from protecting by local trials inhabitants whom the Commissioners suspected of the crime. Rhode Island courts, we have seen, were factionally controlled; but more important, they were heavily prejudiced against the Crown's interest when that interest interfered with Rhode Islanders.

Several disputes in the past had demonstrated how futile the

Crown's cause was when cases involving it were tried by colonial judges. For instance, George Rome, an Englishman living in Newport and an agent for a large London mercantile firm, had good reason to criticize the colony's judicial system since his job was to collect debts in Rhode Island owed to his employer. Rome was painfully aware of political bias in the courts, but his chief complaint was that they were prejudiced against people like himself who represented English creditors. Exasperated, by 1767 he was reluctant even to sue Rhode Islanders, because, he exclaimed, "the perversion of their iniquitous courts of justice is so great." Once after a successful appeal to the Privy Council had armed him with the King's decree for demanding his money, he wrote, "we have danced after their courts and assemblies . . . *in vain.*" George Rome warmly recommended that the Crown abolish the whole court system and establish in its place a new one with judges appointed in London.[29]

Freebody *v.* Brenton is another example of how judges elected by the Assembly deliberately ignored even the King's demands. Originally the issue at stake in this case was a creditor's refusal to accept depreciated old tenor money in payment of a mortgage debt. After almost twenty years of litigation, when a second appeal to the Privy Council was returned in the plaintiff's favor—the first having been ignored—the Superior Court voted three-to-two to go along with His Majesty. But a month later at the annual election (1770), the freemen chose a new legislature which promptly replaced three judges on the bench, and the new Chief Justice was Stephen Hopkins, an outspoken supporter of the defendant (the paper money side of the dispute). Hopkins' court reheard the case, and ambitious Henry Marchant, a young lawyer from Newport, argued for acceptance of the old currency according to the long established laws of the colony. Marchant declared with eloquence that the King and Council had decided the issue "contrary to law, reason, equity and justice, and when the King and Council made up said judgement, the King was no King, and therefore the Court ought to set aside said judgement and make up a judgement of their own according to law." Hopkins' court reversed the decision of the former judges and by a three-to-two vote set aside the King's decree for the second time as contrary to the customs and laws of the colony. Rhode Islanders explained to their friends that the prerogative judges had been replaced by persons of "republican inclinations."[30] Freebody *v.* Brenton, which had begun as a paper money dispute in 1752, was identified in the early 1770's with the patriot cause by colonists who were not inclined to accept interference in their internal affairs by the government abroad.

But a Royal Commission with power to investigate the burning of the *Gaspee,* preparatory to sending the offenders to England for trial, dwarfed republican justices and by-passed customary court procedures, bringing the colonists face to face with the supreme authority of the British government.

The immediate reaction was bitter and noisy. Can anyone be secure, asked the *Newport Mercury,* in the enjoyment of his natural and constitutional rights? "To be, or not to be," the *Mercury* continued, "that's the question. Whether our unalienable rights and privileges are any longer worth contending for, is now to be determined.—" The Commission was promptly labeled a Court of Inquisition more horrible than anything that had ever occurred in Spain and Portugal. *"How long O LORD—How long!"*[31] This matter, Henry Marchant wrote home to a friend in England, "has opened Consequences more alarming to America, than the news of the greatest Armament that France or Spain ever boasted of being upon our coasts. . . ."[32]

Official reaction was less boisterous. Confronted as they were with a wholly new situation, the members of the Assembly discreetly played a waiting game. Even when Chief Justice Stephen Hopkins asked them to instruct him respecting the Commission, the members remained silent. According to Ezra Stiles, Hopkins informed them "that if the Commissioners should apply to him to apprehend any persons for delivery to the Admiral, that he would not do it, and would use his Authority in hindering every Officer in the Colony from doing anything to this End."[33] Hopkins spoke very boldly before the legislature which elected him, but on the third day they met in Newport, he appeared before the Commissioners and assured them he was "ready and willing to aid and assist" in the exercise of power with which they were invested for discovering the culprits. Moreover, when requested to give a "full and particular account" in writing of all he had done so far to bring the guilty persons to justice, he promised to do so "without loss of time."[34]

The Assembly's conduct which some critics reported was "to do nothing respecting the Commissioners Court" must have infuriated many people. At least it did Nathanael Greene, later a prominent General in the Continental Army. Greene was a member from Coventry of the silent Assembly, and although the "new-fangled court" alarmed him, he was more shocked by the legislature which, he observed, "seems to have lost all that spirit of independence and public virtue that has ever distinguished them since they have first been incorporated, and sunk down into tame submission and entire acquiescence to ministerial mandates."[35]

The Commissioners summoned many people to appear before them; some appeared and some did not. After two sessions of inquiry the judges had uncovered practically nothing. The people of Providence and its environs were understandably silent about the facts of the *Gaspee's* destruction. About the middle of June the Commissioners met with four of the judges of the Superior Court and presented the meager evidence they had been able to collect. The court—surprising no one—unanimously agreed that it was insufficient to warrant any seizures, and after making a report to the King the Royal Commission adjourned for good.[36]

Daniel Horsmanden, Chief Justice of New York, and one of the Commission, corresponded with the Earl of Dartmouth during and after his residence in Newport. Horsmanden admitted that the evidence was negligible and concluded that the burning of the *Gaspee* was "committed by a number of bold, daring, rash enterprising sailors, collected suddenly from the neighborhood, who banded themselves together, upon this bold enterprize; by whom stimulated for the purpose" he did not know. This remarkable piece of information the Chief Justice could have got from most any Rhode Islander several months earlier. Respecting the *Gaspee* the colony came off fairly well in Horsmanden's reports. As to the colony's government— "if it deserves that name"—he observed, "it is a downright democracy" and operates in a state of anarchy. He called the Governor a cipher who was annually elected, having no authority or power but "entirely controlled by the populace." Men of property and good sense—doubtless the Tory Junto in Newport—he reported, had long wished the King would bring the government more closely under his protection. The colony disregarded the injunction in its charter, Horsmanden commented, against enacting laws contrary to those of England. Rhode Islanders had never sent these laws home for royal approbation, "nor indeed, by their charter were they obliged to do so." He recommended that Rhode Island and Connecticut be joined in a Crown Colony but confessed that "as to the people, it would require a gentleman of very extraordinary qualifications and abilities, to adventure upon the first arduous task, for modelling them into due subordination and decorum."[37]

But Daniel Horsmanden returned to New York, and Rhode Islanders heard no more from him. After all, reports like his had been sent home before, and nothing had happened. And now even a Royal Commission admitted defeat in attempting to crack the colony's stubborn determination to handle its own affairs. The business of the schooner, *Gaspee,* Henry Marchant wrote to a friend, "however inexcuseable in the Individuals, Yet will wind up by no Means to the Discredit of the Colony—It is so thought by all People."[38] The "licentious republic" had been shaken a little, but it had not surrendered.

Although the Assembly refused to clash with the Commission over the latter's jurisdiction in Rhode Island, it co-operated with the other governments in general opposition to this glaring innovation by the home government. But it was the Virginia House of Burgesses which provoked the Assembly to act, not the members themselves. On March 12, 1773, the Old Dominion appointed a provincial Committee of Correspondence to obtain information about Parliament's activities respecting the colonies and particularly to investigate the "principles and authority, on which was constituted a court of inquiry, said to have been lately held in Rhode Island." Believing the Commission to be a "flagrant attack upon American liberty in general,"[39] most of the colonies, including Rhode Island, sooner or later followed Virginia's example. After choosing a Committee of Correspondence containing Stephen Hopkins, Moses Brown, Henry Marchant, and Henry Ward (two from Providence and two from Newport), the deputies questioned the Governor about his appointment to the Commission which was "said to be held in this colony"—as if they did not know. They asked also to see all the papers which were laid before that body.[40] Once the lower house was aware of support from other colonial Assemblies, it dared to take steps which it previously had avoided. Ezra Stiles concluded that the Commissioners would have been much more severe had the Virginians not circulated their plan for Committees of Correspondence, which, he was certain, would *"finally terminate in a General Congress."*[41] The Commissioners retreated without loss of a periwig; but the investigation had alerted the whole continent. The Committees which each colony established were ready for action when tea revived the dispute.

### III

In 1773 Parliament enacted the Tea Act to extricate the East India Company from a near bankrupt state. According to the new act the Company could ship its tea directly to the American colonies and sell it there for less than the colonists were accustomed to pay for it, in fact, at a price below what their fellow subjects could get it for in England. The small print of this new piece of legislation retained, despite the new low price, the threepenny tax held over from the Townshend duties. According to the colonists, the ministry's scheme in this new move was to lure the colonists into paying the tax peaceably, thus keeping Parliament's right of taxation untarnished. At the same time it lowered the price of tea and gave the East India Company a monopoly on its sale in America. The Americans were quick to squint at the small print and magnify it for all to read. In addition, they looked unkindly upon the monopoly and refused to drink even cheap tea for the sake of the nabobs of India.[42]

Rhode Islanders took up the hue and cry raised against the "pestilential herb," and the newspapers reiterated at length their arguments for not using it. By the end of the year three hundred families in Newport alone abandoned "that noxious WEED." When it was reported that two hundred chests of the "pernicious" stuff were expected in Newport from London, the townspeople hastily determined not to receive it. If landed, which was scarcely possible the *Mercury* warned, "it will be reshipp'd on board the LIBERTY, and sent to GASPEE, the first favourable wind and weather."[43] The details of the Boston Tea Party both Rhode Island newspapers faithfully reported, and the patriots of the Bay Colony were enthusiastically applauded.[44] The inhabitants severely denounced forestallers and labeled as enemies to their country those who paid more than the normal price for tea. When an unfortunate dock worker, unloading a small bag of it from a sloop, tripped and fell into the harbor, tea and all, the *Mercury* warned its readers: "Be cautious how you travel with this baneful article about you; for the salt-water seems of late to attract it as a load stone attracts iron." The "hitherto fascinating exotic Plant [was] daily growing more and more into Disrepute."[45] A number of towns from Cumberland to South Kingstown drafted resolves and elected Committees of Correspondence in opposition to the Tea Act and its enforcement in the colony. The newspapers were cluttered with their deliberations from February to May.[46] It was quite clear that Parliament and the East India Company could expect no help from Rhode Island.

News of the Boston Port Bill, one of the Coercive Acts passed by Parliament in retaliation to the Tea Party, arrived in Boston on May 11, 1774.[47] Parliament's act which shut tight Boston Harbor until the tea was paid for shocked not only the Bostonians but all patriots from New Hampshire to Georgia. Six days later the freemen of Providence met in town meeting to express their intense disapproval. They recommended to the Assembly a congress of representatives from all the colonies in order to establish "the firmest union." It was the opinion of the town meeting that each colony was "equally concerned in the event," and a "universal stoppage of all trade" with Great Britain, Africa, and the West Indies would be the "best expedient in this case." Newport followed close behind, and on May 20, in town meeting—Secretary Henry Ward moderator—the freemen resolved that with the "deepest sense of the injuries done to the town of Boston" they considered "this attack upon them, as utterly subversive of American liberty." The Newporters, however, said nothing about a congress.[48]

When the Assembly met in June the members went directly to work to implement the recommendations of the towns, particularly those of Providence. They agreed that a "firm and inviolable union of all the colonies" was absolutely necessary and endorsed the plan of a congress to be held as soon as possible. Before the Massachusetts leaders got around to suggesting that the congress be held in Philadel-

phia in September, the Rhode Island Assembly had chosen its delegates. As a token of esteem to the colony's most distinguished political
leaders, the Assembly chose Stephen Hopkins and Samuel Ward its
representatives to the first Continental Congress.[49] Historians have
pointed to this selection of Ward and Hopkins as final and conclusive
proof that the schism so closely identified with these men was
gloriously and for all time healed.[50] This may very well be true, but
it is doubtful that the members of the Assembly had in mind the
warm glow of a "happy ending" when they chose Ward and Hopkins to represent them. The decision was probably based on a more
practical consideration that the future of Rhode Island and the other
colonies was at stake. A congress was a dangerous but necessary step
to defend the "very being of the colony," and to it Rhode Islanders
sent their best men—men who were well acquainted with the advantages of self-government. It is possible, too, that an obstinate
residue of Ward sympathizers in the Assembly insisted that if Hopkins went, then Ward would go too. With both these men in Philadelphia Rhode Islanders felt at least that the colony was well represented.

Besides empowering the delegates to consult upon reasonable
measures to "ascertain and establish their rights and liberties," the
Assembly instructed Ward and Hopkins to exert themselves to obtain
a "regular, annual convention of representatives from all the colonies" in order to consider continuously the "proper means for
preservation of the rights and liberties of the colonies."[51] This was
to be no fly-by-night affair to remonstrate against a port bill; Rhode
Islanders meant business and were sanguine of a more permanent
union among the thirteen colonies than that which a single meeting
of delegates could produce.

The Assembly acknowledged its "tender commisseration for the
poor in Boston" and at a later session instructed the deputies to
collect the sentiments of their constituents about granting a sum of
money to the sufferers. In addition, the Assembly recommended a
general subscription throughout the colony "to give an opportunity
for a further exertion of the generous and benevolent mind."[52]

By June Rhode Islanders were well acquainted with the other
Coercive Acts and the Quebec Act which tolerated Catholicism among

the French Canadians in Quebec and enlarged that province to include the coveted area between the Ohio and Mississippi Rivers. The newspapers kept up a steady current of criticism. One writer excoriated all the tools of power who discouraged generous aid to Boston and branded them a *"ministerial, toryitical, jesuitical gentry."*[53] Others demanded a "non consumption covenant" against all British goods and suggested that if the Congress failed to organize it, the colonists should meet and choose other delegates.[54] All agreed, however, on the *"hypocrisy, venality* and *corruption,* with all other immoralities, unthought or unheard of," respecting the reigning administration in England.[55]

Rhode Islanders' sympathy for the oppressed of Boston was expressed in more than long words of commiseration. Newporters worked through a subscription committee and by the next spring had raised upwards of £225 in cash which they sent to the suffering town. In addition to collecting a sum of money by taxes the freemen of Providence welcomed Boston refugees who needed shelter. After all, the *Providence Gazette* sanctimoniously reported, "As a Community we would do unto others, as we would that they should do unto us in like Circumstances." By spring, 1775, several families from the Bay town had settled in Providence.[56]

Like Newport and Providence many other towns in the colony reacted generously to mitigate the severe treatment of the Bostonians. Some passed resolves and elected Committees of Correspondence; some sent cash and tender messages. Several country towns drove livestock—mostly sheep—to Boston. The people of Charlestown, Rhode Island, declared that the "Ax is now laid to the root of American liberty"; they promised to unite with hand and heart to "resist the impending strokes." But in order to protect liberty in Massachusetts the freemen of Charlestown denied it at home. They directed their committee to list the names of all the inhabitants capable of contributing to the relief of Boston. If any of the listed people refused to give for this "laudable purpose," they were to be judged and proscribed enemies to their country. Before the freemen wound up their meeting they instructed their deputies in the Assembly to vote against taking any money out of the general treasury to help the poor sufferers at Boston, because they were of the opinion that a tax for that purpose would be a "detriment to American liberty."[57] The ax in the tree of liberty in Charlestown was double bitted. By this time Moses Brown had succumbed to the soft music of George Fox. In helping to solicit donations for Boston from the Quakers of Rhode Island, he suggested that they "ought to be distinct from the general contribution."[58]

### IV

Stephen Hopkins and Samuel Ward set out for Philadelphia in the latter part of August. It would have been a delightful and fitting end to the "intestine broils" had these erstwhile political enemies ceremoniously departed for the historic gathering in Philadelphia with hands firmly clasped and hearts united. Hopkins, however, embarked from Providence; Ward traveled overland from his farm at Westerly.[59] In the City of Brotherly Love the Rhode Island delegates rubbed shoulders with the most distinguished men in America if not with each other. According to Ezra Stiles, Ward and Hopkins were a significant part of this eminent company; the Newport minister listed them among the cardinals of the Congress. Ward he placed in number three spot giving way only to Samuel and John Adams; Hopkins was an honorable thirteenth.[60]

The Declaration and Resolves of the first Continental Congress expressed an official position taken by the united colonies in September, 1774. The colonial Assemblies, the members declared, possessed exclusive power of legislation "in all cases of taxation and internal polity; subject only to the negative of their sovereign." The Congress did cheerfully consent, however, to the acts of Parliament which in good faith regulated trade for the welfare of the Empire.[61] Hopkins and Ward must have realized immediately that the stand taken by the members of the Congress agreed substantially with what Rhode Islanders had maintained for several years, except for the King's right to review the colony's laws. Up to this time Hopkins had outshone Ward as a politician, political theorist, and defender of colonial liberties. His reputation reached outside the borders of the colony, and his writings were printed and read in other governments. But in 1774 Ward took a more advanced stand than Hopkins in respect to the position of the colonies within the

Empire, and at the Congress he denied Parliament's right to regulate trade under any circumstances. The Rhode Island delegates disagreed, too, over the conservative Galloway Plan presented to the Congress, which would have united the colonies in a Grand Council of delegates presided over by a Crown-appointed officer. Hopkins was sympathetic to the plan; Ward was not.[62] At the Continental Congress Ward blossomed into a bold patriot pushing a radical approach to the problems of the colonies. Ward and Hopkins had not agreed at home, nor in some instances did they agree in Philadelphia.

The delegates returned to Rhode Island in November; the Assembly shortly afterwards approved the proceedings and chose Ward and Hopkins to represent the colony again in the second Congress which would meet the next May if the Coercive Acts were not repealed. The Assembly distributed to each town the Articles of Association which provided for a universal nonimportation, nonconsumption agreement to be enforced by local Committees of Inspection.[63] Rhode Islanders responded rapidly, and soon the townspeople were busy throughout the colony acting the parts of their brothers' keepers. Newport, Providence, and other towns appointed large committees which, according to the actual and interpreted rules of the Association, prevented the exportation of sheep, kept a rigid lid on prices, and confiscated goods imported contrary to the agreement, forwarding the profit derived from their sale to Boston for its relief.[64] Violators, such as Samuel Bours of Newport and Thomas Sabin of Providence, suffered the ignominy of exposure in the newspapers and were persuaded to make public confessions of their guilt.[65] Later Abial Cook of Little Compton boldly sold sheep to the *Swan*, British man-of-war, and had the effrontery to insult the committee which reprimanded him. Cook was branded an enemy to his country and the liberties of America.[66] With the help of vigilant Committees of Inspection, Rhode Islanders co-operated much more willingly in the Association than they had in the nonimportation agreements of 1769 and 1770.

V

Before and after the calling of the Congress the Rhode Island newspapers continued a steady barrage of criticism of the British government. That Parliament had anything to do with the colonies was firmly denied. Solomon Southwick, printer of the *Mercury,* declared that "the people of America have as good a right to *legislate* for, & *tax,* the people of Great-Britain, as they [British] have to legislate for, and tax, the Americans."[67] The newspapers liberally served up arguments for permanent colonial union and encouraged their readers to unite and exert bravely their combined strength, for once united, no power on earth could enslave them. "The Preacher" in the *Mercury* was certain that no other scheme but the "AMERI-CAN INDEPENDENT COMMONWEALTH" would secure the rights of the people "from rapacious and plotting tyrants."[68]

In these newspaper attacks the King himself was not spared. Americans had originally entered a covenant with the King, "Tertius Cato," explained; they agreed to be his subjects provided, of course, that they should enjoy all the immunities and privileges of natural born subjects of the Crown. When one side broke the covenant, he warned, the other was discharged from its obligation.[69] Solomon Southwick described the King as a "servant or steward of the people." It was possible, he warned, that a King might "fix himself beyond the power of the people to call him to account without a *dreadful and bloody struggle.*"[70] The power of the King, the *Providence Gazette* declared, was the power of right, not of wrong; when he was unjust he was no King. "If a magistrate," the *Gazette* concluded, "notwithstanding all laws made for the well-governing a community, will act destructive of that community, they are discharged either from active or passive obedience, and are indispensably obliged by the law of nature to resistance."[71] Passive resistance and nonresistance, the same newspaper observed later, were based on the foolish notion of the divine right of Kings. God did not require any obedience whatsoever to tyrannical power. In fact, the "Preaching up or promoting passive resistance is a greater crime than encouragement of *rebellion.*"[72] If the official colonial position respecting the British Empire was loyalty to the Crown and a denial of Parliament's authority in America, then a number of Rhode Islanders were again a few steps ahead, laying the blame for the colonies' difficulties in the lap of the King. It was not a very long jump from an attack on the King to revolution and independence.

The determination to resist was reflected also in a military spirit which swept over the people. The General Assembly voted to revise the militia laws of the colony; it appointed Simeon Potter of Bristol Major General over all the men under arms and authorized the troops to march out and give assistance to neighboring governments when any of them were invaded or attacked.[73] The towns flooded the Assembly with requests for charters establishing independent military companies. The newspapers faithfully described the training and maneuvering of the Light Infantry, the Guards, and the Grenadiers, the Fusiliers, the Hunters, and several other Cadet Companies which mustered and drilled, marched and wheeled throughout the colony before the approving eyes of the inhabitants.[74] Kent County alone boasted 1500 men under arms who were reported to be equal to the King's regulars.[75] On November 7, 1774, the *Newport Mercury* prophetically and uncannily declared that "there is now such a martial spirit running through the country, that 'tis thought, by next April North-America will be the best disciplined of any country in the world." Arbitrary Parliamentary acts had been met by resolves and petitions, angry mobs and violence. In the winter and spring of 1774-1775 it was probable that further encroachment would be met with local militia, in "warlike posture," armed and trained on the parades of Newport and Providence and clothed in American manufactures.

## CHAPTER IX

## REVOLUTION AND INDEPENDENCE

I

AS GEORGE ROME was led off to the Kings County Jail in October, 1773, he probably pondered the popular aphorism which patriots were mouthing, that "Every fool is not a Tory, yet every Tory is a fool."[1] Rhode Islanders who knew George Rome had no question about his Toryism; but those who did business with him undoubtedly admitted that he was no fool. George Rome was an English bachelor who came to the colonies in 1761 as an agent for the house of Hopkins and Haley and later other British mercantile firms in London. His "deep Purse" afforded him considerable farm property on the Island of Rhode Island and a wharf and warehouses in Newport. At his country estate in North Kingstown he lavishly entertained his friends during the holidays in the good old English tradition, even providing bird shooting for the sports and pickerel fishing for his more sedentary guests.[2] Rome had been a member of Martin Howard's Junto, and it was rumored in Newport that he was a correspondent for a secret intelligence office in London, receiving a stipend from the ministry.[3]

But Rome's business activities in America were sufficient to make him exceedingly unpopular. As agent for English firms a large part of his time was taken in trying to collect debts owed his employers in London. A debt to a mercantile house across the ocean was a second class matter to many Rhode Island merchants, and Rome was forced to spend considerable energy in litigation. The Rhode Island judges, it will be remembered, were unsympathetic to British debt collectors, and Rome found little satisfaction in the courts of law.[4]

After a particularly exasperating experience before the Superior Court, Rome sat down just before Christmas in 1767 and unburdened himself to Thomas Moffat, his friend and former member of the Junto in Newport, then in New London. He severely criticized the legislature and the judicial system, charging corruption and perjury. Rome's solution to the difficulty, of course, was a complete reorganization in which the power to appoint judges would be placed in the Crown.[5] Thomas Moffat sent the letter home to the ministry to demonstrate the total depravity of the "licentious republic." The letter lay buried until 1773, when Benjamin Franklin dug it up along with several others from Thomas Hutchinson and Andrew Oliver of Massachusetts. Franklin cannily sent these letters to the patriots in Boston, and a copy of Rome's letter was soon in the hands of the Rhode Island deputies. The *Providence Gazette* printed it in June, 1773.[6]

The whole colony rose up in a rage at George Rome. He was sued in twelve separate actions for defamation, each for £290, just below the minimum value which would allow him to appeal to England.[7] Several towns instructed their deputies to inquire into Rome's grievous charges and to determine whether it was true that "the fountain of justice is shut up" in the colony. If the charges were false then the representatives were directed to exert every effort to make the writer accountable for his "scandalous aspersions" and "vile abuse" of the government.[8]

In August the Speaker of the house, Metcalf Bowler, read the letter before the Assembly, but action was postponed until Bowler could procure the original from Massachusetts, "as no legal process could be had on the copy."[9] Thomas Cushing of the Massachusetts house informed Bowler that unfortunately the original had been returned to London, and no authenticated copy existed.[10] Respect for the finer points of legal process, which stayed the hand of the deputies in August, had faded by the end of October. The Assembly, then meeting in South Kingstown, issued a warrant to the sheriff to bring Rome on the carpet. The Speaker read the document to the house in Rome's presence and then asked him if he had written anything in substance agreeing with what he had heard. Rome's clear answer must have reddened the faces of the most callous deputies. "I do not think," he replied, "on the privilege of an Englishman, that the question is fairly stated, because I do not consider I am to be called here to accuse myself." Rome told the house that he would willingly acknowledge any letter in his own handwriting and grant "all satisfaction they are pleased to require." Bowler aimed again: "Will you or will you not make a direct answer to the question?" And again Rome replied: "I have already made a direct answer, by saying I cannot be legally called to the bar of this house to accuse myself." The deputies voted George Rome guilty of contempt of the house. They issued a warrant for his arrest and committed him to His Majesty's jail where he lay until the house rose.[11] It is possible that one or two deputies in the General Assembly were convinced by this incident that every Tory was not a fool.

Prior to the outbreak of hostilities other Tories within the colony were not dignified by command performances before the legislature. Stephen Arnold, a justice of the Inferior Court and a former sheriff, and several other people were the cause of a serious disturbance in East Greenwich late in 1774. Their "pernicious tory principles" incited a mob which hanged and burned their effigies. Deputy Governor Darius Sessions prevented any violent outbreak when he boldly dispatched the militia of Providence County and two companies of infantry which marched on East Greenwich in the middle of the night and happily settled the differences. Stephen Arnold humbly confessed his mistake and expressed his wishes to obtain the favorable opinion of his fellow men.[12] At the smell of "fish gurry" and feathers a Tory on Block Island promptly recanted his baleful doctrine and again basked in the favor of the townspeople.[13] Not long after Jonathan Simpson, a refugee from Boston, set up his hardware shop in Providence, he "rendered himself exceedingly obnoxious" to the people there by "zealously espousing the cause of Despotism, and reviling the Friends of Liberty." One morning he awoke to find the front of his shop "tarred and feathered in the modern Way." The next day he "prudently returned to Boston." The freemen of Providence resolved in town meeting that their fair town was "not to become the asylum for refugee Tories" and took steps to discourage them from coming there "by every prudent and legal measure."[14]

The circumstances were different in Newport. Owing to the permanent residence of several customs officials and the constant visits of His Majesty's naval officers, there was a nucleus of loyal gentlemen to which Newporters with Tory sentiments adhered. Toryism got a good start in the days of the Newport Junto, and although Howard and Moffat had left, others took their places as the breach between the colony and the mother country broadened.

There was Thomas Vernon, register of the admiralty court, who kept John Robinson in Boston supplied with news of the goings on in Newport.[15] Charles Dudley, John Nicoll, Nicholas Lechmere, and Richard Beale were customs officers and loyal to the British Exchequer. There was Doctor Hallyburton whom Admiral Montague had appointed surgeon of the hospital established in the colony for the reception of seamen from the King's ships in Rhode Island.[16] Doctor William Hunter, whose fine house bordered the harbor, was a member of the Newport Junto and former ally of Howard and Moffat. There were others such as Walter Chaloner, sheriff of the county, whom William Ellery had tried to defeat in the election of 1769, and several Brentons who owned Brenton Point which jutted into Newport Harbor, ideally situated for supplying the crews of the men-of-war when the patriots would have let them starve. There were probably many others whose loyalty grew warmer as the issues became clearer. Moreover, it was probable that Tories spoke out more boldly in Newport than in other towns of the colony owing to the awful presence of His Majesty's ships in the harbor which afforded at least a feeling of protection and even refuge.

Although Solomon Southwick was accused earlier of coddling a "few idle, jacobitish, tory scoundrels," who had hovered around his press since he undertook the printing business,[17] there was no question where his sentiments lay in 1774. It is possible that private interest played some part in his politics, for the harder he blasted the Tories in the *Mercury* the larger his subscription list grew.[18] That there was an active Tory faction in Newport, however, was indicated by the heat and the frequency of the attacks upon it in his newspaper. Occasionally he published their letters, only, it appeared, to comment editorially in answer.[19] Southwick took great delight in ridiculing his Tory enemies by printing such stuff as the Fellowship Club's toast: "A cobweb pair of breeches, a hedge-hog saddle, a hard trotting horse, and continual riding to *all* enemies of America."[20] Doubtless, too, Newporters chuckled over the gentleman suspected of Toryism who, "to convince his townsmen to the contrary, bought a DOG and named him TORY."[21]

George Rome, Thomas Vernon, Stephen Arnold—although a

minor judge—and other inhabitants charged with Toryism were not significant figures in the politics of the colony. Although William Ellery had pointed an accusing finger at Walter Chaloner in 1769, the attack upon the sheriff was not full scale, and the Ward people were unable to prevent his election. In 1774, however, the Tory spectre was seen by many to be shadowing one of the prominent generals in the colony's politics. The campaign in Newport during the spring of that year was closely identified with a bitter controversy between a man named William Sweet and Joseph Wanton, Jr.; it had been going on for some time but came to a head just before the election in that year. Sweet, it seemed, had got into financial difficulty in Philadelphia for which Wanton, Jr., and some others were primarily responsible. Sweet claimed he had suffered at Wanton's hand—even spent some time in jail—but could not force Wanton to do him justice. Both sides agreed to submit the affair to referees in Boston, but through strategic delay Wanton managed to get the decision postponed until after the election. Sweet and Wanton went to battle in the pages of the *Mercury* and angry words were exchanged.[22]

Wanton claimed that the whole business was stirred up for party reasons "in order to make that controversy subservient to the base purposes of a few factious, envious, designing men." In fact, Wanton labored this point and hoped to discredit Sweet by labeling him the deluded "tool of a faction" which was trying to involve the town in "intestine broils and party dissentions."[23] Wanton, of course, was fearful of losing his seat in the Assembly. Knowing how well acquainted Rhode Islanders were with the "evils of party," he hoped to focus the freemen's attention on the factious character of his critics and opponents. Sweet made no bones about wanting to defeat Wanton at the polls, and some of his remarks implied that Ward votes were behind him. In a broadside just one day before the annual town meeting, he leveled a barrage of Tory accusations upon Wanton which even the most judicious voter could not dismiss as mere party spirit.

This was the man, Sweet charged, who coddled the Stamp Master when the townspeople demanded his immediate resignation, at the time when the government was in the hands of a patriot—a remark which subtly suggested that the same was not then true. This was the man, Sweet continued, who "encouraged the sitting of an unconstitutional court of INQUISITION" in the colony, and, what is more, "urged his father to take the chair in that *detested* court." On top of this, Sweet exclaimed, Wanton boasted to the Assembly "that he had thereby saved the charter."[24] A pamphlet writer corroborated Sweet's charge that at the time of the *Gaspee* Commission, Wanton was a "flaming Tory" who "stood ready for Preferment" if the home government altered radically the colony's constitution.[25] Some of Sweet's charges stuck, and Joseph Wanton, Jr.'s, career as a deputy ended with the election of 1774. Although the freemen re-elected his father Governor of the colony for another year, the first glaring hole had appeared in the hitherto impenetrable front of the Wanton-Hopkins political fortress.

## II

As Governor Wanton walked to the Old Colony House to cast his vote on election day in April, 1775, he must have had serious misgivings about what the next few months would bring. For six years the freemen of Rhode Island had elected him Governor, and after Samuel Ward's final challenge in 1770 there had been no opposition. Wanton was an old man of seventy; he was a soft featured, somewhat feminine looking person with a round, dimpled chin, who had lived a good life as a merchant prince in Newport. He was not a politician of the Hopkins stamp nor did he thrive on controversy as Hopkins had for so many years. Wanton had kept out of politics until late in life, and he consented to become Governor only after the fire had gone out of the sectional dispute. Perhaps he would not have agreed to head so many proxes had the bitter party fight continued. But by supporting him, Hopkins, the Browns, and the other party big-wigs were able to discourage opposition and to control the colony's politics. It was a workable combination which had satisfied a large number of the freemen since 1769. But as the election of 1775 approached the peaceful aspect of politics in Rhode Island was considerably altered. A warning had occurred the year before when Tory charges were hurled at Joseph, Jr., costing him his seat in the lower house. In 1775 Toryism was a more grievous charge than it had ever been, and as the third Wednesday in April drew near the accusing finger pointed at the Governor himself.

For the first time in five years a group of freemen organized an opposition movement to Governor Wanton, because, they announced, a "number of persons in *Newport* were well satisfied that he was a Tory."[26] William Ellery, a zealous Ward man, was ringleader of the opposing party, and as he stirred the coals in Newport, he took special care to see that a few sparks landed in Providence. "You must rouse up all that is Roman in Providence," he wrote to a friend. "There is liberty and fire enough; it only requires the application of the bellows. Blow, then, a blast that will shake the country." He warmly suggested that his friends in the northern town immediately plant something in the newspapers to convince the people there "of the danger we are in from a Tory administration, and don't be afraid," he added, "of seasoning it highly. People with weak appetites must be warned." Ellery did his best to "shake the county" in the north, letting it be known that "John Jenckes of Providence drinks tea." What is more— a telling blow—"Mr. Hopkins drank tea at the Governor's, when he was last at Newport," and he a delegate to the Congress. Tea stains followed party lines, and the "great man" (Joseph Wanton, Jr.), according to Ellery, stopped his bullying long enough to promise in private that he and his family would renounce the tea habit. "He was very much afraid," said Ellery, "that he should be posted, and his father turned out."[27] In April a second prox appeared with the motto: "Liberty and no Tories." It was headed by William Greene of War-wick,[28] son of the former Governor Greene and a staunch Ward man. Curiously the Deputy Governor listed—probably without his permission—was Darius Sessions, then in office under Wanton. If we are deluded by Tories, the *Newport Mercury* exclaimed, "the next may be our last free election."[29]

Wanton fought back against these charges with a spirit which became him. He called them false and injurious and "calculated to serve *Purposes of Party*" by misleading the credulous and unwary. Wanton defied his enemies to produce one instance in his administration wherein he had countenanced any invasion whatever of the "invaluable Charter Privileges."[30] Deputy Governor Darius Sessions immediately came to his aid; through a broadside he severely criticized those who opposed the Governor and defended his political principles by assuring the freemen that Wanton had "always manifested an affectionate Regard for your Charter Rights."[31] Moreover, Darius Sessions, who saw that the "Flames of Contention are again blowing up," flatly refused to serve as Deputy Governor, if elected, unless Joseph Wanton was continued in office.[32]

The party spirit which bristled through the colony at this time, pitting "sons of liberty" against "sons of tyranny," was more acutely serious than ever before. Governor Wanton must have wondered whether it was in his power to keep peace between the two extremes. He must have wondered, too, under the circumstances, whether he wanted to be Governor another year. It was probably with great apprehension, then, that Joseph Wanton marked and signed his prox in Newport on election day, April 19, 1775.

In the evening of that same day the news of the courageous stand of the embattled farmers at Concord Bridge arrived in Rhode Island. It sent an electric shock through the people of the colony. Within a few hours a thousand men stood ready under arms "to march at a Moment's warning." Thus, the *Newport Mercury* again prophetically and uncannily announced, "through the sanguinary Measures of a wicked Ministry, and the Readiness of a standing Army to execute their Mandates, has commenced the *American Civil War,* which will hereafter fill an important Page in History."[33] Along with the news from Lexington and Concord the freemen learned that Joseph Wanton was re-elected Governor of the colony.

The question of revolution was met head-on in the Assembly in emergency session three days later at Providence. The decisive issue was the legislature's vote to raise an army of observation of 1500 men "to repel any insult or violence" to the inhabitants and to join if necessary with forces of the other colonies. The decision was not unanimous. The four Newport deputies who were present dissented from the vote of the house; two of them left the session in protest.[34] Governor Wanton, Darius Sessions, and two Assistants, Thomas Wickes and William Potter, also dissented from the Assembly's vote.[35] In so doing Joseph Wanton chose the King instead of his country and confirmed his Toryism to the satisfaction of the legislature.

Wanton's protest prefaced a number of events which followed in rapid succession. When the Assembly met for the general election on May 3—in Providence instead of Newport, owing to the "most

apparent urgent occasion"—Governor Wanton was not present, nor
were five of the six Newport deputies and none from Jamestown or
Middletown.[36] The Governor "affects to be ill," Ezra Stiles commented, and the deputies "intimidated by the Threats of the Men o'
War."[37] Although elected by the freemen, Darius Sessions refused to
become Deputy Governor, and the Assembly promptly chose Nicholas
Cooke of Providence in his place. Three Assistants resigned, and one
had died since the election; the Assembly lost no time in filling their
places. All told, eight of the ten Assistants of the year before were
replaced, and a new Deputy Governor joined them in the upper
house.[38] The government's decision to go to war had produced a radical change in the council.

With the upper house settled the Assembly turned its attention to
Joseph Wanton who remained in Newport. As Governor, Wanton
had no veto power over the acts of the Assembly. He had hoped, however, to block the act for raising troops by refusing to sign commissions for the officers to command them, and so he stayed at home. The
Assembly scored his refusal to attend the general election and take
the oath required by law. By refusing to sign the officers' commissions
for the new army, it charged, he demonstrated his "intentions to
defeat the good people of these colonies, in their present glorious
struggle. . . ." As a consequence the Assembly forbade anyone to give
Wanton the oath of office "unless in free and open General Assembly . . ." and with the members' consent. (This last violated the
charter which directed that the Governor could be engaged before
two or more of the Assistants.) The members resolved that any act
by Wanton in the "pretended capacity as Governor" would be null
and void before he took the oath as prescribed. They empowered
Henry Ward, the Secretary, to commission the army officers and
authorized Nicholas Cooke, the new Deputy Governor, to convene
the Assembly when and where necessary. Notwithstanding his election as Governor, Joseph Wanton was stripped of power until he
should act in accordance with the wishes of the Assembly.[39]

Wanton did not remain silent: he claimed his ill health prevented
his attendance in Providence; he pleaded for "respectful behavior
towards His Majesty and both Houses of Parliament"; he warned
against levying war on the King; he defended his right to disagree

with the Assembly about raising troops; he insisted that his actions were based on a defense of the charter liberties which, he claimed, were "of too much importance to be forfeited." Since he protested the vote to establish the army of observation—"a measure pregnant with the most fatal consequences"—he could not, he argued, sign commissions for the "execution of a measure, which . . . was subversive of the true interest of this government."[40] When the Assembly met at East Greenwich in June, Wanton attended, expecting to take over the reins of the government. But the members resolved that he had not given satisfaction to the Assembly and refused to administer the oath. He returned, said Stiles, to Newport the next day "in Infamy."[41] "Our Wanton appears Very open now in opposition to the american measures," Cooke wrote to the delegates in Congress in July; he has "Capt Wallace [*Rose*, man-of-war] often at his house to dine &c."[42] Wanton stood around in Newport, a Governor without a chair, until November when the Assembly met in Providence and agreed that his whole conduct, "ever since the battle of Lexington," was "inimical to the rights and liberties of America." After declaring the office vacant the Assembly chose Nicholas Cooke, Governor, and William Bradford of Bristol, Deputy Governor, under him.[43] Darius Sessions craved forgiveness for protesting the act to raise troops and was voted into "favor and friendship."[44]

Had the battle at Lexington and Concord occurred a week earlier, probably the freemen would not have re-elected Wanton Governor of Rhode Island, for doubtless he would have shown his hand by the time they went to the polls. Unaware that hostilities had begun the voters believed he was a safe bet for another term. For a number of years the colony had stiffly resisted British encroachment in defense of a liberal charter and the many practical advantages derived from a factional system of government. No one was louder in this cause than Joseph Wanton. But in 1775 there was a difference of opinion as to how the charter and the colonists' accustomed liberties should be defended. Wanton conscientiously believed that loyalty to the King was the best method to keep Rhode Island intact as a self-governing colony. He turned his back on revolution in order to protect the charter; in fact, he believed revolution was the surest way to lose the charter. According to a majority of Rhode Islanders and to the General Assembly, Wanton's solution fell far short at the time of crisis in 1775. They were convinced affairs had come to such a state that revolution was the *only* way to preserve their self-governing colony. They got rid of a Governor who disagreed with them.

The party which had carried Wanton to victory since 1769 was carried by him to collapse in 1775. The decision to fight revealed to Rhode Islanders that the front rank of the party was shot through with Toryism. The Assembly vigorously chose revolution and just as vigorously chucked Wanton. In a sense this was a revolution in itself.

The turn of events in Rhode Island must have given Samuel Ward a smile and Stephen Hopkins a red face. It was an ironic end to the political career of Joseph Wanton whom Hopkins, the patriot and statesman, the author of *The Rights of Colonies Examined,* the member of the Continental Congress, had helped to keep in office since 1769. It gave a queer twist to the end of the Wanton-Hopkins regime which Samuel Ward alone could fully appreciate.

The Assembly's choice of Nicholas Cooke as Governor was admirable, for he brought strength and tough-mindedness to the job which were badly needed. Although the Ward-Hopkins controversy was supposedly dead, the rise of Cooke's star suggests that the Assembly was not blind to the ability of Ward's friends. Cooke was not in the government when the Assembly drafted him. In fact, he had not held office since 1768 when the Ward party chose him Deputy Governor in the coalition of that year. Ward was extremely pleased when the Assembly rescued Cooke from oblivion and pulled him into the government. He wrote to his daughter, "it is vastly happy that Sessions resigned and We have the Place filled with so good a Man as M$^r$. Cook."[45] Other evidence to show that Ward supporters were active in politics is the fact that Ward himself was chosen to go to Philadelphia along with Hopkins. In the next few years the colony had opportunity to elect three more delegates to the Congress; all three were from Newport. Two were Ward braves from earlier days, William Ellery and Henry Marchant.[46] It is possible that revolution agreed with the Ward people.

### III

The drift toward independence in the winter and spring of 1776 lacked the spectacular quality of the election and succeeding events of

1775. Rhode Island had shot its bolt when it pried the Governor out of his chair and chose in his place a fighting patriot. But despite the firm leadership of Nicholas Cooke, Henry Ward, and Samuel Ward (in Philadelphia), the inhabitants lived through melancholy days of confusion and unrest. On Nicholas Cooke's shoulders rested all the problems of the colony—patriot and Tory, civilian and military.

Chief among these was Captain James Wallace and his fleet of warships which kept the people of Newport and the lower Bay in a state of frenzy with constant threats and marauding tactics. Wallace commanded the *Rose,* man-of-war, and in November, 1775, there were at least ten armed vessels under him which made life miserable for Newporters and all Rhode Islanders whose business depended upon trade.[47] Seized molasses was sent to Boston for adjudication—except that belonging to Joseph Wanton, Jr., and other fast friends of the home government. Small boats were stripped and turned adrift. Ferries were boarded, the mail seized.[48] Livestock and other supplies for the ships' use and for the British army in Boston were demanded by threatening the town with destruction. Newporters lived in constant fear of having their town burned down around them or shelled to ruins while they lay in their beds.[49] Defenseless Bristol was raked with cannon fire for refusing to satisfy Wallace's demands.[50] Early in December the Captain and a company of two hundred marines plundered Jamestown, burned over a dozen houses, and carried off all the movables they could conveniently get away with.[51]

Once hostilities began the men-of-war redoubled their efforts to interdict trade in order to seize supplies for General Gage's troops in Boston and to prevent Rhode Islanders from supplying their own forces. Shortly after the battle at Lexington, the King's men captured John Brown and several hundred barrels of flour in a packet in Narragansett Bay. They sent Brown to Boston early in May where he was questioned by Admiral Graves and General Gage. The seizure of one of the colony's most distinguished citizens caused considerable excitement. Brown's friends and relatives—particularly brother Moses, Hopkins, and Wanton—applied for his release and were immediately successful. It later became clear that John Brown's quick return to Providence was the result of some conciliatory pledges made by him and his brother in Boston which he promptly repudiated by suing Wallace when he arrived home. Moses Brown was embarrassed; his good name was impeached by his brother's disregard of the round promises they had both given to the Admiral and General. The legislature debated the plans of conciliation with the assistance of Ward and Hopkins who delayed their departure for the Second Congress pending disposition of Wanton and the John Brown affair. In a warm debate over dispatching a committee to negotiate with General Gage, Hopkins and Ward split. Hopkins supported the plan; Ward did not. Speaker Metcalf Bowler turned the tie in the lower house for the motion, but the council under Governor Cooke's control scuttled the plan with a firm veto. And so the matter ended. Brown was free, and the Tories chagrined.[52]

Rhode Islanders fought back sporadically with indifferent success against the hit-and-run tactics of Wallace's men. They often beat the British to the draw and took off livestock from the islands and pastures which lined the Bay, driving them inland out of reach of the plundering seamen.[53] Armed resistance was risky and probably would have provoked Wallace to more frightening attacks upon the town. A Newporter named Coggeshall had his own way of expressing his dislike of the warships in the harbor. One morning he ventured out on Long Wharf "and turned up his backsides towards the bomb-brig" lying at anchor just off the town, accompanying the spectacle with several insulting words. The brig's crew promptly answered his greeting with two four-pound shots which missed Coggeshall but tore through Hammond's store and lodged in Sam Johnston's distill-house. Prudish Newporters had Coggeshall "taken up, and sent out of town."[54]

The distress of the people of Newport was acute. Everyone suffered, the indigent in particular. "The vast number of Poor," Samuel Vernon, Jr., reported, "that are destitute of almost every necessary of Life . . . cannot subsist Long [;] their case is to be pitied."[55] Many were reduced to water and bran boiled together with a little bread, and some, it was reported, were lucky to get that at times.[56] Ward and Hopkins warmly recommended evacuation.[57] After a particularly severe threat by Wallace in October, large numbers of people began the slow journey northward seeking places of refuge. Carts, wagons, chaises, and trucks jammed the highways. Streams of people and goods lined the roads in a general migration from the town and off the island. By early November Moses Brown estimated that more than half of the inhabitants—mostly women and children—had moved out.[58] The General Assembly did what it could for the sufferers, voting £200 for their support in November and another £200 in January "for removing such poor persons from Newport as are not able to remove themselves."[59] But, as Mary Callender told Moses Brown, they were moving from one distress to another. Where could they find jobs? Who would feed, clothe, or even receive them?[60] The Quakers under Moses Brown and some other groups generously sent aid and comfort to the poor and destitute.[61] Solomon Southwick moved his print shop for fear of being shot up by the men-of-war. He reduced the size of the *Mercury* because he could not collect sufficient cash to buy paper. In November he suspended regular publication and for a time ran off only "small occasional papers."[62]

In the fall of 1775 Wallace made new demands upon Newport for supplying his ships. A truce was negotiated and with the advice and consent of the colony's government and a committee of the Continental Congress, the people of Newport agreed to supply the fleet with beef, beer, and other provisions provided Wallace abandoned his practice of molesting the ferries, market, fish, and wood boats. A company or two of the colony's militia—lately camped in Newport under General Esek Hopkins—withdrew from the town at Wallace's request.[63] It was an uneasy truce; Tories and patriots bickered over violations.[64] General Nathanael Greene in camp near Boston reported that the Newporters were determined to observe a strict neutrality during the winter and "join the strongest party in the Spring."[65]

The defection at Newport sapped the colony's strength, and it was reflected in a flagging of spirit in some of her citizens and fighting men. After the initial burst of patriotism enlistments came slowly, particularly in Kings County where, Henry Ward complained, the disaffected people "have given such Discouragements to the Service that the Officers notwithstanding all their Exertions" were unable to get two-thirds of the men needed for their companies.[66] "No Publick Spirit prevails," General Greene lamented; "I fear the Colony of Rhode Island is upon the decline." His recruiting officers "got scarcely a man and Report that there are none to be had there." The General hoped Ward and Hopkins would soon come home "to spirit up the People."[67] Despite the dwindling enthusiasm Governor Cooke courageously reported to the delegates in Congress that "considering how heavily the War hath fallen upon us, it is wonderful that we have been able to manifest such a Spirit and exert so great a Force."[68]

The next problem confronting Cooke and the Assembly was what to do with the Tories in the colony, that is, if anything could be done. It was reported in Connecticut that even before the shooting started the Tory party in Newport had gained so much ground "a Whig dared not open his mouth in favor of liberty."[69] In the middle of July Governor Cooke admitted that they were so strong "nothing can be said or done in the colony that they have immediate intelligence of it." To aggravate the problem the patriots were abandoning the town; the Tories, Cooke added, "will have the Rule there soon."[70]

As "these demons" became stronger the patriots found it increasingly difficult to prevent them from clandestinely supplying the fleet and sending provisions to the King's army in Boston. George Rome was a notorious offender who repeatedly defied the warnings of the patriots. Early in June, 1775, hungry Newporters with mounting anger watched seventy barrels of flour trucked to his warehouse, destined for the King's troops. The timid Committee of Safety failed to act, but the Sons of Liberty waited on Rome and demanded every barrel. Rome refused and got Wallace to send his marines ashore for protection. Jahleel Brenton, now openly in the King's service, "behave'd very rideculas," and marched the marines up from the wharf "with a Pistall in each Hand," repeatedly commanding them to fire on the people. They refused and the flour ended up in the granary under guard of the Sons of Liberty. Newport patriots claimed that Wallace's bluff was called, and "seeing such a number of resulate men, who came under Armes," he promptly ordered his marines back to the ships.[71]

Later that year the Committee of Safety ordered Rome taken into custody, but the gallant of bachelors' hall escaped to Wallace's *Rose*. He cheated the patriots only of his obnoxious presence, however, for the colony had the last laugh when it confiscated his extensive holdings along with those of Thomas Moffat and the Brentons.[72] Aaron

Lopez, who already had suffered the Newporters' displeasure, increased his unpopularity when he and George Gibbs spent frequent merry evenings aboard the men-of-war in the harbor enjoying the salty hospitality of Captain Wallace and other "tools of power."[73]

Providence presented a different picture. "The Love of Liberty triumphs in this Town over all other Considerations," Ward wrote Benjamin Franklin. Every danger despised, every difficulty surmounted, and at the same time the people were zealously attentive to the "general Interest of America." It is a question whether "every thing for the common Defense" would have been pursued with such "immense Ardor" had Wallace and his fleet anchored off Fox Point at the head of the Bay instead of Long Wharf in Newport.[74]

In the fall of 1775 the Continental Congress enacted vigorous resolutions respecting Tories. Ward and Hopkins passed these on to Governor Cooke suggesting that he take them with a grain of salt owing to the ticklish situation in Newport.[75] A wrong move at this time might have brought the whole town down around the people's heads—Whigs and Tories. The Assembly abandoned its reserve when news arrived in August of the King's proclamation declaring the colonies in a state of rebellion and withdrawing his protection from them. It promptly enacted a law punishing with death and confiscation of estates anyone who held "traitorous correspondence" with the enemy or supplied him with provisions or warlike stores—making careful exception, however, of the Newport Town Council's truce with Captain Wallace.[76] Samuel Ward was as pleased as punch at the "judicious and decisive Conduct" of the Assembly, which, he said, did "great Honor to the Colony." He had the proceedings read in Congress where they were highly approved. Ward's stock in the radical camp soared when one of the Adamses, Eliphalet Dyer of Connecticut, and several others exclaimed that the Rhode Islanders "had sett them all a noble Example."[77] Moses Brown, suffused in the soft glow of Quakerism, denounced the act as the "great disgrace of Christianity." He cried out for repentance and "mutual Benevolence" instead of a studied attempt to bring "Distress & Misery" down upon them all.[78]

The Assembly next moved in on Charles Dudley demanding of him all the silver, gold, and paper bills in the Customs House belonging to the Crown. Dudley, of course, refused, but General Esek Hopkins forbade his removal of a shilling at the peril of his life and property. Dudley fled to the *Rose,* trusting, he said, in the justice and power of the government he had the honor to serve.[79]

The turning point in the careers of several Tories occurred about Christmas time, 1775, when General Charles Lee, a big-wig in the Continental Army, arrived in Newport with much fanfare to talk over plans for fortifying the town. The General's presence, Ezra Stiles commented, "struck Awe through the Tories," who were "obsequious & submissive as possible." Several "obnoxious persons" were brought before him and asked to take an oath of fidelity to the country. Joseph Wanton, Jr., Nicholas Lechmere, and Richard Beale refused, and the troops dragged them off to headquarters on the island and later to Providence.[80] The patriots of Newport rested more comfortably in their beds that night. A few days earlier Wanton's Negroes had piloted Wallace's crew about the island pointing out the houses to burn. According to Nathanael Greene, Wanton deserved arrest "as much as any Tory upon the Contenent."[81] In June, 1776, the Assembly ordered all suspected males to subscribe to a declaration or test of their loyalty.[82] Some people believed that the tide was changing in Newport; patriotism seemed to become more popular as both Congress and the colony acted decisively.

But the Tory problem, which seemed to have eased slightly, thrust the colony into a bitter struggle at election time in 1776. Owing to a dearth of patriots in Newport the friends of liberty were scared to death the Tories would dominate the town's government. The Assembly came to the patriots' rescue and permitted all refugees to return to their respective towns for the purpose of voting. With this encouragement the Whigs of Newport earnestly appealed to all former residents begging them to come home for town meeting and prevent the Tories from taking over. The situation in Newport approached a crisis, they exclaimed. The Tory Junto was scheming to elect deputies unfriendly to the American cause and in this way counteract every measure proposed in the Assembly to promote American liberty.[83] It was reported that they had already laid plans to replace the "superanuated" Hopkins in Congress with Joseph Wanton or someone of similar principles.[84] The contest resembled the "intestine broils" of earlier days, but the battle in 1776 was a life and death struggle.

Yet, despite the dramatic circumstances, the election of 1776 created less flurry than the one the year before. Owing to preoccupation of the freemen with the war, political organization and discipline were less rigorous. Three men set up for Governor, but the voters, overwhelmingly patriotic and apparently embarrassed by a wealth of candidates, almost unanimously re-elected Nicholas Cooke.[85] If the Newport Tories had intended to reshape the government in their favor, they were disappointed. A Tory Assistant from that town lost his seat in the council. Newporters chose three new deputies, but it is doubtful if any was an extremist on either side—probably their moderation was the reason for electing them.[86] Events which followed demonstrated a strong patriotic spirit in the administration which took office in May.

IV

The movement toward independence developed rapidly in the winter and spring of 1775-1776, stimulated by the tireless efforts of Samuel Ward. (Ward's prestige had continued to rise; the Congress repeatedly elected him chairman of the committee of the whole.)[87] Early in November, 1775, he settled the question for himself and wrote to his brother: "I want nothing more but am ready to declare Ourselves independent."[88] By the end of the month Ward's position on the subject was no secret in Rhode Island. Ezra Stiles recorded in his diary that Ward, among other delegates, was "clear" for independence, while Hopkins was still somewhat uncertain.[89] Ward's influence was felt at home, particularly by his brother, Henry, who, during the same November, exclaimed, "The Die is cast—The union of the Colonies with Great Britain is at an end."[90] Thomas Paine's *Common Sense* in January, 1776, helped to clear the heads of the stragglers. The pamphlet was advertised by both of the colony's printers.[91] But in the last week of March the swift current of opinion received a momentous check when Samuel Ward died suddenly in Philadelphia from smallpox. A zealous Philadelphian lamented: "One, at least, of the mighty advocates for American Independency is fallen in M[r]. Ward, to the great grief of the *protopatriot* [Samuel] Adams."[92]

Despite Ward's death, the movement continued to accelerate. Hopkins wrote home from Philadelphia asking instructions respecting the great debate in Congress which would soon shape up.[93] Had Ward

been with him there probably would have been no question. Doubtless, too, Ward's steady radicalism would have spurred the Assembly
at home to take a definite stand on the question. A majority of Rhode
Islanders and the members of the legislature were undoubtedly ripe
for independence. A final push was lacking; it was shortly supplied
by the general election of 1776.

It was customary for each elected officer to take an oath—an engagement it was called—swearing allegiance to the King before taking up his new duties. Such an engagement stuck in the throats of the
officers, and the Assembly found it absurd to administer oaths of
allegiance to a King whose troops the colony had been battling for
more than a year. To overcome this difficulty the Assembly took a decisive step. On May 4, 1776, the members renounced the colony's
allegiance to George III and struck his name from all commissions,
writs, and processes at law.[94] Rhode Island had done with the King
of England. There were but six dissenting votes;[95] these might well
have been cast by the deputies from Newport.

The Assembly debated instructions to its delegates in Congress—
the members had re-elected Hopkins and chosen William Ellery in
Ward's place.[96] The deputies were all for "taking the sense of the inhabitants at large" on the subject of independence and voted a bill to
that effect. The Assistants saw the danger of this costly delay and
argued that owing to it their delegates would lose their voice in the
pending debate in Congress. When Hopkins and Ellery received a
"Copy of the Act renouncing Allegiance" and the other instructions
just drafted, the council declared, they "could not possibly entertain
a Doubt of the Sense of the General Assembly." This satisfied the
deputies and they dropped their motion.[97] The Assembly's action also
satisfied Hopkins who shortly wrote to Cooke that there was "little
room to doubt what is the opinion of the colony I came from."[98] The
Assembly's instructions to the delegates suggest that the colony was
as ready to defend itself from the possible encroachment of Congress
as it had been against the actual encroachment of Great Britain. Hopkins and Ellery were warned that in their actions in Philadelphia they
should take great care to secure to the colony in the "most perfect
manner, its present established form, and all the powers of government" relating to its internal affairs, civil and religious. Independence

in 1776 meant to Rhode Island independence from *any* interference, foreign *or* domestic.[99] These instructions once again confirmed the colony's constant determination to be politically self-sufficient.

The Congress "cooly discussed" a proposed resolution for independence on June 8-10 but postponed the decision for three weeks.[100] Needless to say, the resolution *was* approved during the first week of July. Two weeks later the Assembly met in Newport—Wallace had left, and the Tories were subdued—where the members immediately ratified the resolution of Congress. One vote was cast against it, said Ezra Stiles, "and he was expelled the House for refusing the Test."[101] With cannon, musketry, and a colorful array of militia, the Declaration of Independence was read to the assembled inhabitants, and the State of Rhode Island and Providence Plantations was proclaimed.[102]

The Revolution brought a fundamental change to Rhode Island politics—a change which began with the decline of Newport and which eventually affected the whole colony. Newport was hard hit by the fortunes of war. Once hostilities commenced, its exposure to the guerrilla tactics of Captain Wallace and his marines resulted in the exodus of a large number of inhabitants who found life in the southern town dangerous and frustrating. After Wallace's departure the town was again in the hands of the rebels, and there followed a voluntary and in some cases a forced exodus of a number of Tories whose lives were made miserable by the official and unofficial badgering of the patriots. The British occupation of Newport, beginning in December, 1776, completed the distress of the town and for a time cut it off altogether from the rest of the state. All these factors contributed to the diminution of Newport and substantially altered the pattern of politics which had prevailed for so long.

Nevertheless, the act of revolution and the declaration of independence produced no change in the structure of government, for none was desired. The fact that the government was already satisfactory to a great many inhabitants goes a long way to explain why there was no attempt to change it, and why the charter of 1663, so affectionately regarded, served as a state constitution until 1842—with the King's name scratched out. Rhode Islanders went to war in April, 1775, to force Great Britain to recognize their self-governing colony. In May, 1776, they declared their independence from the mother country as a final step in defense of their political self-sufficiency.

But to say that Rhode Islanders joined the Revolutionary movement merely to preserve a liberal charter which sustained self-government does not do justice to the political genius of the people of Rhode Island. Factional government, based on a number of local issues, was a stage in political growth which Rhode Island experienced earlier than most colonies owing to its large degree of political independence and the peculiar conditions which existed there. Government by faction was a stage in political growth which was characteristic of English politics as well at the same time. By 1760 Rhode Islanders had reached a surprising level of political maturity; in fact, their history in this period explains a good deal about political behavior in the eighteenth century and is significant if only for that.

To say, too, that Rhode Islanders revolted to protect the wide area of freedom they were accustomed to enjoy does not really get to the bottom of the causes for resisting England. When Parliament, ministry, and King encroached upon self-government, they encroached upon a system of party politics which was not only mature but profitable. Self-interest was a spring for constitutional appeal, not hypocritically but naturally. Taxation and legislation by a Parliament in England—besides intruding on local political habits—intruded also on local property, and a defense of property, in good old Whig terms, was traditionally a defense of liberty. Sensitive to the real danger from abroad, Rhode Islanders joined their fellow colonists and revolted on the broad grounds of constitutional right to keep Rhode Island safe for liberty and property—and the benefits of party politics.

# ABBREVIATIONS

*ALRI—Acts and Laws of the English Colony of Rhode-Island and Providence-Plantations in New-England in America,* Newport, 1767.

BUL—Brown University Library, Providence, R.I.

JCBL—John Carter Brown Library in Brown University, Providence, R.I.

NHS—Newport Historical Society, Newport, R.I.

NYPL—New York Public Library

*RIAR—Acts and Resolves of the Colony of Rhode Island*

R.I. Arch.—Rhode Island Archives, State House, Providence, R.I.

R.I. Col. Recs. (Ms)—Rhode Island Colony Records, R.I. Archives, State House, Providence, R.I.

RIHS—Rhode Island Historical Society, Providence, R.I.

*Recs. Col. R.I.—*John R. Bartlett, ed., *Records of the Colony of Rhode Island and Providence Plantations in New England,* 10 vols., Providence, 1856-1865.

# NOTES

## NOTES TO INTRODUCTION

[1] Carl Becker, *The History of Political Parties in the Province of New York, 1760-1776* (Madison, Wisc., 1909).

[2] See in particular, Lewis B. Namier, *The Structure of Politics at the Accession of George III* (2 vols., London, 1929) and *England in the Age of the American Revolution* (London, 1930); Richard Pares, *King George III and the Politicians* (Oxford, Eng., 1953); Robert Walcott, *English Politics in the Early Eighteenth Century* (Cambridge, Mass., 1956).

## NOTES TO CHAPTER I

## RHODE ISLANDISM

[1] *The Charter of the Governor and Company of the English Colony of Rhode-Island,* John Russell Bartlett, ed., *Records of the Colony of Rhode Island and Providence Plantations in New England* (Providence, 1857), II, 3-21. (Hereafter cited *Recs. Col. R.I.*)

[2] Letters, A-B (n.p., n.d.), NHS.

[3] For a biographical sketch of Samuel Ward, see Bernhard Knollenberg, ed., *Correspondence of Governor Samuel Ward, May 1775-March 1776* (Providence, 1952), pp. 3-13. See also Clifford P. Monahon, "Genealogy of the Ward Family," *ibid.,* pp. 212-214; *Recs. Col. R.I.,* IV, V.

[4] Monahon, "Genealogy of the Ward Family," p. 212; *Recs. Col. R.I.,* IV, 88, 168, et passim.

[5] John Russell Bartlett, *History of the Wanton Family of Newport, Rhode Island,* in *Rhode Island Historical Tracts,* Parts 3-4 (Providence, 1878), pp. 23-60; *Recs. Col. R.I.,* III, 522-524, 532, 553, 564, IV, 47-48, 87, 89, 102, et passim.

[6] Governor Joseph Jenckes refused his assent to the bill to emit £60,000 of paper money in 1731. The Assembly took the position that under the charter the Governor had no power to veto an act of the legislature. Upon an appeal to England, judgment was given that the Assembly was right; the Governor of Rhode Island possessed no veto power, nor could he refuse to have the colony seal affixed to an act of the Assembly. See *Recs. Col. R.I.,* IV, 456-461.

[7] *Ibid.,* 469, 481; William Wanton attacked Ward in a broadside dated Newport, Jan. 3, 1733. See Broadsides, RIHS.

[8] Bartlett, *History of the Wanton Family,* p. 33; *Recs. Col. R.I.,* IV, 495-496, 506, 572, 576, et passim.

[9] *Recs. Col. R.I.,* IV, 576, V, 207, 489, VI, 47, 260. Three of Samuel Ward's children married into the Greene family. Monahon, "Genealogy of the Ward Family," p. 216.

[10] *Recs. Col. R.I.,* V, passim.

[11] James B. Hedges, *The Browns of Providence Plantations, Colonial Years* (Cambridge, Mass., 1952), chs. I, II, et passim.

[12] For an account of Hopkins, see William E. Foster, *Stephen Hopkins, a Rhode Island Statesman, a Study in the Political History of the Eighteenth Century* (2 vols., Providence, 1884); *Recs. Col. R.I.,* V, VI.

[13] *Recs. Col. R.I.,* V, 384-385, 393-394, 427; Stephen Hopkins, *A True Representation of the Plan Formed at Albany* (Providence, 1755), JCBL; Foster, *Stephen Hopkins,* I, 190, 195.

[14] Moses Brown, Some Account of Stephen Hopkins, Esq., in The Letters of Stephen Hopkins, Collected from Various Sources, Sidney S. Rider, ed., Ms copies (Providence, 1881), BUL.

[15] Franklin B. Dexter, ed., *The Literary Diary of Ezra Stiles* (New York, 1901), I, 231. A likeness of Hopkins as an older man hangs in the Rhode Island State Capitol.

[16] William Ellery to Samuel Ward, Newport, Feb. 4, 1769, Ward MSS, Box I, 85, RIHS. There is no portrait extant of Samuel Ward; a painting of his father, Richard Ward, is in the Rhode Island State Capitol.

[17] Hopkins *v.* Ward, No. 101, Worcester County Court of Common Pleas, Nov., 1756-May, 1762, V, 76-92.

[18] *Recs. Col. R.I.,* VI, 68.

[19] Warner Papers, III, #723, #744, RIHS.

[20] James N. Arnold, ed., *The Narragansett Historical Register,* IV (1885-1886), 146.

[21] *Recs. Col. R.I.,* VI, 46, 123.

[22] William B. Weeden, *Early Rhode Island, A Social History of the People* (New York, 1910), pp. 249-250.

[23] Joseph Wanton, Jr., to Moses Brown, Oct. 7, 1770, Moses Brown Papers, I, 116, RIHS.

[24] *The Providence Gazette; and Country Journal,* April 16, 1763.

[25] Elisha Brown to Samuel Ward, North Providence, July 26, 1767, Ward MSS (Knollenberg Transcripts). Through the kindness of Mr. Bernhard Knollenberg of Chester, Connecticut, I have had access to his typed compared copies of a number of Ward letters from RIHS. When reference is made to these transcripts they will be so labeled.

[26] See Lewis B. Namier, *The Structure of Politics at the Accession of George III* (2 vols., London, 1929); Richard Pares, *King George III and the Politicians* (Oxford, Eng., 1953); Robert Walcott, *English Politics in the Early Eighteenth Century* (Cambridge, Mass., 1956).

[27] *Recs. Col. R.I.,* VII, 182-184.

[28] Robert E. Brown, *Middle-Class Democracy and the Revolution in Massachusetts, 1691-1780* (Ithaca, New York, 1955), ch. IV.

[29] For the population of these towns see *Census of the Inhabitants of the Colony of Rhode Island . . . 1774,* arranged by John R. Bartlett (Providence, 1858), p. 239. See also *Recs. Col. R.I.,* VII, 299, for slightly different totals.

[30] *Acts and Laws of His Majesty's Colony of Rhode-Island, and Providence Plantations, in New England in America* (Newport, 1745), pp. 147-148.

[31] *Acts and Laws . . . of Rhode-Island . . .* (Newport, 1752), pp. 12-14.

[32] Ezra Stiles recorded that in Newport in 1761 there were 1244 ratable polls and only six not ratable. Franklin B. Dexter, ed., *Extracts from the Itineraries . . . of Ezra Stiles* (New Haven, 1916), p. 23. The colony government reported that there were 8285 ratable polls in 1762 and 8952 in 1767. Rhode Island Colony Records (Ms), VII, 428, R. I. Arch.; *Recs. Col. R.I.,* VI, 576. These figures were eighteen and seventeen per cent respectively of the estimated population. According to my calculation seventeen per cent of the total population in Rhode Island was adult male. This last figure (17%) was difficult to determine and ought to be explained. From the figures presented by Thomas Jefferson in his notes on Virginia one can determine that adult males were 18.75% of the free inhabitants in that colony. Wil-

liam Peden, ed., *Notes on the State of Virginia* (Chapel Hill, 1955), p. 86. Robert E. Brown believes that the "population of Massachusetts could not have been much different." *Middle-Class Democracy,* p. 52. Probably 18.75% would have been satisfactory for Rhode Island, but according to another method of estimating this figure it was slightly high. Jefferson estimated that of the males over sixteen, twenty-five per cent would be between sixteen and twenty-one, and so the number of adult males would equal the number over sixteen less twenty-five per cent. *Notes on the State of Virginia,* p. 86. Robert E. Brown found that this estimate was also correct for Massachusetts. *Middle-Class Democracy,* p. 49. The census returns of 1755, 1774, and 1790 give the number of males above sixteen years of age. From these figures it was possible to determine that the number of adult males in proportion to the total population was about seventeen per cent in Rhode Island.

[33] Ratemakers' Reports for the five towns in 1757 are in R.I. Arch.

[34] *Recs. Col. R.I.,* VI, 257; Albert E. McKinley, *The Suffrage Franchise in the Thirteen English Colonies in America,* in University of Pennsylvania *Publications,* Series in History, No. 2 (Philadelphia, 1905), p. 462.

[35] Evarts B. Greene and Virginia D. Harrington, *American Population before the Federal Census of 1790* (New York, 1932), pp. 63-69.

[36] Figures for total votes cast are found as follows: 1760, Stiles, *Itineraries,* p. 103; 1764, Miscellaneous MSS, B-814, Box 2, RIHS; 1765, Brown Papers, P-P6, JCBL; 1766, Brown Papers, L&P, 58-70, RIP; 1768, General Assembly Reports, III (1766-1768), 21, R.I. Arch.; 1770, Misc. MSS, B-814, Box 2.

[37] Stiles, *Itineraries,* p. 103.

[38] *Ibid.*

[39] See several letters describing Nicholas Brown's arrangements for buying horses and lumber to send to the West Indies. Brown Papers, Misc. Letters, 1762-1764.

[40] The foregoing information about the colony's economy is taken from the "Remonstrance of the Colony of Rhode Island to the Lords Commissioners of Trade and Plantations, 1764," *Recs. Col. R.I.,* VI, 378-383.

[41] Stephen Hopkins, "An Essay on the Trade of the Northern Colonies," *Prov. Gazette,* Jan. 14 and 21, 1764.

[42] Stiles, *Itineraries,* pp. 89-90.

[43] Petitions, 11-2, 74, R.I. Arch.

[44] *Recs. Col. R.I.,* VI, 546; Stiles, *Diary,* I, 176.

[45] *Prov. Gazette,* Jan. 21, 1764.

[46] *Recs. Col. R.I.,* VI, 381.

[47] Samuel Ward to Joseph Sherwood, Newport, Aug. 6, 1762, Gertrude S. Kimball, ed., *The Correspondence of the Colonial Governors of Rhode Island, 1723-1775* (Cambridge, Mass., 1903), II, 336; Sidney S. Rider, ed., The Letters of Stephen Hopkins, p. 40; *Recs. Col. R.I.,* VI, 347-348; Isaac Backus, *A History of New-England With particular Reference to the Denomination of Christians called Baptists . . .* (Providence, 1784), II, 233.

[48] Gov. Ward to Secretary Joseph Conway, Newport, Nov. 6, 1765, *Recs. Col. R.I.,* VI, 473.

[49] At one time the deputies from the town of Johnston got out of line and voted in the Assembly against the commercial interests of the northern merchants. The Browns of Providence admonished the freemen of that town, expressing surprise that farmers would send to the Assembly deputies who were opposed to the trading interests; for, said the Browns, "it is well known the Farmers get their Estates by Selling the produce of their Farms to Traders." The Browns hoped that this mild rebuke would convince the Johnston freeman "of the necessity of choosing Deputies who are in M$^r$. Hopkins's Interest," for the sake of "Things relative to the Govern-

ment in general" and the northern county in particular. Nicholas and John Brown to the Freemen of the Town of Johnston, n.d., Brown Papers, P-P6.

[50] *The Newport Mercury,* April 3, 1775.

[51] Joseph Wanton, Jr., to Moses Brown, Newport, April 5, 1770, Moses Brown Papers, I, 103; Stephen Arnold to Moses Brown, April ?, 1770, *ibid.,* p. 107.

[52] David Rowland to Ezra Stiles, Providence, April 6, 1767, Ezra Stiles Papers, Yale Univ. Library; Joseph Wanton, Jr., to Nicholas Brown & Co., Newport, April 7, 1765, Brown Papers, L&P, 58-70, RIP.

[53] *Prov. Gazette,* March 19, 1768.

[54] Ezra Stiles to Col. John Hubbard, Newport, Jan. 30, 1764, Stiles Papers, Yale Univ. Library.

[55] *Newp. Merc.,* April 23, 1764.

[56] *RIAR,* Aug., 1760; Election Proxes, RIHS. For a discussion of proxes in Rhode Island, see Howard M. Chapin, "Eighteenth Century Rhode Island Printed Proxies," *The American Collector,* I (Nov., 1925), 54-59.

[57] Election Proxes, RIHS; *Prov. Gazette,* April 18, 1767.

[58] *Prov. Gazette,* April 16, 1764.

[59] Brown Papers, L&P, 58-70, RIP. For a discussion of the financial role of Nicholas Brown & Co. in the Hopkins party campaigns, see James B. Hedges, *The Browns of Providence Plantations,* pp. 190-192.

[60] Nicholas Brown & Co. to Gideon Tripp, April 9, 1767, Brown Papers, P-P6.

[61] Committee to Beriah Brown, Providence, April 10, 1767, James N. Arnold, ed., *The Narragansett Historical Register,* II, 109-111; Brown Papers, P-P6.

[62] Henry Ward to Samuel Ward, n.p., n.d., Ward MSS, Box I.

[63] Stiles, *Itineraries,* p. 103.

[64] Moses Brown to Nicholas Brown & Co., Glocester, April 16, 1764, Brown Papers, P-P6; Nicholas Brown & Co. to Gideon Tripp, April 9, 1767, *ibid.*

[65] *ALRI,* pp. 83-84.

[66] Nicholas Brown to John Grelea, Providence, April 25, 1763, Brown Papers, L&P, 58-70, RIP.

[67] *The Charter, Recs. Col. R.I.,* II, 11.

[68] Account of the Election of 1761, Stiles Papers, Yale Univ. Library; Stiles, *Itineraries,* p. 106.

[69] Journal, House of Deputies, May, 1761, R.I. Arch.; Stiles, Account of the Election of 1761, Stiles Papers.

[70] Stiles, Account of the Election.

[71] *Ibid.;* Journal, House of Deputies, May, 1761.

[72] At the close of his description of the General Election in May, 1762, Stiles recorded: "This Account of the Elect. I write from my own observation chiefly being myself present in the Court house till after the Govr was proclaimed." Stiles Papers; Journal, House of Deputies, May, 1762.

[73] John and Moses Brown to Nicholas Brown & Co., Newport, May 4, 1764, Brown Papers, P-P6.

[74] David Rowland to Ezra Stiles, Providence, April 6, 1767, Stiles Papers.

[75] Romney Sedgwick, ed., *Letters from George III to Lord Bute, 1756-1766* (London, 1939), No. 232; Sir John Fortescue, ed., *The Correspondence of King George the Third* (London, 1927) I, Nos. 143 and 519.

[76] See John Brooke, *The Chatham Administration, 1766-1768* (London, 1956), p. 234.

[77] Edmund Burke, *Thoughts on the Cause of the Present Discontents* (5th edition, London, 1775), pp. 46, 105, 110.

[78] *The Federalist,* No. 10.

NOTES TO CHAPTER II

## MOLASSES BEGINS THE DISPUTE

[1] 3 George III, c. 22, Danby Pickering, ed., *The Statutes at Large* . . . (Cambridge, England, 1763), XXV, 345-351.

[2] *Prov. Gazette,* Sept. 24, 1763.

[3] *Newp. Merc.,* Dec. 26, 1763; Admiral Colville to Gov. of Rhode Island, Oct. 22, 1763, *Recs. Col. R.I.,* VI, 376.

[4] *Prov. Gazette,* Dec. 3, 1763.

[5] Moses Brown Papers, Misc., I, 11.

[6] Jan. 14, 1764. The second half appeared in the next issue, Jan. 21, 1764. *Newp. Merc.* reprinted it in two parts, Feb. 6 and 13, 1764.

[7] *Prov. Gazette,* Feb. 11, 1764.

[8] Moses Brown Papers, Misc., I, 12-13.

[9] *Prov. Gazette,* Jan. 28, 1764; *Prov. Gazette Extraordinary,* April 16, 1764. For an excellent treatment of the background and adoption of the Remonstrance, see Frederick B. Wiener, "The Rhode Island Merchants and the Sugar Act," *New England Quarterly,* III (1930), 464-500.

[10] *Recs. Col. R.I.,* VI, 378-383.

[11] *Prov. Gazette,* Jan. 14, 1764.

[12] New York and Philadelphia merchants corresponded in February, 1764, about joining the New England colonies in "soliciting a discontinuance of the most unjust of all laws." In Philadelphia a committee of merchants was selected to petition the Assembly asking that body to instruct the colony's agent to co-operate with other agents in opposing the act. *Prov. Gazette,* March 17, 1764.

[13] *Prov. Gazette Extraordinary,* April 16, 1764.

[14] *Prov. Gazette,* Aug. 18, 1764.

[15] *Prov. Gazette Extraordinary,* April 16, 1764.

[16] *Ibid.; Recs. Col. R.I.,* VI, 397.

[17] *Prov. Gazette,* Jan. 21, 1764.

[18] Ezra Stiles to Col. John Hubbard, Jan. 30, 1764, Stiles Papers; *Prov. Gazette,* Jan. 21, 1764.

[19] *Newp. Merc.,* Feb. 20, 1764; *Prov. Gazette,* Feb. 25, 1764; Stiles to Hubbard, Jan. 30, 1764, Stiles Papers.

[20] *Recs. Col. R.I.,* VI, 428-430; *Newp. Merc.,* July 16, 1764; *Prov. Gazette,* July 21, 1764; "Copy of a Deposition made by Daniel Vaughan Gunner at Fort George at Rhode Island," Chalmers Papers, Rhode Island, 1637-1785, New York Public Library.

[21] *Recs. Col. R.I.,* VI, 429-430.

[22] Chalmers Papers, Rhode Island, NYPL.

[23] *Recs. Col. R.I.,* VI, 427-428.

[24] *Ibid.,* 444; Gov. Ward to Joseph Sherwood, June 28, 1765, Kimball, ed., *Correspondence of Governors,* II, 366.

[25] *Newp. Merc.,* June 10, 1765; Gov. Ward to Capt. Charles Antrobus, Newport, July 12, 1765, *Recs. Col. R.I.,* VI, 446-447.

[26] *Newp. Merc.,* June 10, 1765; Joseph Redington, ed., *Calendar of Home Office Papers, 1766-1769* (London, 1879), No. 84, p. 26.

[27] Gov. Ward to Antrobus, Newport, June 11, 1765, *Recs. Col. R.I.,* VI, 444.

[28] Redington, ed., *Calendar of Home Office Papers, 1766-1769,* No. 84, p. 26; Gov. Ward to Antrobus, Newport, July 12, 1765, and March 28, 1766, *Recs. Col. R.I.,* VI, 447, 485.

[29] *Recs. Col. R.I.,* V, 447, 485.

[30] Redington, ed., *Calendar of Home Office Papers, 1766-1769,* p. 26.

[31] *Ibid.,* pp. 26-27.

[32] James Munro, ed., *Acts of the Privy Council of England, Colonial Series* (London, 1912), VI, No. 629, pp. 386-387.

[33] 4 George III, c. 15, Pickering, ed., *The Statutes at Large,* XXVI, 35-52; Oliver M. Dickerson, *The Navigation Acts and the American Revolution* (Philadelphia, 1951), p. 180; Edmund S. and Helen M. Morgan, *The Stamp Act Crisis* (Chapel Hill, 1953), p. 24.

[34] *Recs. Col. R.I.,* VI, 414-416.

[35] John Torbuck, ed., *A Collection of the Parliamentary Debates in England from the Year M, DC, LXVIII, To the Present Time* (London, reprinted 1741), X, 443-451.

[36] *Recs. Col. R.I.,* VI, 104, 107; Kimball, ed., *Correspondence of Governors,* II, 275-276; Dorothy S. Towle, ed., *Records of the Vice-Admiralty Court of Rhode Island, 1716-1752* (Washington, D.C., 1936), p. 89.

[37] Joseph Sherwood to Gov. Hopkins, Oct. 31, 1763, Kimball, ed., *Correspondence of Governors,* II, 355.

[38] *Recs. Col. R.I.,* VI, 428; John Robinson and John Nicoll to Gov. Ward, Feb. 22, 1766, Kimball, ed., *Correspondence of Governors,* II, 379-380.

[39] *Prov. Gazette,* Aug. 4, 1764; *Newp. Merc.,* Oct. 8, 1764.

[40] *Newp. Merc.,* Oct. 22, 1764.

[41] *The Rights of Colonies Examined* (Providence, 1764). See also *Recs. Col. R.I.,* VI, 422.

[42] Petition of the Governor and Company of Rhode Island to the King, Nov. 29, 1764, *Recs. Col. R.I.,* VI, 415.

[43] *Newp. Merc.,* Dec. 10, 1764.

[44] *Recs. Col. R.I.,* VI, 458; Robinson and Nicoll to Gov. Ward, Newport, Feb. 22, 1766, Kimball, ed., *Correspondence of Governors,* II, 376-379.

[45] W. Mellish to Governor of Rhode Island, Sept. 14, 1765, *Recs. Col. R.I.,* VI, 457.

[46] Nov. 21, 1765, Kimball, ed., *Correspondence of Governors,* II, 374.

[47] Robinson and Nicoll to Gov. Ward, Feb. 22, 1766, *ibid.,* pp. 394-395; *Recs. Col. R.I.,* VI, 459.

[48] *Recs. Col. R.I.,* VI, 459, 481; R.I. Col. Recs. (Ms), VIII, 408.

[49] Kimball, ed., *Correspondence of Governors,* II, 401 and n.

[50] Stiles, *Itineraries,* p. 204.


## NOTES TO CHAPTER III

## OTHER MOTIVES THAN LOVE OF GOD AND COUNTRY

[1] *Recs. Col. R.I.,* VI, 411, 414.

[2] *Brief Remarks on the Defence of the Halifax Libel, on the British-American Colonies* (Boston, 1765).

[3] *Recs. Col. R.I.,* V, 386; Election Proxes, RIHS. The proxes are not dated, but from the names listed it is clear Martin Howard, Jr., was a candidate in 1761 or

1762, probably the former. Martin Howard, Sr., was a member of the Newport Town Council and an Overseer of the Poor in 1764. *Newp. Merc.,* June 11, 1764.

[4] Ezra Stiles to [Richard Jackson ?], Newport, March 26, 1764, Stiles Papers, Yale Univ. Library.

[5] April 23, 1764.

[6] *Newp. Merc.,* Oct. 22, 1764.

[7] *Ibid.,* Oct. 29, 1764.

[8] *Ibid.,* Sept. 24, 1764.

[9] *Ibid.,* April 23, 1764.

[10] *Ibid.*

[11] Letters, A-B (n.p., n.d.), NHS.

[12] Newport, Feb. 4, 1769, Ward MSS, Box I, 85.

[13] The General Assembly divided the town of Providence and established the twenty-seventh town, Johnston, in 1759. *Recs. Col. R.I.,* VI, 194-195. Providence was again divided in 1765 when North Providence was incorporated. *Ibid.,* pp. 438-441.

[14] From 1761 to 1766 October houses averaged about nine members smaller than May houses. In October, 1767, out of a house of sixty-six, only forty-eight members attended. *RIAR,* 1761-1767.

[15] *Prov. Gazette,* April 18, 1767. Information about the shift in membership of the General Assembly is derived from *RIAR,* May, 1761-May, 1775.

[16] *RIAR,* May, 1761-May, 1767; *Recs. Col. R.I.,* VI, VII, VIII passim.

[17] *RIAR,* May, 1760-May, 1773. The charter did not direct how the Assistants were to be chosen. Nowhere in the records have I found a law or resolve describing their selection. From an occasional letter between the party leaders it appears that each party chose two Assistants from each of the five counties and submitted them to the freemen on election day for approval. See Joseph Wanton, Jr., to Moses Brown, Newport, March 23, 1771, Moses Brown Papers, II, 7.

[18] *ALRI* (Newport, 1767), pp. 266, 98. This volume was usually called the Digest of Laws. The General Assembly had a digest such as this printed every few years to be used as a codified volume of the laws of the colony.

[19] Samuel Ward to Anna Ward, Newport, Dec. 23, 1760, Ward MSS, Box I, 42.

[20] *Recs. Col. R.I.,* VI, 260.

[21] *ALRI,* pp. 94-95.

[22] General Treasurer's Accounts, 1761-1781, Alphabetical Book No. 6, R.I. Arch.

[23] See Lawrence C. Wroth, "The First Press in Providence, a Study in Social Development," American Antiquarian Society, *Proceedings,* LI, 356; *Prov. Gazette,* Aug. 18, 1764.

[24] *RIAR,* Sept., 1762; *Prov. Gazette Extraordinary,* April 16, 1764.

[25] *Prov. Gazette,* April 16, 1763. Elisha Brown, formerly a member of the Committee of War during the French and Indian War, was notoriously late in settling his account with the General Assembly which finally threatened to sue him if he did not promptly return the money entrusted to him.

[26] *RIAR,* May, 1764.

[27] *ALRI,* p. 97.

[28] Misc. MSS, B-814, Box 2, RIHS.

[29] Journal, House of Deputies, May 3, 1764.

[30] *Ibid.,* May 3, 1765.

[31] See letters from some of Hopkins' friends to Beriah Brown, James N. Arnold, ed., *The Narragansett Historical Register,* II, 109-111.

[32] Nicholas Brown & Co. to William Richardson, Providence, Dec. 20, 1767, Brown Papers, P-P6.

33 *RIAR,* May, 1758-May, 1773.

34 Stiles Papers, Yale Univ. Library.

35 *RIAR,* May, 1762. Brown's defeat was a result of his delay in paying to the colony the money entrusted to him as a member of the Committee of War.

36 *Ibid.,* May, 1757-May, 1773.

37 *Recs. Col. R.I.,* VI, 194, 438.

38 *ALRI,* pp. 42-43, 161.

39 *Ibid.,* pp. 96-97.

40 *RIAR,* May, 1761-May, 1767. The precise number of justices of the peace for 1767 is not known. *RIAR* does not list the justices for Providence for that year.

41 *Ibid.*

42 North Providence, May 4, 1767, Moses Brown Papers, I, 72.

43 Journal, House of Deputies, May 3, 1764.

44 *RIAR,* May, 1760-May, 1776.

45 Journal, House of Deputies, May 18, 1760.

46 *Prov. Gazette,* Feb. 23, 1765.

47 General Treasurer's Accounts, 1761-1781, Alphabetical Book No. 6, R.I. Arch.

48 *Recs. Col. R.I.,* VII, 582.

49 *ALRI,* pp. 195, 105.

50 A list of the colony's Naval Officers, taken from the General Assembly Reports, 2, and Accounts Allowed, is available at R.I. Arch.

51 Samuel Nightingale to Samuel Ward, Providence, April 5, 1770, Ward MSS, Box I, 97.

52 *ALRI,* p. 180.

53 Zebedee Hopkins to Moses Brown, Glocester, June 9, 1764, Moses Brown Papers, I, 59.

54 R. I. Col. Recs. (Ms), VII, 384.

55 *RIAR,* June, 1768, p. 20.

56 *Ibid.,* Aug. 1767.

57 R.I. Col. Recs. (Ms), VIII, 568, 148.

58 *ALRI,* p. 93.

59 General Treasurer's Accounts, 1761-1781, Alphabetical Book No. 6, R.I. Arch.

60 Hopkins *v.* Ward, No. 101, Worcester County Court of Common Pleas (Nov., 1756-May, 1762), V, 76-92.

61 Moses Brown to Obadiah Brown & Co., Newport, July 5, 1761, Brown Papers, Misc. Letters, undated to 1761; *Recs. Col. R.I.,* VI, 370-373.

62 R.I. Col. Recs. (Ms), VII, 448-449; General Treasurer's Accounts, 1761-1781, Alphabetical Book No. 6, R.I. Arch.

63 *RIAR,* March, 1757, p. 154.

64 *Ibid.,* May, 1764.

65 Receipt available at R.I. Arch.

66 *RIAR,* May, 1764.

67 *Ibid.,* Oct., 1764, Nov., 1764, June, 1765.

68 Nicholas and John Brown to the Freemen of Johnston, n.d., Brown Papers, P-P6.

69 *Recs. Col. R.I.,* VI, 411.

70 See James Munro, ed., *Acts of the Privy Council of England, Colonial Series,* VI, Nos. 12, 212; Richard Partridge to Gov. Greene, March 7, 1754, Kimball, ed., *Correspondence of Governors,* II, 140-141; Richard Partridge to Gov. Hopkins, May 22, 1756, *ibid.,* p. 215; *RIAR,* March, 1755, p. 89.

71 Edmund S. and Helen M. Morgan, *The Stamp Act Crisis,* pp. 16, 50.

72 Ezra Stiles to [Richard Jackson ?], Newport, March 26, 1764, Stiles Papers; Ezra Stiles to ?, Newport, April 20, 1767, *ibid.*

NOTES TO CHAPTER IV

A MATTER OF PARLIAMENTARY TAXATION

[1] June 10, Sept. 2, 1765.

[2] *Newp. Merc.*, April 9, 1764; *Prov. Gazette*, April 14, 1764.

[3] *Prov. Gazette*, Aug. 18, 1764. This writer may have been Stephen Hopkins. The argument is similar to that of *The Rights of Colonies Examined*, published in Dec., 1764.

[4] Joseph Sherwood to Governor and Company of Rhode Island, April 11, 1765, Kimball, ed., *Correspondence of Governors*, II, 361.

[5] Feb. 23, 1765, *ibid.*, pp. 360-361.

[6] *Newp. Merc.*, May 27, 1765; Stiles, *Itineraries*, pp. 220-221.

[7] William T. Laprade, "The Stamp Act in British Politics," *American Historical Review*, XXXV (1930), 746.

[8] *Recs. Col. R.I.*, VI, 412-413. For text of Hopkins' pamphlet, see *ibid.*, pp. 416-427.

[9] *Prov. Gazette*, Dec. 22, 1764.

[10] April 11, 1765, Kimball, ed., *Correspondence of Governors*, II, 362.

[11] Jan. 3, 1765.

[12] "Extract of a Letter from a Merchant at New York . . .," *Prov. Gazette*, March 2, 1765. The letter writer also acknowledged the colonies' indebtedness to Hopkins for his other patriotic performance, "for they have not only approved of his Plans, but followed the first in dictating their Remonstrances." This refers either to the Rhode Island Remonstrance to the Lords of Trade to which Hopkins contributed, or to "An Essay on the Trade of the Northern Colonies" by Hopkins, printed in the *Prov. Gazette*, Jan. 14 and 21, 1764.

[13] *Prov. Gazette*, May 11, 1765. Goddard published a second edition of *The Rights of Colonies Examined* in 1765. It was reprinted in London in 1766 with the toned-down title, *The Grievances of the American Colonies Candidly Examined*.

[14] Cecil Headlam, ed., *Calendar of State Papers, Colonial Series, America and West Indies, 1732* (London, 1939), No. 367, pp. 204-205, No. 340, pp. 191-192, No. 169, p. 104; *Recs. Col. R.I.*, IV, 456-461.

[15] Munro, ed., *Acts of the Privy Council, Colonial*, VI, No. 470.

[16] *Ibid.*, No. 871, pp. 505-507; RIHS MSS, XII, 21.

[17] RIHS, MSS, XII, 21; Warner Papers, III, No. 734, RIHS.

[18] Gov. Hopkins to Secretary Pitt, Dec. 20, 1760, *Recs. Col. R.I.*, VI, 263.

[19] *Ibid.*, pp. 311-312, 317-320.

[20] London, 1765.

[21] Stiles, *Itineraries*, pp. 52-53. Mr. David C. Adelman has suggested that the Superior Court under Samuel Ward's control refused naturalization to Lopez for political reasons since he was a close business associate of the Browns of Providence who supported Stephen Hopkins. Mr. Adelman assumes that if Lopez eventually received the right to vote he would probably join the northern faction in opposition to Ward and his southern friends. See *Rhode Island Jewish Historical Notes*, I (Dec., 1954), 113-114, and *ibid.*, I (June, 1955), 151-152.

[22] *The Charter, Recs. Col. R.I.*, II, 9.

[23] *Prov. Gazette*, Feb. 23, 1765; Thomas Moffat to Joseph Harrison, London, Oct. 16, 1765, The Chalmers Papers, Rhode Island, 1637-1785, NYPL; Joseph Redington, ed., *Calendar of Home Office Papers of the Reign of George III, 1760-1765* (London, 1878), No. 1959, p. 609.

[24] "A Vindication of a late Pamphlet entitled, The Rights of Colonies Examined, from the Cencures and Remarks contained in a Letter from a Gentleman in Halifax,

to his Friend in Rhode Island, just published at Newport," *Prov. Gazette,* Feb. 23, March 2 and 9, 1765. "A Vindication" is attributed to Stephen Hopkins by William E. Foster, *Stephen Hopkins,* II, 61, 63-64; Moses Coit Tyler, *The Literary History of the American Revolution, 1763-1783* (New York, 1897), I, 75; Lawrence C. Wroth, "The First Press in Providence," American Antiquarian Society, *Proceedings,* LI (Oct., 1941), 371.

[25] *A Defense of the Letter from a Gentleman at Halifax, to his Friend in Rhode-Island* (Newport, 1765).

[26] *A Vindication of the British Colonies, against the Aspersions of the Halifax Gentleman, in his Letter to a Rhode-Island Friend* (Boston, 1765). Samuel Hall advertised this pamphlet in the *Newp. Merc.,* March 25, 1765, as "Just published in Boston, and sold by the Printer hereof."

[27] Boston, 1764.

[28] Newport, 1765. On April 22, Samuel Hall advertised Howard's second pamphlet in the *Newp. Merc.*

[29] Boston, 1765.

[30] For a discussion of James Otis' political apostasy at this time, see Ellen Elizabeth Brennan, "James Otis: Recreant and Patriot," *New England Quarterly,* XII (1939), 691-725.

[31] *A Defense of the Letter.*

[32] *Newp. Merc.,* March 18, 1765.

[33] Moses Brown to Nicholas Brown & Co., Glocester, April 16, 1764, Brown Papers, P-P6.

[34] *Prov. Gazette,* March 30, 1765.

[35] *Ibid.,* Feb. 23, 1765.

[36] Providence, March 25, 1765, Arnold, ed., *The Narragansett Historical Register,* II, 109.

[37] Moses Brown to Mr. Winsor, Jr., April 12, 1765, Moses Brown Papers, I, 62.

[38] Stiles Papers, Election, 1765, Yale Univ. Library.

[39] Hopkins' comment on his own pamphlet is from his letter to agent Joseph Sherwood in London. Samuel Hall printed an excerpt from this letter in the *Newp. Merc.,* March 4, 1765. When the Superior Court dragged Hall before it for printing the *Halifax Letter,* the justices used as their excuse Hall's printing without authority a part of the Governor's official letter to the agent. See *Newp. Merc.,* March 18, 1765.

[40] John Brown to Joseph Winser, April 8, 1765, Brown Papers, L&P, 58-70, RIP. John Brown's plea to "all honest men, who had heretofore kept quiet," indicates further that some people who could vote did not vote.

[41] Brown Papers, L&P, 58-70, RIP.

[42] Stephen Hopkins to Beriah Brown, Providence, March 25, 1765, Arnold, ed., *The Narragansett Historical Register,* II, 109.

## NOTES TO CHAPTER V

### TAXATION WITH REPRESENTATION AND JUSTICE OF THE COMMON LAW IN RHODE ISLAND

[1] R.I. Col. Recs. (Ms), VIII, 433-434.

[2] *Ibid.,* VII, 156-157.

[3] *Ibid.,* pp. 374-375.

[4] *Ibid.,* pp. 387-390.

⁵ *Ibid.;* Journal, House of Deputies, 8-2, Second June Session, 1761.

⁶ Journal, House of Deputies, 8-2, First Oct. Session, 1761; Journal of the Senate (1756-1762), Second June Session, 1761.

⁷ For the struggle between the two factions over taxation, see R.I. Col. Recs. (Ms), VII, 408-410, 428-430; *ibid.,* VIII, 72-74, 146, 243-245, 358-359, 395-396, 406, 420, 423, 433-434, 441, 452-454, 540; Journal, House of Deputies, 8-2, Second June Session, 1761; *ibid.,* 9-3, Dec., 1766; Journal of the Senate (1756-1762), Second June Session, 1761; Petitions, 11-2, 40, 74; *ibid.,* 13-2, 64, R.I. Arch.

⁸ R.I. Col. Recs. (Ms), VIII, 244, 358. For convenience in comparing these tax figures I have eliminated the shillings and pence from each town's rate.

⁹ *Ibid.,* VIII, 395-396, 406, 420, 423, 433-434, 441, 452-453, 540; Journal, House of Deputies, 9-3, June, 1766, Dec., 1766.

¹⁰ R.I. Col. Recs. (Ms), VIII, 452.

¹¹ *Ibid.,* p. 454.

¹² Feb., 23, 1765, Kimball, ed., *Correspondence of Governors,* II, 360-361.

¹³ Actually the distinction between subjects in England and America with respect to the enforcement of stamp taxes was not as precise as Americans claimed. Apparently the colonists were unaware that some violations of the English stamp taxes—which Englishmen had paid since 1694—and specifically the printing or selling of pamphlets and newspapers on unstamped paper had been cognizable since 1711 before two or more justices of the peace and no jury with appeal to the quarter sessions court containing only more justices of the peace. A fundamental distinction still existed, however: American violators of the Stamp Act would be deprived of common law trials which Englishmen at home enjoyed in like offenses. See 10 Anne, c. 19, secs. CXX, CLXXII, Danby Pickering, ed., *The Statutes at Large . . . ,* XII, 378, 388-389; 16 George II, c. 26, sec. V, *ibid.,* XVIII, 134. See also Edward Hughes, "The English Stamp Duties, 1664-1764," *English Historical Review,* LVI (1941), 245-246. In defending the Stamp Act several Englishmen argued that Americans had little to complain about since Englishmen were not entitled to trial by jury either when they violated the stamp acts. See *Correct Copies of the Two Protests against the Bill to Repeal the American Stamp Act* (Paris, 1766) and *The Conduct of the Late Administration Examined* (2nd ed., London, 1767), p. 36. Rhode Island's official complaint against extension of admiralty court jurisdiction under the Stamp Act is in Governor of Rhode Island to Secretary Conway, Newport, Nov. 6, 1765, *Recs. Col. R.I.,* VI, 473, and in Instructions to the Rhode Island Commissioners to the Stamp Act Congress, *ibid.,* p. 450. For the best colonial statement against admiralty court jurisdiction, see the Stamp Act Congress petition to the House of Commons, *ibid.,* p. 469.

¹⁴ See Edmund S. Morgan, ed., *The Stamp Act Crisis, Sources and Documents* (Providence, R.I., 1952), pp. 87-100.

¹⁵ *Recs. Col. R.I.,* VI, 466.

¹⁶ *Ibid.,* p. 470.

¹⁷ *Ibid.,* II, 9.

¹⁸ RIAR, Feb., 1746 (Ms), BUL; *ALRI,* pp. 45-46.

¹⁹ *ALRI,* pp. 204-207.

²⁰ *Ibid.,* pp. 93-96.

²¹ *Recs. Col. R.I.,* VII, 28.

²² General Treasurer's Accounts, 1761-1781, Alphabetical Book No. 6, R.I. Arch.

²³ *Newp. Merc.,* June 1, July 6, Aug. 17, 1772.

²⁴ Petitions, 13-2, 101 (Oct. 27, 1767), R.I. Arch.

²⁵ *RIAR,* 1753-1761.

²⁶ *Ibid.,* May, 1761; Journal, House of Deputies, May 15, 1761.

²⁷ Martin Howard, Jr., *A Letter from a Gentleman at Halifax to his Friend in Rhode-Island* (Newport, 1765).

[28] *Newp. Merc.,* April 23, 1764.

[29] *Ibid.,* Nov. 21, 1763.

[30] *Ibid.,* June 1, June 22, July 6, 1772.

[31] See the discussion of Hopkins *v.* Ward in Chapter I.

[32] Although Simeon Potter was a deputy in the legislature in 1761 when it was dominated by the Ward faction, he did not serve in 1762 under Ward. He reappeared in 1763, however, under the Hopkins government. Potter represented Bristol again for several years in the 1770's during the Wanton-Hopkins regime. For the facts of Simeon Potter's case, see *RIAR,* May, 1761, and June, 1763, pp. 44-45; Petitions, 11-12, 23, R.I. Arch.

[33] R.I. Col. Recs. (Ms), VIII, 135. Joseph Tillinghast was one of several signers in behalf of Samuel Ward of the peace proposals between the two parties in 1767. *Recs. Col. R.I.,* VI, 553-554.

[34] Glocester, May 24, 1764, Moses Brown Papers, I, 58.

[35] Aug. 18, 1769, Ward MSS (Knollenberg Transcripts).

[36] Nicholas Brown & Co. to Edmond Jenney, Nov. 2, 1763, Brown Papers, P-P6.

[37] The Assembly did not act upon the Providence Town Meeting's advice and enacted no law denying admiralty court enforcement of internal taxes in Rhode Island. However, at their next session in September, the members drafted several resolves, one of which declared that the people of Rhode Island had always enjoyed and had never forfeited or given up the right of being governed by their Assembly in the "article of taxes and internal police." Probably "internal police" in this instance included the manner in which taxes were enforced, that is, by the Assembly through the colony's courts. If the Assembly's resolves did not explicitly deny the validity of admiralty court decrees to enforce the Stamp Act, they at least declared what was customary—in fact habitual—in Rhode Island respecting the enforcement of taxes, and that such procedure had been "constantly recognized by the King and people of Great Britain." The Providence Town Meeting Resolves and Instructions are in *Prov. Gazette Extraordinary,* Aug. 24, and *Newp. Merc.,* Aug. 19, 1765. For the Assembly's Stamp Act Resolves, see *Recs. Col. R.I.,* VI, 451-452.

[38] *Newp. Merc.,* April 23, 1764.

## NOTES TO CHAPTER VI

## RIOTS, RESOLVES, AND REPEAL

[1] *Newp. Merc.,* May 6, 1765.

[2] Thomas Moffat, Manuscript account of the Newport riots, Chalmers Papers, Rhode Island, NYPL. That Johnston was a member of the Hopkins faction is explicit in a letter he wrote to Nicholas Brown from Newport prior to the election of 1761. His closing words were: "I find we shall be obliged to fight hard this spring coming, & we must watch all advantages—but D—n then they can't beat us—In the true spirit. I am yrs. A Johnston." Jan. 26, 1761, Brown Papers, Misc. Letters, undated to 1761.

[3] Thomas Moffat, Account of the Newport riots; Thomas Moffat to J. Harrison, London, Oct. 16, 1765, Chalmers Papers, Rhode Island, NYPL.

[4] *Prov. Gazette,* May 11, 1765, Aug. 15, 1766.

[5] Goddard published his newspaper three days before the ringleaders in Newport intended to hang Johnston, Moffat, and Howard in effigy. Although word circulated through Newport on the twenty-fourth—the date of the *Gazette Extraordinary*—that such a spectacle would take place, there was no action which might have in-

timidated Johnston to a declaration. The incidents of the next week and Johnston's reaction to them were, of course, unknown to Goddard on the twenty-fourth.

[6] Italics added.

[7] The information about the Stamp Act riot in Newport is derived from the following sources: Thomas Moffat, Manuscript account of the Newport riots, Chalmers Papers, Rhode Island, NYPL; Thomas Moffat to J. Harrison, London, Oct. 16, 1765, *ibid.;* John Robinson to Commissioners of Customs, Aug. 28 and Sept. 5, 1765, House of Lords MSS, Jan. 14, 1766, Library of Congress transcripts; Augustus Johnston to Commissioners of Stamps, Rhode Island, Aug. 31, 1765, *ibid.;* Abstract, Captain Charles Leslie to Lord Colville, Joseph Redington, ed., *Calendar of Home Office Papers, George III, 1760-1765,* p. 611; *Newp. Merc.,* Sept. 2, 1765.

[8] Johnston to Commissioners of Stamps, Aug. 31, 1765; Moffat to Harrison, Oct. 16, 1765; *Newp. Merc.,* Sept. 2, 1765.

[9] J. Almon, ed., *A Collection of Interesting, Authentic Papers, relative to the Dispute between Great Britain and America, etc., 1764-1775* (London, 1777), p. 13. This volume is often called *Prior Documents.*

[10] Moffat to Harrison, Oct. 16, 1765; *Newp. Merc.,* Sept. 2, 1765.

[11] Johnston to Commissioners of Stamps, Aug. 31, 1765. According to Thomas Moffat and Captain Leslie of the *Cygnet,* Ezra Stiles, minister of the Second Congregational Church in Newport, was responsible for exciting the crowd and helping to continue the riot. They reported that once peace had been restored after Johnston's first note, Stiles came into the street and with a few words altered the whole complexion of the affair. Supposedly Stiles declared to the people that Johnston's "resignation was an artful and base imposition on them." He harangued "copiously to the gaping gathering crowd" claiming that Johnston's note was worthless, and he could execute the office at any time he pleased. The crowd became more and more inflamed with every word the minister spoke when up stepped Samuel Brenton, fixed Stiles with a penetrating stare, and asked him "How he could behave so unbecoming his function?" This shut the minister's mouth for the time being, but the damage had already been done. See Moffat, Account of the riots; Abstract, Leslie to Colville; Johnston to Commissioners of Stamps, Aug. 31, 1765. Stiles, however, denied that he had anything to do with the riot in Newport. See Morgan and Morgan, *The Stamp Act Crisis,* p. 151n.

[12] Johnston to Commissioners of Stamps, Aug. 31, 1765.

[13] Abstract, Leslie to Colville.

[14] Johnston to Commissioners of Stamps, Aug. 31, 1765; *Newp. Merc.,* Sept. 2, 1765.

[15] Moffat, Account of the riots; Moffat to Harrison, Oct. 16, 1765. *Newp. Merc.,* Sept. 2, 1765, claimed that Howard and Moffat sailed for England on September 1.

[16] Gov. Ward to John Robinson and others, Newport, Aug. 31, 1765, *Recs. Col. R.I.,* VI, 454.

[17] Samuel Ward to his wife, Westerly, Jan. 17, 1767, Aug. 2, 1769, Ward MSS (Knollenberg Transcripts).

[18] Robinson to Commissioners of Customs, Sept. 5, 1765. See the correspondence between Gideon Wanton and John Robinson, and Samuel Ward and Robinson in *Recs. Col. R.I.,* VI, 453-456; *Newp. Merc.,* Sept. 9, 1765.

[19] R.I. Col. Recs. (Ms), VIII, 344; *Newp. Merc.,* Sept. 16, 1765.

[20] R.I. Col. Recs. (Ms), VIII, 421.

[21] Joseph Sherwood to Gov. Ward, May 15 and July 25, 1766, Kimball, ed., *Correspondence of Governors,* II, 387-388, 393-394.

[22] R.I. Col. Recs. (Ms), VIII, 421; Governor of Rhode Island to the Earl of Hillsborough, Newport, June 17, 1769, *Recs. Col. R.I.,* VI, 590-592, VII, 200-201, 217, 219.

[23] *Newp. Merc.,* Sept. 9, 1765.

[24] John P. Kennedy, ed., *Journals of the House of Burgesses of Virginia, 1761-1765* (Richmond, 1907), pp. lxvi-lxviii; "Journal of a French Traveller, 1765," *American istorical Review,* XXVI (1921), 745-746.

[25] The Providence Town Meeting Resolves were printed in the *Newp. Merc.,* Aug. 19, 1765; Little Compton Resolves, *ibid.,* Sept. 2, 1765. For Newport Town Meeting's instructions to its deputies, see *ibid.,* Sept. 9, 1765.

[26] R.I. Col. Recs. (Ms), VIII, 344; *Recs. Col. R.I.,* VI, 451-452.

[27] *Recs. Col. R.I.,* VI, 451-452. Unlike the resolves of most of the colonial legislatures against the Stamp Act, the Rhode Island Resolves do not mention the extension of admiralty court jurisdiction nor specifically the Sugar and Stamp Acts. The General Assembly's statement is a declaration of what was true with respect to rights and is not a list of grievances.

[28] *Ibid.,* p. 449.

[29] Jabez Bowen to Moses Brown, Sept. 12, 1765, Moses Brown Papers, I, 65.

[30] *Recs. Col. R.I.,* VI, 449, 451; *Newp. Merc.,* Sept. 16, 1765.

[31] R.I. Col. Recs. (Ms), VIII, 344.

[32] *Proceedings of the Congress at New York* (Annapolis, 1766).

[33] *Recs. Col. R.I.,* VI, 461-462.

[34] *Newp. Merc.,* Jan. 20, 1766.

[35] *Ibid.,* Oct. 21, 1765; *Newp. Merc. Supplement,* Oct. 28, 1765.

[36] *Newp. Merc.,* Oct. 14, 1765.

[37] *Ibid.,* Oct. 28, Nov. 4, 1765.

[38] Joseph Wanton, Jr., to Moses Brown, Moses Brown Papers, I, 65.

[39] *Newp. Merc.,* Nov. 4, 1765.

[40] *Ibid.*

[41] *Ibid.,* Nov. 11, 1765.

[42] *Ibid.,* Nov. 18, 1765.

[43] See Morgan and Morgan, *The Stamp Act Crisis,* Ch. X.

[44] *Prov. Gazette,* Aug. 30, 1766.

[45] *Newp. Merc.,* April 20, 1767.

[46] William Goddard discontinued publication of the *Providence Gazette* in May, 1765, not for fear of the Stamp Act but for want of subscribers. See *Prov. Gazette,* May 11, Aug. 15, 1765.

[47] Records of the Inferior Court of Common Pleas, G (May, 1763-May, 1767), 477-556, Newport County Court House, Newport, R.I.; *Newp. Merc.,* Jan. 6, 1766.

[48] *Newp. Merc.,* Dec. 23, 1765.

[49] Records of the Superior Court of Judicature of Newport County, E (1754-1772), 286-287, Nov. 21, 1765.

[50] Morgan and Morgan, *The Stamp Act Crisis,* p. 176.

[51] *Newp. Merc.,* Nov. 18, Dec. 2, 1765.

[52] *Recs. Col. R.I.,* VI, 476-477.

[53] Nov. 4, 1765.

[54] Charles Lowndes to Governor of Rhode Island, Sept. 14, 1765, *Recs. Col. R.I.,* VI, 460.

[55] "At a Council held at Newport the 23$^d$ day of Decr. A.D., 1765," Ward MSS, Box I, 60 (copy).

[56] *Newp. Merc.,* Dec. 30, 1765.

[57] *Recs. Col. R.I.,* VI, 478.

[58] Governor to Captain Antrobus, March 28, 1766, *ibid.,* p. 485.

[59] *Ibid.,* p. 490.

[60] *Newp. Merc.,* Dec. 5, 1768, May 15, 1769.

[61] *Ibid.,* March 31, 1766; RIHS MSS, XII, 64.

[62] For lists of the committee members, see RIHS MSS, XII, 63, 67.

[63] *Newp. Merc.,* March 31, April 7, 1766; RIHS MSS, XII, 64-70.

[64] *Newp. Merc.,* May 26, 1766.

[65] Feb. 25, 1765, Official Letters from Rhode Island Agents in London, 1746-1769, p. 47, JCBL.

[66] H. Babcock to Samuel Ward, n.d., Ward MSS, Box I, 61.

[67] Samuel Ward to his wife, Westerly, March 6, 1766, Ward MSS (Knollenberg Transcripts).

[68] Nicholas Brown & Co. to Joseph Holley, April 15, 1766, Brown Papers, P-P6.

[69] John Dexter to Nicholas Brown & Co., 1766, Brown Papers, L&P, 58-70, RIP. A "Bank" was an emission of paper money.

[70] Daniel Jenckes to Gov. Ward's friends, South Kingstown, March 1, 1766, Misc. MSS, B-814, Box 2; Moses Brown to Nicholas Brown & Co., Newport, March 25, 1766, Brown Papers, P-P6; Nicholas Brown & Co. to Joseph Holley, April 15, 1766, *ibid.;* Brown Papers, L&P, 58-70, RIP.

[71] *Prov. Gazette,* Aug. 15, 1766.

[72] Morgan and Morgan, *The Stamp Act Crisis,* p. 277.

[73] Henry Cruger, Jr., to Henry Cruger, Bristol, England, Feb. 14, 1766, Massachusetts Historical Society *Collections,* LXIX (1914), 140-141.

[74] Henry Cruger, Jr., to Aaron Lopez, March 1, 1766, *ibid.,* p. 145.

[75] *Newp. Merc.,* May 19, May 26, 1766.

[76] William Ellery to Captain Carr, May 24, 1766, Peck MSS, III, 2, RIHS; R.I. Col. Recs. (Ms), VIII, 393.

[77] *Newp. Merc.,* May 26, 1766.

[78] *Prov. Gazette,* Aug. 8 and 23, 1766.

[79] *Ibid.,* Sept. 6, 1766.

[80] R.I. Col. Recs. (Ms), VIII, 396; Kimball, ed., *Correspondence of Governors,* II, 389-391; Ward MSS, Box I, 67.

[81] *Prov. Gazette,* April 18, 1767.

[82] *Ibid.,* Aug. 30, Sept. 6, 1766.

[83] Silas Downer to Sons of Liberty of New York, Providence, July 21, 1766, Peck MSS, III, 3, RIHS.


### NOTES TO CHAPTER VII

### MORE TAXES AND MORE POLITICS, 1767-1771

[1] Joseph Sherwood to Gov. Ward, May 15, 1766, *Recs. Col. R.I.,* VI, 491-492.

[2] Benjamin Gale to Ezra Stiles, Oct. 15, 1767, Stiles, *Itineraries,* pp. 493-494.

[3] *Newp. Merc.,* Feb. 22, 1766. To "see Men as Trees walking" is obviously an allusion to Shakespeare's *Macbeth:* "till Birnam wood do come to Dunsinane."

[4] Nicholas Brown & Co. to John Brown, Providence, March 17, 1767, Brown Papers, Misc. Letters, 1767, I.

[5] Elisha Brown *et al.* to Stephen Hopkins, East Greenwich, Feb. 28, 1767, Misc. MSS, B-814, Box 2, RIHS; *Recs. Col. R.I.,* VI, 550-551. In addition to Elisha Brown this letter was signed by Nicholas Easton, Gideon Wanton, Jr., Thomas Owen, Stephen Rawson, John Jepson, Nathaniel Searle, John Burton, Hezekiah Babcock, and Othniel Gorton.

[6] March 12, 1767, Brown Papers, P-P6; Misc. MSS, B-814, Box 2, RIHS; *Recs. Col. R.I.,* VI, 551-552. The Hopkins party's proposals were signed by Daniel Jenckes, Ephraim Bowen, Darius Sessions, Benjamin Cushing, Joseph Russell, Nathan Angell, Thomas Greene, Joseph Nash, and Moses Brown.

[7] Newport, March 25, 1767, Misc. MSS, B-814, Box 2; *Recs. Col. R.I.,* VI, 553-554.

[8] Newport, April 7, 1767, *Recs. Col. R.I.,* VI, 550-553.

[9] Nicholas Brown & Co. to Gideon Tripp, April 9, 1767, Brown Papers, P-P6.

[10] Nicholas Brown & Co. to Richard Greene, April 10, 1767, *ibid.*

[11] Nicholas Brown & Co. to Thomas Aldrich, Providence, April 10, 1767, *ibid.*

[12] Elisha Brown to Samuel Ward, North Providence, July 26, 1767, Ward MSS (Knollenberg Transcripts).

[13] Providence, April 6, 1767, Stiles Papers, Yale University Library.

[14] *Prov. Gazette,* April 18, 1767; Brown Papers, P-P6.

[15] *RIAR,* May, 1767.

[16] *Ibid.,* May, 1767, p. 11; *ALRI,* Newport, 1767, p. 24.

[17] *Prov. Gazette,* April 18, 1767.

[18] North Providence, July 26, 1767, Ward MSS (Knollenberg Transcripts).

[19] *Newp. Merc.,* May 11, 1767.

[20] *Ibid.,* July 13, 1767; *Prov. Gazette,* July 11, 1767.

[21] Aug. 7, 1767, Kimball, ed., *Correspondence of Governors,* II, 497. For the Townshend Duties, see Danby Pickering, ed., *The Statutes at Large,* XXVII, 505-512.

[22] *Newp. Merc.,* Oct. 31, 1767.

[23] *Ibid.,* Sept. 28, 1767; Lord Shelburne to Gov. of Rhode Island, Oct. 8, 1767, Kimball, ed., *Correspondence of Governors,* II, 398.

[24] *Newp. Merc.,* Oct. 26, Nov. 30, 1767.

[25] Henry Marchant to George Hazard, London, May 15, 1772, RIHS MSS, VI, 39.

[26] Merrill Jensen, ed., *English Historical Documents,* IX, *American Colonial Documents to 1776* (London, 1955), No. 119, pp. 707-708.

[27] *Ibid.,* p. 708.

[28] *A Discourse Delivered in Providence, in the Colony of Rhode-Island, on the 25th. Day of July, 1768, at the Dedication of the Tree of Liberty From the Summer House in the Tree.* By a Son of Liberty (Providence, 1768).

[29] Thomas Vernon to Charles Russel, March 11 and July 22, 1773, Vernon Papers, Metal Box 3, folder 114, NHS.

[30] Henry Marchant, Journell of Voyage from Newport in the Colony of Rhode Island &c to London, Travels thro' many Parts of England & Scotland—begun July 8th 1771. This manuscript is owned by Miss Alice Clarke of Cohoes, New York; a microfilm of it is in RIHS.

[31] *Recs. Col. R.I.,* VI, 556, 559-561. The petition was dated Sept. 16, 1768.

[32] *Ibid.,* pp. 535-537, 541, 563; *Prov. Gazette,* July 9 and 16, 1768; *Newp. Merc.,* July 25, 1768.

[33] *Prov. Gazette,* Sept. 19, 1767; *Newp. Merc.,* Feb. 13, 1769.

[34] *A Discourse Delivered in Providence, in the Colony of Rhode-Island.*

[35] *Newp. Merc.,* Jan. 11, 1768.

[36] The coalition proposals of 1768 are in seven letters between Ward's and Hopkins' friends bearing dates from March 5 to March 24, 1768, Ward MSS (Knollenberg Transcripts). See also Hopkins' Friends to Ward's Friends, March 17, 1768, Misc. MSS, B-814, Box 2, RIHS; Nicholas Easton to Hopkins, n.p., n.d. (probably 1768), *ibid.; Prov. Gazette,* March 5, 19, April 2, 9, 1768.

[37] Elisha Brown to Samuel Ward, North Providence, April 18, 1768, Ward MSS (Knollenberg Transcripts).

[38] Josias Lyndon to Moses Brown, Newport, April 17, 1769, Moses Brown Papers, I, 94.

[39] Stephen Hopkins *et al.* to Josias Lyndon, Providence, April 7, 1768, Brown Papers, P-P6.

[40] Elisha Brown to Samuel Ward, North Providence, April 18, 1768, Ward MSS (Knollenberg Transcripts).

[41] Nicholas Brown & Co. to Daniel Howland, Providence, April 11, 1767, Brown Papers, P-P6.

[42] Josias Lyndon to Moses Brown, Newport, April 17, 1769, Moses Brown Papers, I, 94.

[43] Ezra Stiles to Dr. Alison, Newport, April 23, 1768, Stiles Papers. "Chh" to Stiles meant Church, his abbreviation for the Church of England.

[44] Elisha Brown to Samuel Ward, North Providence, April 18, 1768, Ward MSS (Knollenberg Transcripts).

[45] On April 23, 1768, the *Prov. Gazette* announced that Wanton carried five towns. However, the election results in the General Assembly Reports show that only three towns had majorities for Wanton. III (1766-1778), 21, R.I. Arch.

[46] April 23, 1768.

[47] Josias Lyndon to Moses Brown, Newport, April 17, 1769, Moses Brown Papers, I, 94.

[48] *RIAR,* May, 1768, et passim. Joseph Wanton (son of Gideon), Peter Philips, and Charles Holden had been sheriffs under Ward—Wanton at four different times.

[49] R.I. Col. Recs. (Ms), VIII, 537-538, 568, 585.

[50] Josias Lyndon to Moses Brown, Newport, April 17, 1769, Moses Brown Papers, I, 94.

[51] Samuel Ward to his wife, Newport, April 11, 1769, Ward MSS, Box I, 87.

[52] Josias Lyndon to Moses Brown, Newport, April 17, 1769, Moses Brown Papers, I, 94.

[53] Elisha Brown to Samuel Ward, Providence, April 17, 1769, Ward MSS, Box I, 88.

[54] *Prov. Gazette,* April 15, 1769.

[55] The breakdown of the coalition and Josias Lyndon's dilemma are explained in two long letters: Lyndon to Moses Brown, Newport, April 17, 1769, Moses Brown Papers, I, 94, and Moses Brown to Lyndon, Providence, April 18, 1769, *ibid.,* p. 93.

[56] Election Proxes, RIHS.

[57] Joseph Wanton, Jr., to Moses Brown, Newport, April 18, 1769, Moses Brown Papers, I, 93.

[58] Elisha Brown to Samuel Ward, Providence, April 17, 1769, Ward MSS, Box I, 88.

[59] Brown Papers, L&P, 58-70, RIP; *Prov. Gazette,* April 22, 1769.

[60] William Ellery to Samuel Ward, Newport, Feb. 4, 1769, Ward MSS, Box I, 85. Walter Chaloner had been a vestryman of Trinity Church, Newport. George C. Mason, *Annals of Trinity Church, Newport, Rhode Island, 1698-1821* (Newport, 1890), I, 104. The General Assembly in 1757 recommended Chaloner, an officer in a Rhode Island regiment, to Lord Loudoun "as a gentleman that may deserve his favor." *Recs. Col. R.I.,* VI, 10-11.

[61] Joseph Wanton, Jr., to Moses Brown, April 22, 1769, Moses Brown Papers, I, 94.

[62] *RIAR,* May, 1769.

[63] *Newp. Merc.,* Aug. 29, 1768, May 29, 1769, Aug. 21, 1769. For early non-importation plans, see Providence Town Council Address to Selectmen of Boston, Nov. 20, 1767, JCBL; also *Newp. Merc.,* Dec., 1767, March 19 and May 7, 1768.

[64] *Newp. Merc.,* Oct. 16, 1769.

[65] *Ibid.,* Oct. 30, Nov. 6, 1769; *Prov. Gazette,* Nov. 4 and 11, 1769.

[66] Merchants of Philadelphia to Merchants of Newport, Nov. 17, 1769, Brown Papers, P-P6.

[67] *Prov. Gazette,* July 22, Oct. 14, 21, and 28, Dec. 9, 1769; *Newp. Merc.,* Oct. 30, 1769. For a discussion of nonimportation in Providence, particularly as it related to the Brown brothers, see James B. Hedges, *The Browns of Providence,* pp. 203-208.

[68] *Newp. Merc.,* Nov. 27, 1769, Jan. 1, 1770.

[69] *Ibid.,* June 4, 1770.

[70] May 26, 1770.

[71] Committee of Providence Merchants to Boston Merchants, June 1, 1770, RIHS MSS, VI, 36; Moses Brown to Committee of Merchants in Boston, Providence, May 23, 1770, Moses Brown Papers, I, 108.

[72] Moses Brown to Joseph Sherwood, Providence, June, 1770, Kimball, ed., *Correspondence of Governors,* II, 420; Moses Brown Papers, I, 111.

[73] *Prov. Gazette,* June 9, 1770.

[74] Josiah Hewes to Messrs. Vernon and Tanner, Philadelphia, June 2, 1770, Vernon Letters (Aug., 1743-March, 1777), p. 42, NHS; Nicholas Roosevelt to Messrs. Samuel & William Vernon and James Tanner, New York, June 1, 1770, Vernon Papers (1770-1789), folder for 1771, NHS.

[75] Joseph Wanton, Jr., to Moses Brown, Newport, July 10, 1770, Moses Brown Papers, I, 112; *Prov. Gazette,* June 30, 1770; Postscript to *Newp. Merc.,* June 7, 1770.

[76] *Newp. Merc.,* June 18, 1770; *Prov. Gazette,* June 30, 1770; Nicholas Roosevelt to Samuel and William Vernon and James Tanner, New York, June 25, 1770, Vernon Papers, Metal Box 7, folder 111, NHS.

[77] *Prov. Gazette,* June 23, 1770.

[78] Joseph Wanton, Jr., to Moses Brown, Newport, July 10, 1770, Moses Brown Papers, I, 112.

[79] Stiles, *Diary,* I, 53-54.

[80] Thomas Vernon to [John Robinson ?], Newport, June 27, 1770, Vernon Papers, Metal Box 3, folder 114, NHS.

[81] Stiles, *Diary,* I, 270.

[82] *Prov. Gazette,* June 30, July 7, 1770.

[83] Moses Brown to Joseph Wanton, Jr., North Providence, July 6, 1770, Moses Brown Papers, I, 112; *Prov. Gazette,* June 30, 1770.

[84] *Prov. Gazette,* July 21, 1770. For a description of the breakdown of nonimportation and New York's role in it, see Arthur M. Schlesinger, *The Colonial Merchants and the American Revolution, 1763-1776* (New York, 1918), p. 217ff.

[85] Sept. 14, 1770, Moses Brown Papers, I, 115.

[86] Oct. 20, Nov. 24, 1770.

[87] Schlesinger, *Colonial Merchants,* pp. 213, 236-239; John C. Miller, *Origins of the American Revolution* (Boston, 1943), pp. 278-279.

[88] Letter to law clients, April, 1772, quoted in Edward T. Channing, *Life of William Ellery,* Jared Sparks, ed., *Library of American Biography* (Boston, 1836), VI, 99-100.

[89] An Act for the Establishment of a College, or University, within this Colony, *Recs. Col. R.I.,* VI, 385-391.

[90] For information about the removal of the college to Providence, see Walter C. Bronson, *The History of Brown University, 1764-1914* (Providence, 1914), pp. 43-49; James B. Hedges, *The Browns of Providence,* pp. 194-197.

[91] *Newp. Merc.,* March 12, 1770.

[92] Stiles, *Diary,* I, 39.

[93] *Newp. Merc.,* March 12, 1770.

[94] Joseph Wanton, Jr., to Moses Brown, Newport, March 6, 1770, Moses Brown Papers, I, 102.

[95] Elisha Brown to Samuel Ward, South Kingstown, Oct. 29, 1769, Ward MSS (Knollenberg Transcripts).

[96] Samuel Nightingale to Samuel Ward, Providence, April 5, 1770, *ibid.*

[97] Edward Sands to Samuel Ward, New Shoreham, April 19, 1770, Ward MSS, Box I, 99.

[98] Henry Ward to John Comstock, Newport, April 13, 1770, Ward MSS (Kollenberg Transcripts).

[99] Joseph Wanton, Jr., to Moses Brown, Newport, April 5, 1770, Moses Brown Papers, I, 103.

[100] April 8, 1770, *ibid.*

[101] April 21, 1770.

[102] Edward Sands to Samuel Ward, New Shoreham, April 19, 1770, Ward MSS, Box I, 99.

[103] Misc. MSS, B-814, Box 2, RIHS; *Prov. Gazette,* April 21, 1770.

[104] Joseph Wanton, Jr., to Moses Brown and Jabez Bowen, Jr., Newport, April 22, 1770, Moses Brown Papers, I, 107.

[105] Election Proxes, RIHS.

[106] *RIAR,* May, 1770.

[107] Henry Marchant to Samuel Ward, Jan. 22, and Feb. ?, 1771, Ward MSS (Knollenberg Transcripts).

[108] *Newp. Merc.,* Oct. 8, 1770; *Prov. Gazette,* Nov. 24, 1770.

[109] Samuel G. Arnold, *History of the State of Rhode Island and Providence Plantations* (New York, 1860), II, 281-282; Clarence S. Brigham, *History of the State of Rhode Island and Providence Plantations* (n.p., 1902), p. 213; William E. Foster, *Stephen Hopkins,* II, 27; Thomas Bicknell, *The History of the State of Rhode Island and Providence Plantations* (New York, 1920), III, 1083; Irving B. Richman, *Rhode Island, a Study in Separatism* (Boston, 1905), p. 178; *Recs. Col. R.I.,* VI, 550.

[110] Moses Brown to Joseph Sherwood, Providence, Dec. 10, 1770, Moses Brown Papers, II, 3.

[111] *Recs. Col. R.I.,* VII, passim.

[112] Joseph Wanton, Jr., to Moses Brown, Newport, March 23, 1771, Moses Brown Papers, II, 7.

[113] Stiles, *Diary,* I, 231.

[114] *RIAR,* 1770-1775.

## NOTES TO CHAPTER VIII

## A FIRM AND INVIOLABLE UNION

[1] Providence, Dec. 10, 1770, Moses Brown Papers, II, 3.

[2] Stiles, *Diary,* I, 270-271; *Newp. Merc.,* Nov. 23, 1767.

[3] *Newp. Merc.,* Aug. 8, Dec. 12, 1768.

[4] *Recs. Col. R.I.,* VI, 413, 587; *Newp. Merc.,* Sept. 18, Oct. 9 and 14, 1769.

[5] Committee of Merchants to Charles Dudley, Sept., 1769, signed by Silas Cooke, Frank Malbone, and Will Wanton, Moses Brown Papers, I, 98.

[6] Sept. 14, 1769, *ibid.*

[7] Stiles, *Diary,* I, 270-271.

[8] July 19, 1771, *Recs. Col. R.I.,* VII, 34-35.

[9] Nov. 2, 1771, *ibid.,* pp. 42-43.

[10] Henry Marchant to George Hazard, London, May 15, 1772, RIHS, MSS, VI, 39.

[11] June 10 and 24, 1769; *Newp. Merc.,* June 12, 1769.

[12] *Newp. Merc.,* May 15 and 22, 1769.

[13] *Ibid.,* July 24 and 31, Aug. 7, 1769; *Recs. Col. R.I.,* VI, 593-596.

[14] Thomas Vernon to [John Robinson ?], Newport, June 27, 1770, Vernon Papers, Metal Box 3, folder 114, NHS.

[15] *Newp. Merc.,* Oct. 14, 1765, Aug. 31, 1767, July 17, 1769.

[16] *Ibid.,* Jan. 18, 1773. See the correspondence of Dudingston, Admiral Montague, and Gov. Wanton, *Recs. Col. R.I.,* VII, 61-66.

[17] *Prov. Gazette,* March 21 and 28, 1772.

[18] Newport, May 20, 1772, *Recs. Col. R.I.,* VII, 66-68.

[19] Newport, Nov. 21, 1772, Henry Marchant, Letter Book, pp. 28-31, NHS.

[20] For documents describing the burning of the *Gaspee,* see *Recs. Col. R.I.,* VII, 68-94; William R. Staples, *The Documentary History of the Destruction of the Gaspee* (Providence, 1845).

[21] *Newp. Merc.,* June 15, 1772; *Recs. Col. R.I.,* VII, 81.

[22] Sept. 4, 1772, *Recs. Col. R.I.,* VII, 103-104.

[23] *Ibid.,* p. 108.

[24] *Newp. Merc.,* April 26, 1773.

[25] *Ibid.*

[26] For the details of this dispute, see Stiles, *Diary,* I, 334, 336; Dartmouth to Governor of Rhode Island, March 3, 1773, Kimball, ed., *Correspondence of Governors,* II, 430; Gov. Wanton to Dartmouth, July 1, 1773, Peck MSS, III, 31, RIHS; *Newp. Merc.,* Jan. 25, 1773.

[27] See Commission and Royal Instructions, *Recs. Col. R.I.,* VII, 108-112. For a revealing letter about the Commission, see Ezra Stiles to Elihu Spencer, Newport, Feb. 16, 1773, Stiles, *Diary,* I, 345-351. See also Stiles's other comments in *ibid.,* pp. 379-380, 382-385, 387.

[28] For an analysis of the constitutional and political implications of the *Gaspee* Commission, see: William R. Leslie, "The Gaspee Affair: A Study of its Constitutional Significance," *Mississippi Valley Historical Review,* XXXIX (1952-1953), 233-256; Eugene Wulsin, "The Political Consequences of the Burning of the Gaspee," *Rhode Island History,* III (1944), 1-11 and 55-64.

[29] George Rome to Thomas Moffat, Narragansett, Dec. 22, 1767, in Wilkins Updike, *A History of the Episcopal Church in Narragansett, Rhode Island,* Daniel Goodwin, ed. (second ed., Boston, 1907), II, 80-89.

[30] James Munro, ed., *Acts of the Privy Council, Colonial* (London, etc., 1912), VI, No. 871, pp. 505-507; Journal, House of Deputies, 1769-1770, May and June sessions. For accounts of Freebody *v.* Brenton, see Joseph Henry Smith, *Appeals to the Privy Council from the American Plantations* (New York, 1950), pp. 336-341; see also David S. Lovejoy, "Henry Marchant and the Mistress of the World," *William and Mary Quarterly,* 3rd ser., XII (1955), 379-381. The court remained adamant until 1774 when it finally gave in and executed the royal decree.

[31] *Newp. Merc.,* Dec. 21, 1772, Jan. 4, 1773.

[32] Henry Marchant to David Jennings, Newport, Jan. 28, 1773, Marchant, Letter Book, pp. 34-38, NHS.

[33] Stiles, *Diary,* I, 337.

[34] *Recs. Col. R.I.,* VII, 125-126.

[35] Quoted in George Washington Greene, *The Life of Nathanael Greene* (New York, 1867), I, 43.

[36] Stiles, *Diary,* I, 387, 391; *Recs. Col. R.I.,* VII, 178-182.

[37] *Recs. Col. R.I.,* VII, 182-185, 187.

[38] Henry Marchant to [——— Dana ?], Newport, March 4, 1773, Marchant, Letter Book, p. 68.

[39] *Newp. Merc.,* Feb. 1, 1773.

[40] *Recs. Col. R.I.*, VII, 226-228. See correspondence between the several Houses of Representatives, *ibid.*, pp. 227-239.

[41] Stiles, *Diary*, I, 384-385.

[42] Miller, *Origins of the American Revolution*, pp. 337-346.

[43] *Newp. Merc.*, Dec. 7, 13, 20, 1773; Jan. 3, 1774.

[44] *Ibid.*, Dec. 20, 1773; *Prov. Gazette*, Dec. 18, 1773.

[45] *Newp. Merc.*, Nov. 22, Dec. 13, 1773, Feb. 14, 1774.

[46] See also *Recs. Col. R.I.*, VII, 272-280.

[47] Miller, *Origins of the American Revolution*, p. 360.

[48] *Recs. Col. R.I.*, VII, 280-281; *Newp. Merc.*, May 23, 1774; *Newp. Merc.*, Supplement, June 13, 1774.

[49] *Recs. Col. R.I.*, VII, 246-247.

[50] William E. Foster, *Stephen Hopkins*, II, 126-127; Samuel G. Arnold, *History of the State of Rhode Island*, II, 336.

[51] *Recs. Col. R.I.*, VII, 247.

[52] *Ibid.*, pp. 250, 257.

[53] *Newp. Merc.*, July 4, 1774.

[54] *Ibid.*, July 11, 1774.

[55] *Ibid.*, Aug. 22, 1774.

[56] *Prov. Gazette*, June 4 and 18, Aug. 15, 1774, April 15, 1775; *Recs. Col. R.I.*, VII, 281-282.

[57] *Newp. Merc.*, July 18, Oct. 17, 1774.

[58] Moses Brown to a Friend, Dec. 1, 1774, Moses Brown Papers, II, 23.

[59] *Newp. Merc.*, Aug. 29, 1774.

[60] Stiles, *Diary*, I, 459.

[61] Worthington Chauncey Ford, ed., *Journals of the Continental Congress, 1774-1789* (Washington, D.C., 1904), I, 68.

[62] Bernhard Knollenberg, ed., *Correspondence of Governor Samuel Ward, May 1775-March 1776* (Providence, 1952), pp. 28-29; Edmund C. Burnett, ed., *Letters of Members of the Continental Congress* (Washington, D.C., 1921), I, 74, 80.

[63] *Recs. Col. R.I.*, VII, 263.

[64] See *Newp. Merc.*, and *Prov. Gazette*, Nov., 1774 to April, 1775, passim.

[65] *Newp. Merc.*, April 10, 1775; *Prov. Gazette*, Feb. 18, 1775.

[66] *Newp. Merc.*, June 26, 1775.

[67] *Ibid.*, March 6, 1775.

[68] *Ibid.*, Feb. 7, March 21, 1774.

[69] *Ibid.*, March 28, 1774.

[70] *Ibid.*, March 6, 1775.

[71] *Prov. Gazette*, March 18, 1775.

[72] *Ibid.*, April 8, 1775.

[73] *Recs. Col. R.I.*, VII, 269-270; *Newp. Merc.*, Dec. 26, 1774.

[74] *Recs. Col. R.I.*, VII, 260-261; *Newp. Merc.*, Nov. 7, 1774.

[75] *Newp. Merc.*, April 10, 1774.

## NOTES TO CHAPTER IX

## REVOLUTION AND INDEPENDENCE

[1] *Newp. Merc.*, Sept. 2, 1771.

[2] Wilkins Updike, *A History of the Episcopal Church in Narragansett, Rhode Island* (Daniel Goodwin, ed., Boston, 1907), II, 78-89; Joseph Wanton, Jr., to Moses Brown, March 30, 1771, Moses Brown Papers, II, 7.

[3] Stiles, *Diary*, I, 65.

[4] See Chapter VIII.

[5] George Rome's letter is printed in Updike, *A History of the Episcopal Church in Narragansett*, II, 80-89.

[6] Stiles, *Diary*, I, 387; *Newp. Merc.*, Aug. 23, 1773; *Prov. Gazette*, June 26, 1773; Thomas Hutchinson, *The History of the Colony and Province of Massachusetts-Bay*, Lawrence Shaw Mayo, ed. (Cambridge, Mass., 1936), III, 283, 291.

[7] Stiles, *Diary*, I, 387.

[8] *Prov. Gazette*, Sept. 20, 1773.

[9] *Newp. Merc.*, Aug. 23, 1773.

[10] Bowler to Cushing, Newport, Aug. 20, 1773, Massachusetts Historical Society *Proceedings*, LVII (1923-1924), 357-358; Cushing to Bowler, Boston, Aug. 23, 1773, *ibid.*, p. 358.

[11] At Rome's request the proceedings of the house were printed in the *Newp. Merc.*, Nov. 8, 1773; see also *ibid.*, Nov. 1, 1773, and *Prov. Gazette*, Nov. 6, 1773.

[12] *Newp. Merc.*, Sept. 2 and 19, 1774.

[13] *Ibid.*, Feb. 13, 1775.

[14] *Prov. Gazette*, Aug. 27, Sept. 3, 1774; *Newp. Merc.*, Aug. 29, 1774; *Recs. Col. R.I.*, VII, 282. For the treatment afforded William Vassal of Boston and Bristol (R.I.), see *Prov. Gazette*, Sept. 24, 1774; *Newp. Merc.*, Sept. 11, 1775; William Vassal to Moses Brown, Sept. 4, 1784, Moses Brown Papers, V, 9.

[15] See letters in Vernon Papers, Metal Box 3, folder 114, NHS.

[16] *Newp. Merc.*, Jan. 18, 1773.

[17] *Ibid.*, Dec. 18, 1769.

[18] *Ibid.*, July 18 and 25, Aug. 15, 1774.

[19] E.g., *ibid.*, Jan. 2, 1775.

[20] *Ibid.*, Jan. 10, 1774.

[21] *Ibid.*, Jan. 23, 1775.

[22] For the details of this controversy see *Newp. Merc.*, April 11 and 18, 1774; *To the Public*, Newport, April 19, 1774 (Broadside), JCBL; *Dialogue Between a Renowned Rhode-Island Colonel and one of his New Converted Lackeys, J - - - - R - - - - - -n; Dialogue Between Mr. R. - - - - - -N and Mr. M - - - - - S* [Newport ?, 1774 ?], JCBL.

[23] *Newp. Merc.*, April 18, 1774.

[24] *To the Public*, April 19, 1774.

[25] *Dialogue Between Mr. R - - - - - N and Mr. M - - - - - S.*

[26] William Ellery, *To the Freemen of the Colony of Rhode-Island*, Providence, April 17, 1775 (Broadside), RIHS.

[27] William Ellery to ?, Newport, March 27, 1775, Mass. Hist. Soc. *Proc., 1858-1860* (Boston, 1860), pp. 381-383.

[28] Election Proxes, RIHS; John E. Alden, ed., *Rhode Island Imprints, 1727-1800*, (New York, 1949), No. 614.

[29] April 3, 1775.

[30] *To the Freemen of the Colony of Rhode-Island*, Newport, April 12, 1775, RIHS.

[31] *To the Freemen of the Colony of Rhode-Island*, Providence, April 15, 1775, JCBL.

[32] This last statement, signed by Darius Sessions, is written on the blank side of the broadside in RIHS, *To the Freemen . . .*, April 15, 1775.

[33] April 24, 1775; *Prov. Gazette*, April 22, 1775.

[34] Acts and Resolves of the Rhode Island General Assembly, 1774-1775 (Ms), p. 75, R. I. Arch. The deputies in their dissent claimed that "such a Measure is unseasonable" and would be followed by the "most dangerous Consequences to the Colony in general and to the Town of Newport in Particular." Respecting the town of Newport, the deputies feared the raising of 1500 troops—an act of rebellion—would provoke Captain Wallace and His Majesty's fleet to declare open war and

destroy the town. Samuel Bours and Thomas Cranston returned to Newport. Stiles, *Diary,* I, 539.

[35] *Recs. Col. R.I.,* VII, 310-311.

[36] *Ibid.,* pp. 312-313; *Prov. Gazette,* April 29, 1775; *RIAR,* May, 1775, p. 2; R.I. Col. Recs. (Ms), IX, 192.

[37] Stiles, *Diary,* I, 544.

[38] *RIAR,* May, 1775, p. 3; *Prov. Gazette,* May 6, 1775.

[39] *Recs. Col. R.I.,* VII, 325-326; *Prov. Gazette,* May 20, 1775.

[40] See the correspondence between Governor Wanton and the General Assembly, *Recs. Col. R.I.,* VII, 332-337.

[41] *Ibid.,* p. 336; *Prov. Gazette,* June 17, 1775; *Newp. Merc.,* June 19, 1775; Stiles, *Diary,* I, 572.

[42] "Revolutionary Correspondence of Governor Nicholas Cooke, 1775-1781," American Antiquarian Society *Proceedings,* XXXVI (1926), 256; Knollenberg, ed., Governor Ward *Correspondence,* p. 64.

[43] Cooke, "Correspondence," p. 287; *Recs. Col. R.I.,* VII, 392-393, 404; *RIAR,* Oct., 1775, pp. 173-174, 194; *Newp. Merc.,* Nov. 13, 1775; Stiles, *Diary,* I, 633.

[44] *Recs. Col. R.I.,* VII, 398-399.

[45] Philadelphia, Oct. 19, 1775, Knollenberg, ed., Governor Ward *Correspondence,* p. 106. There is a portrait of Nicholas Cooke in the Rhode Island State Capitol.

[46] *Recs. Col. R.I.,* VII, 538, VIII, 220, 388.

[47] For an account of Rhode Island's difficulties with Captain Wallace and his fleet, see William G. Roelker and Clarkson A. Collins, 3rd, "The Patrol of Narragansett Bay (1774-1776) by H.M.S. *Rose,* Captain James Wallace," *Rhode Island History,* VII-IX (1948-1950), serialized.

[48] *Newp. Merc.,* Aug. 7, 14, Sept. 18, 1775; Massachusetts Provincial Congress to Governor Nicholas Cooke, Watertown, Aug. 14, 1775, Cooke, "Correspondence," p. 266; Governor Cooke to Benjamin Franklin, Providence, Aug. 15, 1775, *ibid.,* pp. 266-267.

[49] *Newp. Merc.,* June 19, July 24, Nov. 13, 1775; *Prov. Gazette,* July 22, 1775.

[50] *Newp. Merc.,* Oct. 9 and 16, 1775; *Prov. Gazette,* Oct. 14, 1775.

[51] *Newp. Merc.,* Dec. 11, 1775.

[52] For a detailed treatment of John Brown's capture and release, see Roelker and Collins, "The Patrol of Narragansett Bay," *Rhode Island History,* VIII, 45-63; Stiles, *Diary,* I, 544, 548.

[53] *Newp. Merc.,* Oct. 9, 1775; *Prov. Gazette,* Oct. 7, 1775.

[54] *Prov. Gazette,* Nov. 11, 1775.

[55] S. Vernon, Jr., to Isabel Marchant, Newport, March 20, 1776, Vernon Papers (1770-1789), NHS.

[56] Mary Callender to Moses Brown, Newport, Jan. 24, 1776, Moses Brown Papers, II, 48; Philip Wanton to Moses Brown, Newport, Jan. 24, 1776, *ibid.*

[57] Stiles, *Diary,* I, 539; Ward and Hopkins to Nicholas Cooke, Philadelphia, Oct. 9, 1775, Peck MSS, Box III, 47, RIHS.

[58] *Newp. Merc.,* Oct. 9, Dec. 4, 1775; Moses Brown to John Pemberton, Nov. 7, 1775, Misc. MSS, B-814, Box 5, RIHS.

[59] *Newp. Merc.,* Nov. 6, 1775, Jan. 12, 1776; *Prov. Gazette,* Jan. 27, 1776.

[60] Newport, Jan. 24, 1776, Moses Brown Papers, II, 48.

[61] *Ibid.;* Mary Callender to Moses Brown, Newport, Feb. 7, 1776, *ibid.,* p. 50.

[62] *Newp. Merc.,* Oct. 16, Nov. 6, 1775.

[63] Correspondence between Newport Town Council and Governor Cooke, Newport, Oct. 16, and Cambridge, Mass., Oct. 21, 1775, Cooke, "Correspondence," pp. 280-281; *Prov. Gazette,* Oct. 14, Dec. 9, 1775; Stiles, *Diary,* I, 643; Newport Town Meeting to Committee of General Assembly, Dec. 20, 1775, RIHS MSS, XII, 112.

[64] *Prov. Gazette,* April 13, 1776.

[65] General Greene to Ward and Hopkins, Prospect Hill, Dec. 10, 1775, Knollenberg, ed., Governor Ward *Correspondence,* p. 138.

[66] Henry Ward to Samuel Ward, Providence, May 30, 1775, *ibid.,* p. 42.

[67] General Greene to Samuel Ward, Prospect Hill, Dec. 10, 1775, *ibid.,* p. 138.

[68] Providence, Dec. 4, 1775, *ibid.,* p. 136.

[69] *Newp. Merc.,* Jan. 23, 1775.

[70] Cooke to Ward and Hopkins, Providence, July 18, 1775, Cooke, "Correspondence," p. 256.

[71] Rebecca Clarke to Joseph Clarke, Newport, June 4, 1775, Misc. Letters, folder 10, R.I. Arch.; *Newp. Merc.,* June 5, Aug. 28, 1775.

[72] RIHS MSS, XII, 118; *Prov. Gazette,* Dec. 2, 1775; *Newp. Merc.,* Nov. 13, 1775; *Recs. Col. R.I.,* VII, 376-377, 394, 499, 549.

[73] Enclosure in letter from Job Hawkins to Nicholas Cooke, Dec. 19, 1775, Cooke, "Correspondence," pp. 296-297.

[74] Providence, Aug. 12, 1775, Knollenberg, ed., Governor Ward *Correspondence,* p. 75.

[75] Philadelphia, Oct. 9, 1775, Peck MSS, Box III, 47, RIHS; Knollenberg, ed., Governor Ward *Correspondence,* p. 97.

[76] *Recs. Col. R.I.,* VII, 388-389; Governor Cooke to Governor Jonathan Trumble, Providence, Nov. 14, 1775, Cooke, "Correspondence," p. 287.

[77] Samuel Ward to Henry Ward, Philadelphia, Nov. 16, 1775, Knollenberg, ed., Governor Ward *Correspondence,* p. 122.

[78] Moses Brown to John Pemberton, Providence, Nov. 7, 1775, Misc. MSS, B-814, Box 5, RIHS.

[79] Charles Dudley to Governor Cooke, Custom House, Newport, Nov. 14, 1775, Cooke, "Correspondence," pp. 288-289; *Prov. Gazette,* Nov. 18, 1775.

[80] Stiles, *Diary,* I, 646-647; *Prov. Gazette,* Dec. 30, 1775.

[81] General Greene to Samuel Ward, Prospect Hill, Dec. 18, 1775, Knollenberg, ed., Governor Ward *Correspondence,* p. 147.

[82] *Recs. Col. R.I.,* VII, 566-568; *Prov. Gazette,* June 22, 1776.

[83] *Prov. Gazette,* April 6, 1776; *Newp. Merc.,* April 8, 1776.

[84] Mary Ellery to Isabel Marchant, Providence, March 17, 1776, Vernon Papers, Metal Box I, folder 3, NHS.

[85] For a Mr. Babcock's prox, see Howard M. Chapin, "Eighteenth Century Rhode Island Printed Proxies," *The American Collector,* I (1925), 56. Nicholas Cooke's and Josiah Arnold's proxes are in the collection at RIHS. John E. Alden, *Rhode Island Imprints, 1727-1800,* No. 681, lists Arnold's prox as of 1777. One of Arnold's proxes is in RIHS MSS, XIII, 42, and on the blank side is written: "June 25, 1776 the Salt Company to John Wells Dr." This would seem to fix it as printed in 1776. Stephen Hopkins to Governor of Rhode Island, Philadelphia, May 15, 1776, *Recs. Col. R.I.,* VII, 527.

[86] For behind the scenes politicking over Newport County's Assistants, see William Greene to Governor Cooke, Warwick, March 26, 1776, Cooke, "Correspondence," pp. 311-312. Samuel Dyre of Newport was replaced as an Assistant. For his Toryism see Stiles, *Diary,* II, 134. Newport's new deputies were Samuel Fowler, George Sears, and Gideon Wanton. Stiles listed Sears as a Whig and Thomas Freebody, who was re-elected, a Tory. *Ibid.*

[87] John Adams to James Warren, Philadelphia, Oct. 25, 1775, Knollenberg, ed., Governor Ward *Correspondence,* pp. 114-115.

[88] Philadelphia, Nov. 2, 1775, *ibid.,* p. 116.

[89] Stiles, *Diary,* I, 635-636.

[90] Henry Ward to Samuel Ward [?], Nov. 27, 1775, Knollenberg, ed., Governor Ward *Correspondence,* p. 141.

[91] *Prov. Gazette,* Feb. 17, 1776; *Newp. Merc.,* March 18, 1776.

[92] *Prov. Gazette,* April 6, 1776; Dr. Thomas Young to Henry Ward, Philadelphia, March 27 [26], 1776, Knollenberg, ed., Governor Ward *Correspondence,* p. 203.

[93] Stephen Hopkins to Governor of Rhode Island, Philadelphia, May 15, 1776, *Recs. Col. R.I.,* VII, 527; Governor Cooke to Stephen Hopkins, Providence, May 7, 1776, Cooke, "Correspondence," pp. 323-324.

[94] "An Act repealing an act, entitled 'An act for the more effectually securing to His Majesty, the allegiance of his subjects, in this his colony and dominion of Rhode Island and Providence Plantations'; and altering the forms of commissions, of all writs and processes in the courts, and of the oaths prescribed by law." *Recs. Col. R.I.,* VII, 522-523; *Newp. Merc.,* June 10, 1776. The action of the General Assembly in this matter is puzzling. The act which was repealed was passed in 1756 (*Recs. Col. R.I.,* V, 554-556); actually it did not prescribe allegiance to the King of England. It was enacted during the first year of the French and Indian War and empowered a number of the colony officers to "tender the oaths of allegiance and abjuration unto" persons suspected of disloyalty to the King. It further enacted that a person who declared, maintained, or affirmed "that the Kings and Queens of Great Britain, with and by the authority of Parliament, are not able to make laws and statutes of sufficient force and validity to limit and bind the crown of Great Britain, with the dominions thereof . . . shall incur the danger and penalty of a praemunire," etc. Rhode Islanders had declared and maintained this for some time. Nevertheless, the repeal of this act was considered a flat revocation of allegiance to George III. The repealing act directed also that the King's name be struck from all writs, commissions, etc. The preamble reads like an undersized Declaration of Independence in Lockean terms implying that the King had broken his end of the compact. The Journal of the Senate (May, 1776, No. 20) refers to this act in one line: "Vote of the Lower House altering the Forms of Commissions Writs &c. was read & Concurred (Repeal of allegiance)." In a letter to Stephen Hopkins, Nicholas Cooke cited the repealing act as "discharging the Inhabitants of the Colony from Allegiance to the British King." Providence, May 7, 1776, Cooke, "Correspondence," p. 323. Despite the actual meaning of the original act, there was no doubt how Rhode Islanders interpreted its repeal. May 4 is now a legal holiday in Rhode Island.

[95] Governor Cooke to Stephen Hopkins, Providence, May 7, 1776, Cooke, "Correspondence," p. 323.

[96] *Recs. Col. R.I.,* VII, 519, 538; Journal of the Senate, May, 1776. William R. Staples has pointed out that in 1776 the Assembly elected delegates, Hopkins and Ellery, in grand committee as other colony officers were chosen. *Rhode Island in the Continental Congress* (Providence, 1870), p. 71. Ward and Hopkins, then, were elected in 1774 and 1775 "by concurrent vote of both houses." In March, 1777, the Assembly decided that in the future the freemen should choose the delegates to the Congress in their annual town meetings, and beginning with the election of 1777 the delegates' names were listed on the proxes. A delegate to Congress, then, became a general officer in the government, elected each April by the freemen, like the Governor, Secretary, and Assistants. *Recs. Col. R.I.,* VIII, 179; Election Proxes, RIHS; Staples, *Rhode Island,* p. 129.

[97] Governor Cooke to Stephen Hopkins, Providence, May 7, 1776, Cooke, "Correspondence," pp. 323-324.

[98] Philadelphia, May 15, 1776, *Recs. Col. R.I.,* VII, 527.

[99] May 6, 1776, *ibid.,* pp. 526-527; Staples, *Rhode Island,* pp. 71-73.

[100] William Ellery to Governor Cooke, Philadelphia, June 21, 1776, Cooke, "Correspondence," p. 326.

[101] Stiles, *Diary,* II, 30.

[102] *Recs. Col. R.I.,* VII, 581-582.

# BIBLIOGRAPHICAL ESSAY

AN ENCOURAGING factor about research in early Rhode Island history is that most of the sources rest within a small geographical area. Rhode Island as a colony was no larger than it is as a state, and the papers and documents which have remained there or which have since been collected there are available within a limited radius. The John Carter Brown Library, the Rhode Island Historical Society, the Brown University Library, and the State Archives, all in Providence, and the Newport Historical Society, less than thirty miles to the south, contain the bulk of manuscript and printed sources which were necessary for the preparation of this book. History does not write itself, nor do musty letters in crabbed writing and public records in official style scream interpretations in their margins. But when the letters and records are collected in a handful of places within walking distance of one another or at most within an hour's drive, geography, at least, has given the historian a welcome assist. To Roger Williams and the founders I am grateful for their restrained and tidy pretensions.

## PUBLIC RECORDS

*Manuscript:* Rhode Island should be proud of the splendid manner in which its early records have been preserved in the Rhode Island Archives at the State House in Providence. The present archivist, Miss Mary T. Quinn, graciously presides over a magnificent collection of manuscripts, a number of which form a substantial basis for this volume. Miss Quinn's knowledge of these documents is only outdone by her ability to put her finger upon them at a moment's notice. Of first importance are the Rhode Island Colony Records, Journal, House of Deputies, and Journal of the Senate (Council), which are necessary for piecing together the intricate procedures, customs, and political habits of the Governor and Company of the Colony of Rhode Island. The Journals of the upper and lower houses give an intimate picture of the relations between the two houses, often including texts of messages passed and reasons for concurrence or nonconcurrence with the other's doings. Yet, important as these volumes are, I often found their content not altogether comprehensible until I had examined the General Assembly Papers and also the Reports of that body; the General Treasurer's Accounts and the Accounts Allowed; the Ratemakers' Reports; and particularly the Petitions to the General Assembly— granted and ungranted. Helpful, too, were the Acts and Resolves of the Rhode Island General Assembly which stand, in the governmental process, half-way between the Journals of the houses and the more elaborate Colony Records. All the above manuscripts are found in the Rhode Island Archives in the State House, Providence.

Court records in both Newport and Providence were examined in connection with the colony's reaction to the Stamp Act, particularly the Records of the Superior Court of Judicature of Newport County and the Inferior Court of Common Pleas, Newport County, both of which are in the Newport County Court House. Papers relating to the libel case brought by Stephen Hopkins against Samuel Ward in 1757 are in Records of the Worcester County Court of Common Pleas, Court House, Worcester, Massachusetts.

Many of the documents describing the burning of the *Gaspee* and the Commission which followed are printed (see below) but see also an important manuscript collection called Gaspee Commission in the John Carter Brown Library (JCBL).

*Printed:* Not many of the official records have been published; primary among those in print are *Records of the Colony of Rhode Island and Providence Plantations in New England* (*Recs. Col. R.I.*), ed. John R. Bartlett (10 vols., Providence, 1856-1865). Unfortunately, Bartlett selected only portions of the manuscript material to be printed, and the results do not give a complete picture of what occurred in the General Assembly. Although his volumes are handy— and I must admit that I used them constantly, as one can see from the notes to the text—they do not tell the whole story. They do not contain all the legislation enacted by the Assembly, omitting often acts, resolutions, and official documents which would help explain the factional goings-on within the legislature. There are other shortcomings: the indexes are incomplete and sometimes inaccurate, there are typographical errors, and the spelling has been modernized. Despite these difficulties, which can be overcome only by frequent use of the manuscript records, what Bartlett did print is still extremely useful, since he collected from various sources considerable official correspondence and reports not easily available elsewhere.

The colony itself published its laws in two separate forms. After each session of the legislature it was the Secretary's duty to see printed *Acts and Resolves of the Colony of Rhode Island* (*RIAR*) for distribution to the towns. It was these "Schedules," as they were called, which Secretary Henry Ward was often slow in sending to towns which voted against his brother. Before 1746 these documents were circulated in manuscript. Brown University Library (BUL) has both manuscript and printed "Schedules." Periodically the General Assembly ordered to be printed digests of the laws, called *Acts and Laws of the English Colony of Rhode-Island and Providence-Plantations in New-England in America* (*ALRI*), in order to keep its members and the town clerks up-to-date. The 1745 and 1752 editions have slightly different titles. For this study I have used most frequently the 1767 (Newport) edition which, like the earlier ones, is prefaced by the colony's charter. Occasionally helpful but limited to an earlier period are *Records of the Vice-Admiralty Court in Rhode Island, 1716-1752,* ed. Dorothy S. Towle (Washington, D.C., 1936).

*Other Printed Records: Proceedings of the Congress at New York* (Annapolis, 1766), the Stamp Act Congress; *Journals of the House of Burgesses of Virginia, 1761-1765,* ed. John P. Kennedy (Richmond, 1907); *Journals of the Continental Congress, 1774-1789,* ed. Worthington Chauncey Ford, *et al.* (34 vols., Washington, D.C., 1904-1937). For British documents bearing on the colonies at this time, see *The Statutes at Large, from Magna Charta to the End of the Eleventh Parliament of Great Britain,* ed. Danby Pickering (46 vols., Cambridge and London, 1762-1814); *A Collection of the Parliamentary Debates in England, from the Year M, DC, LXVIII, To the Present Time,* ed. John Torbuck (21 vols., London, 1739-1742); and *Acts of the Privy Council of England, Colonial Series,* eds. William L. Grant and James Munro (6 vols., Hereford and London, 1908-1912).

British naval officers and customs officials stationed in Rhode Island often sent reports home to England describing conditions; frequently they complained about abuses they had suffered and the colony's conduct at times when resistance to England grew violent. Some of these letters and reports are in *Recs. Col. R.I.*, VI; digests of others can be found in *Calendar of Home Office Papers of the Reign of George III, 1760-1765*, ed. Joseph Redington (London, 1878) and *ibid., 1766-1769* (London, 1879). Digests of documents relating to the Governor's right to veto acts of the General Assembly in 1731 and the judgment of the King's Attorneys in this issue are in *Calendar of State Papers, Colonial Series, America and West Indies, 1732*, ed. Cecil Headlam (London, 1939).

## LETTERS, DIARIES, AND JOURNALS

*Manuscript:* Equally important as the manuscript records in the Rhode Island Archives were the rich collections of letters and papers in the Rhode Island and Newport Historical Societies (RIHS and NHS) and JCBL. Chief among these are the Ward Manuscripts, the Moses Brown Papers, and the Brown Papers from which a sizable proportion of the material for this volume was taken. The Ward Manuscripts (RIHS) are a large collection of letters relating in part to the time of Samuel and Henry Ward and were particularly useful for the light they shed on the colony's politics and the Ward faction. They describe, too, in intimate fashion, the religious, social, agricultural, and business interests of one of the most significant families in early Rhode Island history. Mr. Bernhard Knollenberg of Chester, Connecticut, who has edited and published a portion of these letters relating to Samuel Ward and the Revolution (see below), lent me typed copies of some of Ward's earlier correspondence which I found very helpful. These are labeled "Knollenberg Transcripts" whenever referred to in the notes to the text.

Also in RIHS are the Moses Brown Papers, containing letters to, from, and about Moses Brown, one of the four Brown brothers of Providence. I have relied heavily upon these papers for considerable information about his role in the colony's politics and the growing conflict with Great Britain. Much of the correspondence respecting politics between Brown and Joseph Wanton, Jr., of Newport is collected here. Moses Brown was a remarkable individual with ubiquitous interests, many of which are reflected in this splendid collection of his papers.

In JCBL are the Brown Papers, one of the largest and most distinguished collections of its kind in the United States. These manuscripts are the meticulous record of the rise and progress of a notable mercantile family whose early history has been so well written by Professor James B. Hedges in *The Browns of Providence Plantations, Colonial Years* (Cambridge, Mass., 1952). The Browns were public servants, politicians, and patriots, as well as merchants and manufacturers, and these letters and papers, besides describing in great detail their business and trading interests, are a valuable source of information about local politics and the merchant attitude toward the restrictive colonial policy of Great Britain. Moreover, the Browns, good Yankees that they were, never discarded a scrap of paper with writing on it. Their papers are a sumptuous preserve of the stuff from which history is made.

Other collections in RIHS, containing material bearing on Rhode Island politics and resistance to Great Britain and which supplement the major collections already mentioned, are: the Rhode Island Historical Society Manuscripts; Miscellaneous Manuscripts; the Peck Manuscripts; and the Warner Papers. Each of these, the first two in particular, added several chunks of information which were invaluable.

At NHS I found a good deal of material vital to an understanding of the times. Among the manuscripts examined there were the Vernon Letters and Vernon Papers, both liberally charged with political and Revolutionary ammunition; Henry Marchant's Letter Book containing copies of several letters relating to the *Gaspee* and the Commission; and Letters, A-B (n.d.), which are miscellaneous bits of correspondence bearing on politics.

Letters to and from the colony's agents in London were particularly important, and although some of these have been printed in *Recs. Col. R.I.,* and *Correspondence of the Colonial Governors of Rhode Island, 1723-1775* (see below), a number in manuscript are collected in JCBL under the title, Official Letters from Rhode Island

Agents in London, 1746-1769. See also in BUL, Manuscript Papers of Joseph Sherwood, Agent for the Colony of Rhode Island in London, 1764-1765, compiled by Sidney S. Rider.

Several scattered manuscript sources were of great value. I am indebted to Yale University for permission to examine the Ezra Stiles Papers which are dotted with pithy observations and eyewitness reports germane to the lives and times of Rhode Islanders. (See the description of the election of 1761 in Chapter I of this volume.) In the Miscellaneous Letters in the Rhode Island Archives I found documents describing the distress of Newport during Captain Wallace's violent visit in 1775. A major part of the description of the Stamp Act riot in Newport in 1765 (Chapter VI) is based on a number of letters and reports in the Chalmers Papers, Relating to Rhode Island, 1637-1785, in the New York Public Library and the House of Lords Manuscripts, January 14, 1766, from Library of Congress Transcripts. There are no Stephen Hopkins manuscripts as such; according to William E. Foster, his papers were lost in the "great storm" of 1815. See *Stephen Hopkins, a Rhode Island Statesman, a Study in the Political History of the Eighteenth Century* (Providence, 1884), I, xiii. In 1881 Sidney S. Rider had copies made of several Hopkins letters and compiled what he called the Letters of Stephen Hopkins, Collected from Various Sources, which is in BUL. Unfortunately it is not a very extensive collection; included, however, is a short sketch of Hopkins by Moses Brown written many years after the former's death.

Helpful, too, for a description of the problems confronting a Rhode Island agent in Great Britain was Henry Marchant, Journell of Voyage from Newport in the Colony of Rhode Island &c to London, Travels thro' many Parts of England & Scotland—begun July 8th 1771. This manuscript is in possession of the owner, Miss Alice Clarke of Cohoes, New York. A microfilm of it is in RIHS.

*Printed:* Most significant of the printed letters is *Correspondence of the Colonial Governors of Rhode Island, 1723-1775,* ed. Gertrude S. Kimball (2 vols., Cambridge, Mass., 1902-1903). This work helps to supplement Bartlett's *Recs. Col. R.I.;* it includes a wealth of official material and a number of personal letters.

Splendid sources for Rhode Island religious and social history in the period studied are *The Literary Diary of Ezra Stiles* (3 vols., New York, 1901) and *Extracts from the Itineraries . . . of Ezra Stiles* (New Haven, 1916) both edited by Franklin B. Dexter. Stiles had an eye for detail about Newport in particular and New England in general which makes these works tremendously important to the historian. Some of the Ward Manuscripts have been published in *Correspondence of Governor Samuel Ward, May 1775-March 1776,* ed. Bernhard Knollenberg (Providence, 1952). These are letters to and from Ward in the last year of his life and relate to the Revolutionary movement and Ward's contribution to it as a member of the Continental Congress. Other letters pertaining to the colony's problems during the war can be found in "Revolutionary Correspondence of Governor Nicholas Cooke," American Antiquarian Society *Proceedings,* XXXVI (1926); "Revolutionary Correspondence from 1775 to 1782," Rhode Island Historical Society *Collections,* VI (1867); and *Letters of Members of the Continental Congress,* ed. Edmund C. Burnett (8 vols., Washington, D.C., 1921-1938). Excellent source material for Rhode Island's economy is in *Commerce of Rhode Island, 1726-1800,* Massachusetts Historical Society *Collections,* LXIX-LXX (2 vols., Boston, 1914-1915). *The Narragansett Historical Register,* ed. James N. Arnold (9 vols., Providence, 1882-1891) contains among other documents several revealing letters about politics. A striking description of Patrick Henry's presentation of the Virginia Stamp Act Resolves, which served as models for other colonies, is in "Journal of a French Traveller in the Colonies, 1765," *American Historical Review,* XXVI (1921), 729-747.

Helpful for a view of contemporary English politics are *The Correspondence of King George the Third from 1760 to December 1783,* ed. Sir John Fortescue (6 vols., London, 1927-1928); *Letters from George III to Lord Bute, 1756-1766,* ed. Romney Sedgwick (London, 1939); Edmund Burke, *Thoughts on the Cause of the Present Discontents* (5th edition, London, 1775).

## NEWSPAPERS, PAMPHLETS, BROADSIDES, AND ELECTION PROXES

*Newspapers:* The colony's two newspapers, *The Newport Mercury* and *The Providence Gazette; and Country Journal,* are better sources of information about the colony's attitude toward Great Britain and its resistance to imperial policy than about local politics. They contain countless letters debating the vital issues of Parliamentary taxation and legislation and numerous documents reflecting the consensus of the inhabitants. It was usual to find the colony's most radical opinions as to the power of Parliament and the British government in the form of letters to the printer. The sentiments expressed were on many occasions several steps ahead of the colony's official position respecting the Revolutionary movement and Rhode Island's place in the Empire. One cannot depend completely on the *Mercury* and *Gazette* for an explanation of local politics. Although political issues were frequently aired and election results annually recorded, an intimate picture of the factional tug-of-war depends on more than what the newspapers offer in news, letters, and editorial comment. Rhode Island's newspapers in this period—and I suspect this is true of those of other colonies as well—were not printed for posterity but for the people who bought and read them. They do not tell the historian all he wants to know. And yet, in a larger sense, they are probably the best all-round source of information available.

Samuel Hall and later Solomon Southwick printed the *Newport Mercury* during the period of this study, and since Newport was the heart of the Ward party's home territory, the *Mercury,* particularly under Hall, was susceptible to a Ward bias in politics. Had it not been, Hall doubtless would have had to close shop. Printer Hall made the mistake of trying to keep the *Mercury* neutral during the Stamp Act crisis; he made himself extremely unpopular by providing considerable space for the writings of the Tory Junto. Moreover, he printed Martin Howard's *Halifax Letter* and was yanked before the Superior Court for his trouble. Southwick in the early 1770's was accused of Tory sympathy, but as the Revolutionary movement accelerated he gave unquestionable evidence to the contrary by blasting the colony's enemies in high fashion in the columns of his paper.

Stephen Hopkins was instrumental in bringing William Goddard to Providence to set up the *Gazette* in 1762. The Hopkins party needed a newspaper to combat successfully its rival in Newport and Goddard's *Gazette* answered bountifully. A lack of subscribers interrupted publication in the spring of 1765, but the paper was revived within a few months and carried on by Goddard's mother, Sarah Goddard, and later John Carter. There was no doubt where the *Gazette* stood with respect to local politics and imperial affairs. Goddard himself was a severe critic of the Ward faction and a personal enemy of Henry Ward who had cheated him out of a share of the government's printing. Tory sentiments, if they existed in Providence, never found their way into the *Gazette* which was wholly patriotic. No Tory Junto arose in Providence to stir up the inhabitants and enliven the columns of the northern town's newspaper.

NHS has an excellent collection of original copies of the *Newport Mercury* while photostat copies can be found in JCBL. Original issues of the *Providence Gazette* are preserved in RIHS and on microfilm in BUL.

*Pamphlets:* Pamphlet writing was common practice during the growing dispute between the colonies and the mother country, and occasionally a political issue, which could not be settled in the confining columns of a newspaper, was dignified in pamphlet form by a writer or a faction with the price. When Stephen Hopkins returned from Albany in 1754, he found the government of Rhode Island fixed solidly against the Albany Plan of Union blocked out by Benjamin Franklin and agreed to by Hopkins and a number of his colleagues at the Congress. Just before the colony's next election Hopkins published *A True Representation of a Plan Formed at Albany* (Providence, 1755), JCBL, and cleverly used the issue over colonial union to promote his own election as Governor a few weeks later. The problem of Parliamentary taxation of the colonies produced a first-rate pamphlet controversy beginning with Hopkins' statesmanlike *Rights of Colonies Examined* (Providence, 1764) in which he took an advanced position about the authority of Parliament in America. (The pamphlet was later reprinted in England and entitled *The Grievances of the American Colonies Candidly Examined,* London, 1766. Under the original title it is included in *Recs. Col. R.I.,* VI, 416-427.) Martin Howard, Jr., of Newport ably answered Hopkins with *A Letter from a Gentleman at Halifax to his Friend in Rhode-Island* (Newport, 1765), often called the *Halifax Letter,* in which he boldly defended Parliamentary supremacy. The controversy continued with a long essay by Hopkins in three issues of the *Providence Gazette* (Feb. 23, March 2 and 9, 1765) called "Vindication of a late Pamphlet entitled, The Rights of Colonies Examined, etc.," which Howard answered with *A Defense of a Letter from a Gentleman at Halifax, to his Friend in Rhode-Island* (Newport, 1765). Meanwhile James Otis of Boston joined the dispute and contributed *A Vindication of the British Colonies, against the Aspersions of the Halifax Gentleman, in his Letter to a Rhode-Island Friend* (Boston, 1765) and *Brief Remarks on the Defense of the Halifax Libel, on the British-American Colonies* (Boston, 1765). Other Stamp Act pamphlets which were useful were *The Rights of the British Colonies Asserted and Proved* (Boston, 1764) by James Otis; the Reverend David S. Rowland's sermon, *Divine Providence Illustrated and Improved. A Thanksgiving Discourse . . . Occasioned by the Repeal of the Stamp Act* (Providence, 1766), BUL; and *A Discourse, Addressed to the Sons of Liberty At a solemn Assembly, near Liberty-Tree, in Newport, February 14, 1766* (Providence, 1766), BUL.

Silas Downer took a radical stand against Parliamentary power in 1768 when he published *A Discourse Delivered in Providence . . . at the Dedication of the Tree of Liberty . . .* (Providence). William Goddard, first printer of the *Providence Gazette,* accounted for much of his career as a printer in *The Partnership: or the Rise and Progress of the Pennsylvania Chronicle . . .* (Philadelphia, 1770). Just before the election of 1774 Joseph Wanton, Jr., was anonymously attacked for his Tory sympathies in *Dialogue Between a Renowned Rhode-Island Colonel and one of his New Converted Lackeys, J----- R------n;* and *Dialogue Between Mr. R---N and Mr. M-----S* [Newport ? 1774 ?] bound as one pamphlet in JCBL. Wanton lost the election.

*Broadsides:* When it came to printing broadsides Rhode Islanders lacked imagination; they were always about politics, they were published just before elections, and most of them bore one of two headings: *To the Public* or *To the Freemen of the Colony of Rhode-Island.* There was nothing unimaginative, however, about their content, for usually they were strong attacks on political rivals expressed in colorful and sometimes bitter language. William Wanton blasted Richard

Ward over colonial self-determination in 1733 and explained to the public that Ward's conduct tended to hasten the ruin of the colony (Newport, in RIHS). Samuel Ward and Stephen Hopkins each presented the "facts" about the other and his gang to the freemen just prior to the election of 1764 (Newport, in RIHS). William Sweet helped bring Joseph Wanton, Jr.'s, political career to an ignominious end with a particularly damaging broadside in 1774 (Newport, in JCBL). In the election campaign of 1775 the Tory smear was handsomely applied, and not so handsomely removed, producing three broadsides, all with the title: *To the Freemen of the Colony of Rhode-Island*—one by William Ellery (Providence, in RIHS), another by Darius Sessions (Providence, in JCBL), and the third by Joseph Wanton (Newport, in RIHS). In addition to the publications already mentioned, see Miscellaneous Collections of Rhode Island Broadsides, collected by Sidney S. Rider, in BUL.

*Election Proxes:* A prox or proxy was a party ticket on which candidates for the general offices of the colony were listed. The freemen used these as ballots and after signing their names on the reverse side, turned them in (proxed) at their town meetings annually on the third Wednesday in April. The best collection of proxes is in RIHS. See also Howard M. Chapin, "Eighteenth Century Rhode Island Printed Proxies," *The American Collector,* I (1925), 54-59.

*Documentary Collections:* The following collections of documents were consulted—the first for specific material bearing on Rhode Island and the remaining for general information respecting the Revolutionary movement: *The Documentary History of the Destruction of the Gaspee,* ed. William R. Staples (Providence, 1845)—see also under manuscript records, Gaspee Commission, JCBL; *A Collection of Interesting, Authentic Papers, Relative to the Dispute between Great Britain and America, etc., 1764-1775,* ed. John Almon (London, 1777), often called *Prior Documents; Principles and Acts of the Revolution in America,* ed. Hezekiah Niles (Baltimore, 1822); *Sources and Documents Illustrating the American Revolution, 1764-1788,* ed. Samuel Eliot Morison (Oxford, Eng., 1929); *English His-*

*torical Documents,* IX, *American Colonial Documents to 1776,* ed. Merrill Jensen (London, 1955); *The Stamp Act Crisis, Sources and Documents,* ed. Edmund S. Morgan (Providence, 1952).

## SECONDARY WORKS

*Histories of Rhode Island:* There is no history of the origin and progress of the Revolution in Rhode Island. To fill half of this gap is the purpose of this volume. There are several general histories of the colony and state, none of which was particularly useful for this study, since none focused primarily upon the Revolutionary period and no attempt was made in any to relate the internal politics of the colony to the Revolutionary movement. Probably the best of them is the earliest, Samuel G. Arnold, *History of the State of Rhode Island and Providence Plantations* (2 vols., New York, 1859-1860), but this work suffers from a meticulously chronological organization which makes choppy reading as the author jumps from one topic to another. Other Rhode Island histories are, in order of publication: Clarence S. Brigham, *History of the State of Rhode Island and Providence Plantations* (n.p., 1902); *State of Rhode Island and Providence Plantations at the End of the Century: a History,* ed. Edward Field (3 vols., Boston and Syracuse, 1902); Irving B. Richman, *Rhode Island, a Study in Separatism* (Boston, 1905); William B. Weeden, *Early Rhode Island, A Social History of the People* (New York, 1910); Thomas W. Bicknell, *The History of the State of Rhode Island and Providence Plantations* (5 vols., New York, 1920); Earl C. Tanner, *Rhode Island, a Brief History* (Providence, 1954).

*Biographies:* There are no modern biographies of Rhode Island's political and Revolutionary leaders. A *Life of Samuel Ward* by William Gammell appeared in *The Library of American Biography,* second series, IX (Boston, 1846), ed. Jared Sparks. Bernhard Knollenberg has written a biographical sketch of Ward as an introduction to his recent publication of *Correspondence of Governor Samuel Ward, May 1775-March 1776* (Providence, 1952). See also, appended to this volume, Clifford P. Monahon, "Genealogy of the Ward Family." The only full length life of Stephen Hopkins is William E. Foster, *Stephen Hopkins, a Rhode Island Statesman, a Study in the Political History of the Eighteenth Century,* published in *Rhode Island Historical Tracts,* No. 19 (2 vols., Providence, 1884). This is useful work for the facts of Hopkins' career, but it is over-documented, heavily weighted in Hopkins' favor, and for the most part uncritical of his role as political boss of the colony. Foster describes many of the details of the Ward-Hopkins controversy but never really determines what was in dispute. Edward T. Channing wrote a *Life of William Ellery* which was published in Jared Sparks's *Library of American Biography,* VI (Boston, 1836). Valuable for several Nathanael Greene letters is George Washington Greene, *The Life of Nathanael Greene* (3 vols., New York, 1867-1871). For biographical material about the Wantons of Newport, see John R. Bartlett's undocumented account, *History of the Wanton Family of Newport, Rhode Island* in *Rhode Island Historical Tracts,* Nos. 3-4 (Providence, 1878).

*Books and Articles on Specific Aspects of Rhode Island History:* Wilkins Updike, *A History of the Episcopal Church in Narragansett, Rhode Island* (first ed., New York, 1847; second ed., revised and enlarged, by Daniel Goodwin, 3 vols., Boston, 1907). This work contains much original material including George Rome's notorious letter to Joseph Harrison written in 1767. George C. Mason, *Annals of Trinity Church, Newport, Rhode Island, 1698-1821* (2 vols., Newport, 1890); William R. Staples, *Rhode Island in the Continental Congress* (Providence, 1870) and *Annals of the Town of Providence* (Providence, 1893); Walter C. Bronson, *The History of Brown University, 1764-1914* (Providence, 1914). Bronson was not fully aware of the political implications of the removal of Rhode Island College to Providence in 1770. James B. Hedges, *The Browns of Providence Plantations, Colonial Years* (Cambridge, Mass., 1952), an excellent account of the intercolonial and international economic interests of the first family of Providence.

Following are several articles which were valuable in contributing to a picture of Rhode Island in the period prior to the Revolution: William Davis Miller, "The Narragansett Planters," American Antiquarian Society *Proceedings,* XLIII (1933), 49-115; Lawrence C.

Wroth, "The First Press in Providence, a Study in Social Development," *ibid.*, LI (1941), 351-383; Howard M. Chapin, "Eighteenth Century Rhode Island Printed Proxies," *The American Collector,* I (1925), 54-59. Two good articles on the *Gaspee* are William R. Leslie, "The Gaspee Affair: a Study of its Constitutional Significance," *Mississippi Valley Historical Review,* XXXIX (1952), 233-256, and Eugene Wulsin, "The Political Consequences of the Burning of the Gaspee," *Rhode Island History,* III (1944), 1-11, 55-64. Frederick B. Wiener, "The Rhode Island Merchants and the Sugar Act," *New England Quarterly,* III (1930), 464-500, and "Notes on the Rhode Island Admiralty, 1727-1790," *Harvard Law Review,* XLVI (1932), 44-90. A description of the inhabitants' difficulties with the British Navy is in William G. Roelker and Clarkson A. Collins, 3rd, "The Patrol of Narragansett Bay (1774-1776) by H.M.S. *Rose,* Captain James Wallace," *Rhode Island History,* VII-IX (1948-1950). For an account of a Rhode Island agent's problems in London, see David S. Lovejoy, "Henry Marchant and the Mistress of the World," *William and Mary Quarterly,* 3rd ser., XII (1955), 375-398.

    *Other Secondary Works Consulted:* Thomas Hutchinson, *The History of the Colony and Province of Massachusetts-Bay,* new edition, Lawrence Shaw Mayo, ed. (3 vols., Cambridge, Mass., 1936) proved useful for contemporary events in Massachusetts. Robert Rogers, *A Concise Account of North America: Containing a Description of the Several British Colonies on that Continent* (London, 1765). The famous ranger saw very little that was admirable in Rhode Island. Isaac Backus, *A History of New-England, With particular Reference to the Denomination of Christians called Baptists . . .* (3 vols., Boston, 1777-1796); Thomas Jefferson, *Notes on the State of Virginia,* ed. William Peden (Chapel Hill, 1955), offers census figures and suffrage requirements for comparison with those of Rhode Island.

    Lorenzo Sabine, *Biographical Sketches of Loyalists of the American Revolution* (Boston, 1864); Moses Coit Tyler, *The Literary History of the American Revolution, 1763-1783* (2 vols., New York, 1897); Albert E. McKinley, *The Suffrage Franchise in the Thirteen English Colonies in America,* University of Pennsylvania *Publications,* Series in History, No. 2 (Philadelphia, 1905); Carl Becker, *The History of*

*Political Parties in the Province of New York, 1760-1776* (Madison, Wisc., 1909); Arthur M. Schlesinger, *The Colonial Merchants and the American Revolution, 1763-1776* (New York, 1918); Charles MacLean Andrews, *The Colonial Period of American History* (4 vols., New Haven, 1934-1938); John C. Miller, *The Origins of the American Revolution* (Boston, 1943); Oscar Zeichner, *Connecticut's Years of Controversy, 1750-1776* (Richmond, Va., 1949); Henry Joseph Smith, *Appeals to the Privy Council from the American Plantations* (New York, 1950); Oliver M. Dickerson, *The Navigation Acts and the American Revolution* (Philadelphia, 1951); Edmund S. and Helen M. Morgan, *The Stamp Act Crisis: Prologue to Revolution* (Chapel Hill, 1953); Robert J. Taylor, *Western Massachusetts in the Revolution* (Providence, 1954); Robert E. Brown, *Middle-Class Democracy and the Revolution in Massachusetts, 1691-1780* (Ithaca, N.Y., 1955); Ellen Elizabeth Brennan, "James Otis: Recreant and Patriot," *New England Quarterly,* XII (1939), 691-725.

For a description of English politics prior to the Revolution, I have relied upon the following secondary accounts: Lewis B. Namier, *The Structure of Politics at the Accession of George III* (2 vols., London, 1929) and *England in the Age of the American Revolution* (London, 1930); Richard Pares, *King George III and the Politicians* (Oxford, Eng., 1953); Robert Walcott, *English Politics in the Early Eighteenth Century* (Cambridge, Mass., 1956); John Brooke, *The Chatham Administration, 1766-1768* (London, 1956); William T. Laprade, "The Stamp Act in British Politics," *American Historical Review,* XXXV (1930), 735-757.

Some population figures for Rhode Island are in *Census of the Inhabitants of the Colony of Rhode Island . . . 1774,* ed. John R. Bartlett (Providence, 1858); and Evarts B. Greene and Virginia D. Harrington, *American Population before the Federal Census of 1790* (New York, 1932).

*Bibliographies: Bibliography of Rhode Island, a Catalogue of Books and other Publications Relating to the State of Rhode Island,* ed. John R. Bartlett (Providence, 1864); *Bibliography of Rhode*

*Island History,* ed. Clarence S. Brigham (Boston, 1902). An extremely helpful guide to the material printed in Rhode Island in the eighteenth century is *Rhode Island Imprints, 1727-1800,* ed. John E. Alden (New York, 1949). All colonial historians owe a debt of gratitude to Clarence S. Brigham for his *History and Bibliography of American Newspapers, 1690-1820* (2 vols., Worcester, 1947).

# INDEX

Date Due